UFOS ARE COMING
WEDNESDAY

UFOS ARE COMING WEDNESDAY

Eric Sykes

First published in Great Britain in 1995 by
Virgin Books
an imprint of Virgin Publishing Ltd
332 Ladbroke Grove
London W10 5AH

A catalogue record for this book is available from the British Library

ISBN 1 85227 597 9

Typeset by TW Typesetting, Plymouth, Devon
Printed and bound in Great Britain by
Mackays of Chatham, Lordswood, Chatham, Kent

Dedicated to Norma, my manager

CONTENTS

CONTENTS

FOREWORD

Unidentified Flying Objects have, throughout the centuries, been observed by people of Earth. It is a fact that we now accept these UFOs; we accept that they are from a distant planet and that they are products of a much higher intelligence than our own. Strangely, in the latter half of this century, with international communications now highly sophisticated and extremely efficient, a blanket appears to have been drawn over sightings and reportings.

Ordinary citizens of this world do not seem particularly worried by this. Indeed, space vehicles are regarded as amiable, friendly and good fun for comic strips. People would be more concerned, however, if they knew of the importance that governments all over the world attach to these extraterrestrials and their interest in planet Earth.

Eric Sykes

UFOS ARE COMING WEDNESDAY

PART ONE

SWINEGAP, NEAR BIRMINGHAM

CHAPTER

ONE

A part from the people who are born or die on the 4th of May, there is nothing significant for anyone in the date itself. It is not a bank holiday, nor a Saint's day, it isn't even the longest or shortest day, it's simply the 4th of May. It was, however, an auspicious day for the people of Birmingham, or to be more exact, Swinegap, a thriving new town a few miles to the west.

Before dawn letters were delivered to the homes of four prominent citizens. The envelopes were properly addressed and marked *Strictly Private and Confidential*.

Councillor Blackstone OBE, leader of the Tory Council, was the first of the four to discover the letter on his doormat. He was halfway through his breakfast before he slit open the envelope. He was not only a councillor but also the town's leading solicitor and accustomed to scanning quickly through long and complicated documents – but before he had reached the bottom of page one of the letter he started it again, reading slowly and more carefully. The message was so world-shattering that his first reaction was that it could only be an elaborate hoax. But suppose it were to prove genuine? His mind flashed along several paths and he began to feel the cold awakenings of panic. Ashen faced, he rose unsteadily to his feet. His wife popped her head in from the kitchen and, regarding her husband's general demeanour, thought it must be the egg again. As he walked stiff legged to the bathroom clutching the letter, she assumed it was.

At the home of the Opposition leader, Councillor Sharp, results were just as devastating, except that Sharp was slightly more fortunate in that he read the letter whilst still in bed which, if you're going to pass out, is the best place to be. His aged mother was unable to prise the letter from his grasp, but by laying her head sideways on the eiderdown she tried to read what she could. Fortunately, before she could start making sense of the piece that was

3

visible her son revived, puzzled as to why his mother was apparently listening to his knee.

Three streets away the mayor, unable to find his own glasses, asked his wife to read it out to him. The fact the letter was marked *Strictly Private and Confidential* was irrelevant as he considered his wife barely able to understand 'wish you were here' on a holiday postcard, so whatever secrets the letter contained would be beyond her comprehension. She was a slow reader and at first he wondered idly whether she would be finished by lunchtime, but as he listened to her stumbling dissertation his interest and pulse quickened. If the letter was genuine, it would without a doubt be the most stupendous happening in the history of the town, even in the history of the world. His palms began to sweat. Frantically, he snatched the glasses from her face in order to read the letter for himself. Unfortunately he had underrated his wife's capacity for understanding and only half noticed her sliding sideways out of her chair and on to the floor with what later turned out to be a mild heart attack.

The mayor's thoughts were racing incoherently through his head too fast for him to keep up. Was the letter genuine, and what action should he take? With some relief, he saw on his second reading that copies of the letter had also been sent to three of his colleagues. That eased the burden a little, and being a Class 1 bureaucrat he immediately came to a decision – 'See what the others think first.' That was his standard ploy: to nod wisely through the debate, then always vote with the majority. It was the surest way to attain high office, an index-linked pension and, in all probability, a knighthood. Striding over the prostrate figure of his wife he made for the phone. It wasn't that he was an uncaring man, but he knew where his priorities lay, and that pathetic bundle on the floor came way down the list.

The last man to receive the letter was the local police inspector. Being a professional he read the letter in a detached, unemotional way. In the past he'd had many things pushed through his letterbox: petrol followed by a match which fortunately went out before hitting the floor; threatening and obscene letters practically every week; and of course dog droppings, or what he assumed to be dog droppings – he had never had them analysed. So this latest *Strictly Private and Confidential* load of bumph was just par for the course – the sooner they brought back hanging the better. He only had to read the first few lines to realise that it was a load of codswallop. Crumpling the letter, he was just about to sling it into the fireplace when the phone rang. He picked up the receiver and barked 'Yes?' (He used to give his full title but criminals, cranks and members of the public phoning to complain about rising crime figures had led him to become more secretive.) He was relieved to hear the mayor's voice asking him if he had received an anonymous letter. The inspector's initial reaction was to deny all knowledge of any such letter but something in the mayor's voice intrigued him. He replied that he had received one but that he hadn't had time to digest its contents. As he spoke he hunched his shoulder to hold the phone against his ear while he desperately tried to straighten out the letter. It was only then he became aware that copies had also been sent to the other officials. He listened to the mayor with half his mind but picked up enough to know that a meeting was arranged in the town hall in twenty minutes' time when all four of them would discuss the missive and its implications. He was about to ask 'What implications?' but the mayor had already broken the connection. He fumed all the way to the town hall at this disruption of his day and half an hour later he was seated, with ill grace, in the mayor's parlour.

They were all seated at a round table to avoid the risk of a breach of protocol, but in spite of this Councillor Blackstone OBE was quick to assume the chair.

'We've all read the letter, I assume,' he began.

The inspector nodded, although he hadn't had time to read it all. In any case, it was difficult to follow the letter while he ironed it, a wise precaution as it turned out because Councillor Blackstone OBE suggested that they place the letters before them to ascertain that they were all identical. He cleared his throat.

'I think it is safe to say that this morning we have all received a shock, to put it mildly. It's not every day that four prominent citizens receive notice that a spacecraft from an alien planet will be landing on Wednesday, with even the location of its landing site – Tenkly Common, not two miles from where we sit.'

The inspector was not listening, he was reading the letter quickly to try to find out what all this fuss was about. The letter purported to come from a planet called Androm, headquarters of the Inter-Galactic Peacekeeping Force. This force had been initiated to monitor the delicate mathematical structure of the Inner Galaxies and the Supreme Powers were gravely concerned about the way in which Earth people were conducting their affairs. The inspector pushed the letter away.

'We're not going to take this seriously are we? This is *Boy's Own Paper* stuff. It's a joke,' he sneered. 'Inter-Galactic Peacekeeping Force? Concerned for us, are they? Well, I'm sure we're all concerned about the state of things nowadays, but what motive would *they* have for coming here?'

Councillor Blackstone OBE eyed him coldly. 'It's quite obvious to me that you have only given the letter a cursory glance. Paragraph four states quite clearly their motives. May I read it to you?'

' "The Supreme Council on Androm are deeply concerned by the proliferation of nuclear weapons on planet Earth. In fact, the situation has gone from merely grave to critical and Earth is in danger of being utterly destroyed sooner rather than later." '

Councillor Sharp decided that it was time he put his fourpence worth in. 'We all know that,' he said testily, 'but that's up to us, isn't it? It's nothing to do with anyone else.'

'In any case,' broke in the inspector, 'if this did come from outer space, somebody human on this planet must have typed the letters and shoved them through our letterboxes.'

Councillor Blackstone OBE sighed and looked at the ceiling. 'Not necessarily,' he said. 'May I draw your attention to paragraph eight?'

They all turned over their top sheets.

'Paragraph eight,' continued Blackstone OBE, 'states categorically that men from Androm, having assumed human form, have been infiltrating every country on this planet for thousands of years, in which case the delivery could have been made by a citizen of Androm.'

This last observation intrigued the mayor. If such was the case, any one of his colleagues could be from Androm, he mused idly. His thoughts were broken by a discreet tap on the door and a young girl pushed it open with her back, edging in carrying a tray on which were four cups of coffee, a jug of milk and a sugar bowl. They suspended their discussion whilst she placed a cup of coffee in front of each of them. The mayor, watching her covertly, continued his train of thought. Was she one of the aliens? No, he smiled to himself. If she had assumed human form she would have done a lot better than a spotty face and a king-sized hooter. And look at those legs. Oh, dear Lord, if he had a pair like that he wouldn't be wearing a mini-skirt, he would be hopping around in a sack. She couldn't be an alien in a million years, but then again it could be a perfect disguise.

He looked up to see that the inspector was staring at him, in fact they were all staring at him.

'Well,' snapped Councillor Sharp, 'do you or don't you?'

The mayor hadn't the foggiest idea what he was on about, but he nodded and said, 'I would have to give it some thought. It's not as simple as it sounds.'

They all looked at each other with baffled expressions. Sharp sighed and jerked his thumb towards the young girl. 'This young lady would like to know if you want milk.'

'Oh, er, no thanks.' He recovered himself. 'I was miles away thinking about this document.' He tapped the letter in front of him. 'Yes,' he said as an afterthought, 'I will have some milk,' but by that time the girl had gone.

The inspector took a quick sip of his lukewarm coffee and pushed it aside with disgust.

'Let's collate the facts,' he began. 'We each get a letter marked "Strictly Private and Confidential". It claims to come from an unknown planet called Androm and we are informed that one of their space modules will be landing on Tenkly Common on Wednesday.' He paused. 'Right so far?'

They nodded.

'We are then told,' he continued, 'that the four of us are to wait, maintaining the strictest confidence, for the alleged landing whereupon we will be taken aboard for instruction.'

'Instruction for what?' blurted Councillor Sharp. 'Fretwork, clog dancing, the theory of relativity?'

Councillor Blackstone OBE stopped his flow. 'As long as it's not Marxism.'

'Now then, now then,' soothed the mayor. This was his domain and there would be no political in-fighting in his office. He made his contribution to the discussion.

'What happens if we get on board and the spacecraft takes off?' As soon as he'd said it he wished he hadn't.

The inspector chuckled and said drily, 'We'd better remember to take our passports.'

Councillor Blackstone OBE sighed once again. 'They give their reason for their anxiety on page two.' He read once more:

'"Although the self-destruction of planet Earth is of no consequence in itself, the great fear is that this very action of self-

7

destruction will affect the planets of the solar system and the consequences of this are too horrific to contemplate." ' He took off his glasses and sat back in his chair.

The inspector had had enough. 'If you want my opinion,' he said slowly, 'I think it's a load of codswallop.'

Councillor Blackstone OBE steepled his fingers. He was a solicitor and viewed most things from a legal standpoint. 'It's all very well to dismiss this as codswallop,' he said gravely, 'but do you realise that we would be shirking our duties in ignoring this situation?'

He glared at the inspector as though he were a hostile witness.

'All I am saying,' said the inspector, 'is that we should wait and see what happens.'

'That's a very slipshod attitude, if I may say so,' interposed Councillor Sharp. 'If we all adopted that philosophy this town would still have horse-drawn trams.'

Councillor Blackstone OBE went on as if there had been no interruption. 'We can, of course, sit back and keep silent in the hope that this is all a gigantic hoax. But on the other hand, have you considered the possibility that if this Peacekeeping Force, or whatever it calls itself, does land on Tenkly Common next Wednesday the consequences are liable to be disastrous for each one of us?'

There was silence around the table. They looked at each other uneasily, not quite understanding. Blackstone OBE now had his audience and continued: 'Think about it – aliens from another planet land in our country and we, having had prior knowledge of their arrival, did nothing about it.'

Still their faces remained blank. Councillor Blackstone OBE shook his head.

'Don't you see? England would be invaded and because we withheld the information we could become accessories after the fact. In effect, we could be guilty of treason.'

There was yet more silence around the table as they all digested this seemingly simple truth. Treason was an ugly word. After only a few moments the mayor's face brightened. He had the answer.

'Ah, well, that's taking it a step further. If I read you right, this isn't a local problem at all; it's of national importance and as such it is our bounden duty to override the confidentiality of this document and pass it on to a higher authority.'

They all nodded vigorously. That was the obvious solution. It was the right and proper course to take. Councillor Blackstone

8

OBE, as senior member, was unanimously appointed to place the whole matter in the hands of their local Member of Parliament, and that was when the snowball really started to roll down the slippery slope.

TWO

Charles Tupping was a rookie back-bencher. Due to the death of his predecessor, he'd retained the seat in a by-election. It was a safe Tory stronghold and from a majority of 25,000 he managed to scrape home by 800 votes. He was now a Parliamentarian of some eight weeks' standing and although he hadn't yet made his maiden speech he felt that already he was being noticed. On one or two occasions the Prime Minister had nodded to him as they had passed in the corridors of Westminster and once he'd sat at the next table in the tea room. Oh, yes, it was only a matter of time before they were exchanging Christmas cards and from there the path to the Cabinet lay open, and perhaps eventually – why not? – the door to Number 10. But in the meantime there was work to be done.

Tupping was dictating a letter to a shared secretary when his train of thought was interrupted by the telephone. It was Security at the Main Gate to tell him that a Councillor Blackstone OBE wished to see him most urgently on a matter of extreme importance. Tupping said he'd be right down and, dismissing the secretary, he hurried outside to the gate. He could easily have obtained a pass for the town councillor to come inside, but he was deeply embarrassed by the little cubby hole he had been given as an office.

Outside it was bitterly cold and Tupping wished he'd worn his overcoat, but then he remembered that very few MPs wore overcoats outside when being interviewed on television, whatever the weather.

'Hello, Blackstone,' he said; 'sorry I can't take you in. I'm in a meeting of the Back-Bench Committee and I'd have to get security clearance for you and all that rigmarole, so if it's not going to take too long, I thought we might have our little discussion out here.'

Councillor Blackstone OBE shrugged and silently handed over

the letter. He had never liked the pompous little twit and had voted against his adoption as the Parliamentary candidate. Tupping hurriedly scanned the pages. God, that wind was cold. He could barely read the printed pages for the tears in his eyes. Finally he lowered the letter and stared at the councillor.

'It couldn't be a joke, could it?'

Blackstone groaned inwardly. He wouldn't have been down in London freezing to death outside the Houses of Parliament if he thought it was a joke.

'That was our first impression,' he said, 'but we felt we couldn't dismiss it outright, and if it is genuine then the consequences don't bear thinking about.'

'Hmmm,' said Tupping. He felt his nose beginning to run but he was reluctant to use the nicely folded silk handkerchief in his top pocket. He turned away and sniffled.

'I see. Well, let me sleep on it and I'll let you know in the morning.'

Blackstone was exasperated.

'With due respect, Mr Tupping, I feel that time is not on our side. After all, if they're coming, they'll be here next Wednesday.'

'Yes, I realise that. It's just that we have a rather heavy schedule what with the Health Service cuts and everything. Still, leave it with me, I'll see to it. Got a meeting with the Minister for Ag and Fish and I can't keep him waiting. George here will get you a cab.' He nodded towards the commissionaire, who immediately turned away. He had better things to do with his time and he wasn't even called George.

Blackstone watched the disappearing back of his MP. Pompous prat, he'd run him around the next time he came up for his weekly surgery.

Tupping was glad to be back in the warmth of his small office. Outside he'd been too cold to give the letter much attention so he read it again and with a sickening lurch of his stomach he suddenly realised why Councillor Blackstone OBE had travelled all the way down from Birmingham to hand it to him personally. It was called 'passing the buck'. After all, the town council, the mayor and the police inspector were mature people, older and presumably wiser than he was, so why had they dumped this on him? Was it a test of some sort? Was it a trick to measure his aptitude as an MP . . . or did they really believe that spaceships would be landing next week? He stared unseeing at the letter.

Suddenly a cheery voice bellowed, 'Bad news, old boy?'

Tupping jerked upright like a badly manipulated puppet. He didn't actually lose control of his bowels, but it was a close thing. Thankfully, it was his cousin Gerald, a Parliamentary figure of high esteem. Indeed, he was respected enough to be Parliamentary Private Secretary to the Prime Minister. Tupping sighed with relief. Since entering the House his cousin, some twenty years his senior, had taken him under his wing and his intervention at this precise moment seemed like a monumental slice of good fortune. Without a word he handed over the letter. If the Prime Minister's PPS couldn't advise him on this one, then who could? He wiped his sweaty palms down the sides of his trousers as his cousin read through the letter before throwing it down on the desk.

'Good grief, Charles,' he said, 'is that all that's bothering you? You'll be getting more outrageous letters than that in this job, I can tell you.'

Tupping smiled shakily. 'I wasn't really worried, Gerald. As a matter of fact, I think it's rather funny.' He was immensely relieved by his cousin's reaction and admiration shone from his face in a dazzling beam of hero worship.

Gerald patted him on the shoulder. 'Don't give it another thought. Put it in the shredder where it belongs,' and with that he swept out of Tupping's office in a cloud of expensive aftershave. Almost immediately the door opened again and Gerald reappeared. 'On second thoughts, let me have the letter. I'll show it to God; he needs a laugh. Hasn't had much to cheer him up lately!'

Alone again, Tupping smiled shamefacedly at his momentary panic. Little did he realise that he had just handed over the stick which would be waggled about in a gigantic hornets' nest.

A few hundred yards away in the Cabinet Room at Number 10 the daily briefing had passed off without incident. The PM was in a lighthearted mood, cheered by the opinion polls that morning. He wasn't too far behind the Opposition leader. More importantly, in five days' time it had been arranged that he attend a top-level summit meeting in the Bahamas – which couldn't be bad. He was looking forward to the trip – sunshine, white private beaches, banquets and fine wines. Of course, there would be talks as well, but he didn't anticipate these being too taxing. And when he stepped off the plane on his return he would cheerfully announce that the discussions had gone exceedingly well, etc., etc. His homecoming speech was already written, in fact he had memorised most of it already. So today was one of the few occasions on which the PM felt he could relax and enjoy the perks of power.

His Cabinet went along with his euphoric frame of mind. Secretly they would be glad to see the back of him. He'd had a rough passage over the past few months and they feared he was close to a breakdown. Perhaps six days in the sun would be just the break he needed to top up his batteries.

The PM smiled benignly as he imagined his wife, Mary, in some of the light dresses she had purchased for the trip. He was relaxed and content. It was a mistake. He, of all people, should have known never to drop his guard – it's the quickest way of inviting a sucker punch and, sure enough, it was about to be unleashed.

Sensing the almost boyish exuberance of his master, Gerald deemed it an opportune moment to broach the subject of the letter. He began with a soft chuckle. The PM looked across at him.

'Well, Gerald,' he said, 'whatever it is let's all share it.'

'Oh, it's nothing really, Prime Minister. My cousin has received a letter and it was rather amusing to see his reaction.'

'Is it a funny letter?' prompted the PM, smiling.

Gerald ventured a grin. 'No, as a matter of fact it's rather serious. I was enjoying more the expression on my cousin's face when I burst in on him.'

He handed the letter to the Prime Minister, silently congratulating himself on his skilful passing of the buck. He watched the PM's face covertly while pretending to rummage in his briefcase, ready to burst out laughing or look statesmanlike, depending on the reaction of his leader. But things didn't seem to be going according to plan. The PM should have dismissed the letter with a smile by now, but instead his expression was becoming increasingly grave and it was obvious that he was giving it his utmost attention. The letter was read and re-read in an icy silence; the drop in temperature was almost tangible and Gerald wondered for a moment whether he had handed over the right letter. He hoped to God it wasn't the one he'd received that morning accusing him of being a 'poofter'.

As the PM continued his reading, the PPS began clipping pens in his inside pocket and coughed discreetly. 'I'm sorry to rush you, Prime Minister, but we're due at the House in thirty minutes and the press and TV are outside.'

The PM looked at him blankly. 'Press?' he echoed.

'Yes, sir. You said you'd have a statement for them concerning the Child Allowance Bill.'

13

The PM rose and, scowling, thrust the letter back at his PPS.

'I haven't time to read it now,' he snapped and strode towards the door.

Gerald's heart sank. He knew that the PM had read enough to be perturbed and by handing the letter back he had cleverly returned the buck. But why was this such a hot potato? Good grief, UFOs had been spotted for years – saucer shape, round, elliptical, static, moving at the speed of light, little green men with three heads – so what was all the panic about? He cursed his cousin for dropping him in it but was appalled by his own stupidity. He should have learned by now that it was always the messenger who took the bullet.

THREE

I t was true that the letter had affected the Prime Minister and with each step as he slowly descended the staircase to the hall in No. 10 his gloom deepened. Only himself, the Foreign Secretary and a handful of senior civil servants were privy to the secret agenda of the Bahamas Summit headed 'UFOs'. He had not attached too much importance to this until now. Over the years every major government in the world had assembled mountains of information concerning Unidentified Flying Objects. All these sightings came from reputable witnesses: airline pilots reporting near misses, police alarmed at strange lights too powerful to be earthly, skimming at roof-top height over main roads. The CIA had only recently submitted a dossier presenting evidence that aliens from outer space had already infiltrated several countries on Earth. Even more immediate, two unidentified spacecraft had crashed in the Andes. This sighting had been verified by unimpeachable sources but inspection of the crash site was impossible for the moment due to the high levels of radiation. On his own patch, the Government had received notice from GCHQ Cheltenham of the increased volume of radio traffic in outer space.

The fear now amongst world leaders was that the likelihood of extraterrestrial intervention in Earth's business was now at a critical stage and, therefore, was it not his duty to inform his colleagues at the Bahamas Summit of the contents of that letter? He groaned softly. He hadn't really taken the Bahamas trip seriously; for him it was a junket, a week in the sun, but if the letter was authentic, his duty was plain. He would have to be in Britain with his own people on Wednesday, not swanning about in the Caribbean. Mary was going to be bitterly disappointed about cancelling the trip. Damn the letter and damn Gerald for showing it to him. Then, just as suddenly as the gloom had descended, he brightened. What letter? He hadn't read any letter. No such letter existed. That was the answer! Having convinced himself, he was greatly cheered. He squared his shoulders and stepped out of the famous front door to meet the press and was greeted by a barrage of flashbulbs.

'Good afternoon, ladies and gentlemen,' he said.

There was a murmured reply from the assembled 'News at 10 Downing Street' mob. The Prime Minister pointed to a bespectacled harridan from one of the tabloids.

'Yes, Miss Curshaw,' he politely solicited a question.

He was proud of his name-dropping. He was under the impression that it made him more approachable, a man of the people, one of the lads.

But the woman reporter flared at him, 'It's Ms Jackson, actually.'

There was a ripple of laughter and the PM smiled with them. 'Clever bitch,' he thought. Did they expect him to remember all their names? He was the Prime Minister, for God's sake, not a telephone directory.

Ms Jackson continued. 'Can the Prime Minister assure us that there will be no cut in child allowance for single-parent families?'

The PM answered easily. He had been well briefed for such a question and spoke with a confident evasion. He did not like Ms Jackson, he knew her of old, a rabid left-winger. He could imagine her bedroom full of pictures of Harold Wilson and a lock of Denis Healey's eyebrow under her pillow. Before Ms Jackson could nail him with a follow-up question, he pointed to a man at the back.

'Yes, sir?'

The man at the back spoke loudly and clearly.

'Prime Minister,' he began, 'is there any truth in the rumour that on Wednesday next a spacecraft will be landing near Birmingham?'

There was a stunned silence as all the media people turned to stare at the man. He was a stranger in that tight clique. This was an entirely new departure from the agreed line of questioning but it was infinitely more interesting than single-parent allowances. There was a rustle as pages were flipped over in notebooks. They waited eagerly for the reply. Those with microphones thrust them forwards and television lenses zoomed in on the PM's face. It bore the look of a man struck violently over the back of the head with a sock full of cold porridge. In fact, for the moment he was brain dead, but with the skill of the consummate politician that he was, his mouth switched to automatic pilot.

'I'm sorry,' he blurted. 'I didn't hear the question. Can you repeat it please?'

It was a standard retort to give himself time to get up off the ropes. The assembled reporters turned round again but the stranger was nowhere to be seen. The damage, however, was done. In millions of homes viewers would be able to watch a badly shaken Prime Minister floundering in front of the cameras. His stricken face would appear on millions of TV screens at six o'clock and pictures would be plastered all over the morning editions of every newspaper. The fan was already beginning to revolve and the Prime Minister sensed that something really nasty would hit it when he reached the House of Commons.

FOUR

Q uestion Time began with the usual exchanges of traditional platitudes. A Conservative member congratulated the Prime Minister on last month's trade figures. A Labour member posed a question that was deftly fielded by the Prime Minister although it was only realised later that he had answered a question that had not yet been asked. It was a normal Question Time . . . but the bomb had been primed and was about to explode.

There was a question from a Labour back-bencher.

'Mr Speaker,' he began. 'I was about to ask the Prime Minister a question relating to car manufacture in Birmingham but in the light of recent information to the effect that a landing vehicle from outer space seems imminent in the area, would the Prime Minister . . .'

The rest of his words were drowned by cries from the Government benches – 'Disgraceful', 'What landing vehicle?', 'Out of order', etc., etc., and from the Opposition came cries of 'Explain', 'Resign', 'Take more water with it'.

The uproar was unprecedented and the Speaker was inaudible as he frantically sought to gain control. The Prime Minister was rattled; this wasn't just a leak, it was Niagara Falls. How had the contents of the letter fallen into Opposition hands?

The answer was simple. Unknown to the PM, Councillor Sharp, niggled by the way in which Councillor Blackstone OBE had taken over their conference, had decided that if the document had any relevance as a matter of National Importance, it should be an all-party matter. Before Councillor Blackstone OBE had even boarded the train for London, Sharp had faxed his copy of the letter to a prominent Labour back-bencher. He knew the man slightly, having scraped an acquaintance at the Party Conference in Blackpool.

The Labour MP had read the fax, more amused than anything

else, with half his attention on his portable television. Hearing the reporter's question and seeing a close-up of the PM's face, he'd read the faxed letter again. His pulse quickened and in less than an hour he'd advised a great many of his Labour colleagues of the strange letter. It was a little gold mine. At the very least it would embarrass the Government if it could somehow be worked into the afternoon questions. The Labour benches could not have hoped in their wildest dreams for the effect it was now having on the Prime Minister.

The PM appeared to be in a coma. It was momentary, however, and he soon sprang to his feet.

'Will the honourable member . . .' He tried again. 'Will the honourable member . . .' but it was no good. The cacophony was now at such a level that had Concorde flown through the chamber, no one would have heard it. Spittle flecked the corners of his mouth and his eyes were wild. The question had not been tabled and he should have left it to the Speaker to censure the man – but the Prime Minister was beyond reason.

The Opposition were out for blood. Cries of 'Androm' and 'Take me to your leader' were thrown across the floor of the House. The Speaker was no help – he had collapsed, but there were plenty of doctors in the Commons so nobody was particularly perturbed.

'Will the honourable gentleman,' the Prime Minister yelled again, but the noise was still too great. The Foreign Secretary took the back of the PM's jacket and tried to pull him down, but the leader slapped his hand away.

'We have been aware of the impending landing for some weeks now,' he ranted and the baying subsided to normal levels. The Opposition sensed they were about to hear something momentous and the Government benches were eager to hear what they were supposed to have been aware of for weeks.

'Oh, yes,' the PM went on hysterically. 'My colleagues and I have had constant discussions along with the Joint Chiefs of Staff.'

His Cabinet colleagues stared at him aghast. What was he on about? Discussions about what, for God's sake? As for the Joint Chiefs of Staff, they'd not been seen in the Cabinet Room since the Falklands. The PM babbled on manically, committing the cardinal sin of making policy on the hoof. On the bench behind him, Gerald groaned as he listened to the PM digging himself deeper and deeper into a dark and friendless pit. Gerald was under no illusion as to his own future. That stupid letter! And, worse, he'd even chuckled as he'd handed it across the desk. He looked over his shoulder to his cousin on the back benches, his face shining with patriotic fervour as he drank in the words of his Prime Minister. Gerald's teeth ground together, panic turned to anger. If he was about to get the boot he wouldn't go down alone. No, by God, he'd take that prat of a cousin with him even if it came to murder.

Mercifully, Question Time came to an end and the Government front bench couldn't wait to leave the chamber. They hustled their spluttering Prime Minister out before he could break into 'Mary Had A Little Lamb'. Most of them were totally ignorant of the existence of the letter and were totally mystified by the taunts about Androm and spacemen from the Opposition benches. Of one thing they were certain, especially when the whips informed them there was to be a full Cabinet meeting at eight o'clock: they were all on the verge of a major crisis.

That evening lights burned in the Cabinet Room at No. 10. The first hour had been tempestuous, to put it mildly. As the Prime Minister apprised them of the facts, his ministerial colleagues listened with growing incredulity and alarm. After all, the letter was anonymous. Why hadn't the PM ignored it, laughed it off for goodness' sake? Aliens from an unknown planet landing on Wednesday, and near Birmingham of all places! Why not Hyde Park or the Champs Élysées? With mounting terror they realised how deep was the hole the PM had dug for himself and in order to save his face they had no option but to jump in after him. Wild thoughts of revolt flashed around the Cabinet table, but they were only thoughts. They were too astute and wily to speak out and there might come a time when their words would be remembered and used against them.

Openly, they had no option but to back the PM's actions and a damage limitation conference ensued. After Wednesday, the knives would be out. There would be time before the next General Election to have the PM certified. The Chiefs of Staff from the Air Force and the Army were ushered in and some of the Cabinet Ministers were ushered out.

Amongst those who remained, a war council was established. The Prime Minister was in an impossible situation. He could apprise the military of the letter, but not his concerns about the

Bahamas Summit. The summit agenda was too secret, so all he had to justify his performance in the Commons was the letter.

It was no wonder that the military men were aghast. They were expected to come up with a plan to counter a full-scale alien invasion on the basis of an anonymous letter. Various plans and stratagems were discussed and it was finally agreed that from 24.00 hours on Tuesday the surveillance wing of the Royal Air Force would monitor air space over Birmingham. Traffic control at Birmingham Airport would not be involved, and would be told that the increased RAF presence was due to a large-scale routine exercise. The RAF planes would fly thousands of feet above the commercial lanes and would be in contact with an elite force of ground troops. On landing, the aliens would be apprehended by the ground force and taken to a secret rendezvous where they would be interrogated. It was a hastily cobbled-up plan but it was the best they could do in the short time available. It wasn't exactly 'Overlord' but then Churchill, Eisenhower and their top brass had had nearly a year to prepare for that show. Good grief, if they had had less than a week, we would all be speaking German. As dawn took over the burden from the Downing Street lights, the military hurried away to set the wheels in motion. Secretly they were convinced that the man running their country was definitely losing his marbles.

The PM had time for a shower and a change of suit whilst a TV crew set up cameras and lights in the Cabinet Room. At ten o'clock that morning, the Prime Minister was to appear in a special news flash on all channels. It was now almost thirty hours since he had slept and he was full of black coffee and benzedrine, heavily made up to hide the dark patches under his eyes. It was through this grotesque mask that he smiled at the nation. He appealed to the British people to stay calm and carry on as normal. The likelihood of a spacecraft actually landing was extremely remote. It was all a storm in a teacup and he urged that Wednesday be treated as a normal working day. There was much more of this, all in the same vein, and in view of the circumstances it was a creditable performance – he sounded quite sane and statesmanlike. Any fears that the people may have had regarding invasion should now be dispelled – but he had greatly underestimated the man in the street.

CHAPTER

FIVE

On Monday the traffic roared up and down the M1. It was a normal, average, horrendous day on the motorway but very few people noticed that the turn-off slip roads to Birmingham were taking an above-average volume of traffic. As a result, by midnight Birmingham was at a standstill.

It was now obvious to the Birmingham traffic police that the main bulk of the vehicles were making tracks to Tenkly Common, so cars were diverted – down side streets, up alleyways – anywhere to get the damn things out of the centre of the city. Anywhere would do as long as it cleared the main streets. The Automobile Association was out in force and yellow signs marked 'Tenkly Common' were displayed all round Birmingham.

At this point the mood of the crowd was orderly. Some were apprehensive and others reverent but mainly there was a happy holiday atmosphere. There were exceptions: for instance, when two traffic control police returned to their parked car they found it jacked up and the wheels missing.

On Tuesday, however, on D minus one, the good humour of over 100,000 motorists had evaporated. By midday all vehicles heading for Tenkly Common had come to a standstill. Cars, buses and lorries continued to pull up behind the stationary traffic, and before long there was a tailback as far as Watford. On the southbound lane the jam stretched as far north as Carlisle. Desperate appeals were made by radio and television for people to avoid the motorways unless in an absolute emergency; but they were bolting the stable door when the horse was long gone.

Airports ground to a halt as the foreign media arrived along with the thousands of sightseers. Many planes from overseas were diverted to France, Holland and Belgium. The railways suffered the same fate. The platforms were now so jammed with people that passengers arriving at Birmingham New Street were unable to alight and had no option but to stay on to London. Eventually, in the interests of public safety, the trains stopped running altogether.

Inevitably some people managed to get through to the landing site but they had arrived on foot and so tightly were they packed, the majority had to sleep standing up. Oddly enough there were few locals present. With so many strangers in town they felt it best to stay put and keep an eye on their possessions. In any case, the restaurants, garages and hotels were enjoying the biggest boom since any of them could remember. Most of the ordinary householders had put bed and breakfast signs in their front windows, and weary travellers who couldn't afford the £100-plus per night spent three or four days in the open air. Oh yes, the locals welcomed the strangers with open arms all right. Nothing was too much trouble and nothing was cheap; even water was expensive and luckily it didn't rain. A bonanza of tax-free money was finding its way under floorboards and mattresses were growing lumpy. By next week many of the local inhabitants would be buying time-share villas in more exotic places.

However, for the rest of the country the outlook was bleak. By Wednesday afternoon business in England was practically nonexistent. Factories closed due to widespread absenteeism and industry was unable to move its products. Inevitably shares on the Stock Exchange fell dramatically; the pound was pathetic beside the dollar and the Deutschmark, and to all intents and purposes Britain had ceased to function as a trading nation. Millions of people were totally unaware of this as they waited for the arrival of the beings from outer space.

From the onset of darkness on Wednesday a tense feeling of expectancy pervaded the atmosphere. People began to converse in whispers, eyes scanned the blackness for some visible sign of the arrival, and speculation was rife as to where the aliens would actually land. The designated site, being so densely packed, was now out of the question. In fact, the whole area for miles around was now jammed into a solid phalanx and a landing was impossible.

Throughout the night millions of eyes searched the heavens but it was a fruitless vigil. Low cloud blotted out the stars, even the navigation lights of commercial aircraft would have been a welcome diversion; but, alas, the airport had been closed since mid-afternoon. It was a long night.

23

With the dawn the skies lightened promising a fine Thursday, but there was still no sign of any alien spaceships. The monitoring aircraft circling miles above the cloud base had no information to beam down to the special forces, which was just as well because the elite ground troops weren't even in position. Owing to the tremendous press of people, there had been no place for the military helicopters to land. The backup plan, considering the situation, was simply fatuous. The helicopters would make height sufficient for the special forces to descend by parachute. Fortunately the major in charge of the operation was a realist and countermanded the order. He only had to look down on the white mass of up-turned faces to visualise the carnage below as two sticks of para-troopers in full battle gear landed feet first amongst them. So, on his own initiative, he ordered the choppers to land in a farmyard some twelve miles short of Tenkly Common. It was the nearest point but then a forced march of twelve miles was merely a constitutional for a seasoned force of combat troops, and they swung out of the farmyard in fine fettle.

From then on their troubles began. The crowds thickened and in four hours they had only covered half a mile and were trapped in a seething mass of sightseers. Some of them took off their balaclavas. These masks were supposed to provide anonymity, but what did that matter now? They had become separated from each other and in any case the balaclavas were frightening the children.

For the whole of Thursday nothing moved. None of the crowd could have gone home even had they wanted to and after suffering for the last three days, they were loath to miss anything now. Rumours floated around like the evening midges: 'The spaceships have landed in Manchester', 'The spaceships are orbiting Earth waiting for the crowd to disperse', and some people had heard on their car radio that two flying saucers had crashed in the Channel. As the hours went by children became fractious. Many were desperately hungry and to cap it all it started to rain – that was the last straw. As the rain got heavier, people turned round and tried to move in all directions to where they'd left their cars. But it was hopeless. The cries of the young and the admonitions of their parents were augmented by engine noise as cars were started up. The exodus seemed to have begun, but it was to be many hours before they would begin to disperse.

The police, the AA , the RAC, in fact all the authorities connected with transport were pressed into service to unsnarl the biggest jam in road history. The whole operation was overseen, literally, by the Minister of Transport fluttering up and down the motorways in a helicopter to the extent of its fuel load, a quick filling of the tanks and up again. It was very impressive, except that the Minister slept most of the time. Finally his chopper alighted and he leaped down, refreshed, announcing to the waiting media that the motorways were now running normally, and any hold-ups were now due to the usual roadworks.

Inevitably there was a heavy price to pay for the last week, both financially and politically. The centre of England was littered with discarded beer cans, coke cans, containers of every description, papers, articles of clothing and three bodies. In fact it was a forty-odd square mile rubbish tip, and the compensation claims on the Government were horrendous although the army of cleaners off-set this to some extent by causing a drop in the unemployment figures.

The real battle in the House of Commons became a no contest as the Opposition brought their 16-inch guns to bear against the sticks wielded by the Government front benches. It was carnival night, birthday and Christmas as political points were scored one after another. It was too easy, it was trawling in a fish hatchery, but the Opposition party was relentless. 'Would the Prime Minister deny that the whole disgraceful episode had been manufactured in order to divert attention from the shambles of the Health Service?' 'Was he aware of the widespread damage both at home and abroad this mischievous malicious hoax had caused?' 'Did the Prime Minister realise the enormity of the danger in leaving the country virtually defenceless during the last week?' There was more, and the Government's responses were pathetically defensive.

In the event, by some miracle, the Government survived. This was largely due to the prompt and decisive action taken by the Prime Minister: he sacked most of his Cabinet. It wasn't a pretty sight. The corridors of power resembled a bowling alley, so many heads were rolling. It wasn't just a reshuffle, it was breaking open a whole new deck.

Surprisingly, outside Parliament the whole affair died a quick death. People seemed reluctant to discuss it and, of course, nobody would admit to being on the motorways – they'd watched the whole thing on television. Everybody knew it was a joke from the start, and most of the people who had besieged Birmingham were obviously foreigners ... Ah well, what can you expect? What's the weather forecast for tomorrow? And what are the chances of Spurs winning the Cup? And did you see *Neighbours* yesterday? The country slipped into its normal lethargic routine – and that was fatal. The bell was about to ring for round two.

SIX

In a small Welsh town a few miles north of Cardiff, the two leading councillors, the mayor and chief constable received letters marked *Strictly Private and Confidential*. The contents were identical in every respect to the Swinegap letters, except that the location of the landing site would not now be on grassland but in the playground of a children's school. This small target would require pinpoint navigational skill and, in the interests of public safety, it was imperative the area be isolated. There must be no recurrence of the shameful behaviour of sightseers on Tenkly Common. And, as before, the time of arrival would be Wednesday next.

The dignitaries, on receiving the letters, not unmindful of the prosperity that worldwide notoriety had brought upon their predecessors, ignored the strictly private and confidential nature of the missives and immediately despatched them to the Government. And to make doubly sure of their windfall, they also leaked the letter to the dailies before they could be issued a 'D-notice' forbidding them to print the story. The townspeople were excitedly discussing the contents of the letters even before the Government received them. Of course the aliens wouldn't land in a little town near Birmingham. That was a try-on. This was different, this was Wales, boyo. Oh yes, there'd be a welcome in the valleys for the little green men. Since the pit closure some years ago they hadn't had much to sing about but they hadn't let it bring them down. They were, to a man, God-fearing chapelgoers and here was their just reward. Never mind a week in Swansea for a holiday, it would be the Costa del Sol from now on. Anxiously they awaited the morning papers, but they needn't have worried. News of the spacemen was headlined on every front page, perhaps not as enthusiastically as the first time, but nevertheless the front pages carried it: *Daily Mail* – WAS TENKLY A REHEARSAL?; *Daily Express*

– HERE WE GO AGAIN; *Daily Mirror* – A WELSH WELCOME FOR SPACE-MEN; and from *The Times* – TROUBLE IN ZIMBABWE.

It was enough to inspire the little Welsh town to drooling point in their preparations to reap the riches. Hotel charges were trebled, the two restaurants vied with each other to see how high they could raise their prices. It was ludicrous: £2.50 for a bread roll and in case customers came in just for the bread, each establishment now had a £10.00 cover charge. Extra tables were crammed in to the extent that some customers would have to eat in the kitchen. Spare rooms in private cottages were scrubbed out and bed and breakfast signs sprouted like mushrooms in a damp bedsit. Ordinary sightseers would not be able to afford the prices, but there was always the expense account media personnel, many of whom had already arrived and were doubled up some three or four to a small back room. Cardiff wasn't too far away, with much better accommodation, but they had learned from the Birmingham fiasco that if you weren't right on the spot it was a wasted journey. The foreign press arrived only to find the little town already booked out and resigned themselves to spending a week in the open. But the astute council gave the delighted children two weeks' holiday and turned their school into a hostel. Hospital patients were also sent home and their beds commandeered for the makeshift hostel, with the price of a bed at £500.00 per night, breakfast not included. No one complained. After all, as the mayor lightheartedly mentioned in his welcome speech, when the spaceships landed they couldn't be better placed. School desks which had been turfed out were placed in a circle round the school yard, and would be used to give the town dignitaries a ringside seat on the night.

Not surprisingly, ordinary sightseers with traumatic memories of the horrendous three or four days at the last lot, stayed home and traffic was comparatively light. In any event the police acted quickly and road blocks were installed every twenty miles or so on the main highways leading to Wales. Motorists who could not produce a specific reason to cross the border were turned back. Naturally some got through to arrive at the little Welsh town, and wished they hadn't. Every small space that could hold a bed was already booked although sleeping bags were available for hire at £50.00 per night. Alternatively, if one decided to spend the night in the car, it was just as expensive in parking fees.

The Government decided to stay out of this one but the

Bahamas high-level conference was once again postponed. The Prime Minister declared during Question Time they were keeping a watchful eye on the proceedings, and more than that he could not say as it would not be in the national interest. It was a political answer that meant nothing in Parliament but satisfied the electorate. This time no military aircraft would be circling the airspace over Wales, and special forces would not be on the ground. It was just as well because Wednesday passed without incident, and when Thursday came and went so did most of the media, leaving the inhabitants of the little Welsh town counting considerably more than just their blessings.

SEVEN

Perhaps the Joker or whoever was sending the letters was over-playing his hand, or maybe the letters were genuine. Whichever the case, exactly two weeks later in a little town not far from Scarborough the by now familiar letters were received by the four leading citizens. This time, however, there were no headlines, although most dailies printed the information in the middle pages. The inhabitants of the little town, being hard-headed Yorkshire folk, were thankful not to be splashed all over the media. They had had enough with foreigners tramping over their patch with expensive cameras clicking at everything. 'Excuse pliss, did Emiry Blonte live here?' 'Say buddy, how far is Ilkley Moor?' and 'Was this the place they made *All Creatures Great and Small*?'

Outwardly the locals appeared to treat the arrival of the space-men with indifference, but this was merely a facade. They knew in their hardhearted Yorkshire way that if the spacemen did land they would be treated like any other visitors, with courtesy and plain honest-to-God Yorkshire hospitality. In any case, if they came they came, and if they didn't there was always the football pools.

On the Wednesday the media drifted into town. They were bored, blasé, and had seen it all before. Nor were they the top names in the media; in fact the newspaper reporters were way down the pecking order – the ones who usually covered weddings, anniversaries and local obituaries. For television, the occasion was used as a test for new, aspiring directors. The overseas correspondents didn't turn up at all.

The Government chose to ignore the whole thing, and very wisely too, because again it was a non-starter. And as the media circus packed its equipment, the consensus of opinion was that spaceship news was box-office poison and the next time they dashed off to some little town in the middle of nowhere, it would be after the aliens landed and not before.

Over the next ten months several other small towns received letters marked *Strictly Private and Confidential*, but in most cases they found the waste-paper basket. The whole thing was becoming a bore, although on the occasions when it was made public there were still the inevitable sightseers, extraterrestrial societies, wandering layabouts and the usual people who appear on the scene whenever there's a chance of a television camera being present. In fact, one old-age pensioner became a celebrity merely by holding up a placard which read 'Hello Mother'.

EIGHT

C hief Inspector James, one of the most experienced investigative officers in Scotland Yard, had been assigned the task of finding the Joker and after nearly a year was still completely baffled. He had had several meetings with the Prime Minister, each one more uncomfortable than the last. He remembered the last encounter which took place in Downing Street. It was horrendous to say the least. The Prime Minister's paranoia was evident.

'I want him, chief inspector,' ranted the Prime Minister. 'I want the miserable bastard who perpetrated this nonsense, and I want him not now but yesterday!'

He thumped the desk and a picture of his wife and children crashed to the floor. The chief inspector bent to retrieve it.

'Leave that rubbish where it is!' yelled the Prime Minister. 'You're a high-ranking police officer, not a dustman!'

It was a painful interview. His anger flared as he recalled the meeting. He was one of the Met's most respected policemen, after all, and he had been taken off a multi-million-pound drugs bust for this – finding some Joker who wrote anonymous letters. It was a Noddy job, for God's sake, one for PC Plod. All he'd done so far was ordinary 'Bobby on the beat' stuff. He'd interviewed the original recipients of the letter, Blackstone OBE and his cronies. He'd examined their medical histories for signs of instability, malicious or violent tendencies, but apart from the fact that Sharp was homosexual and the mayor a reformed alcoholic, there was nothing to suggest they had any part in the original hoax.

The chief inspector had done all he could and he was still no closer to an arrest. He'd even had the PM relate to a police artist a description of the man who had posed the question at the Downing Street press conference. An Identikit picture was drawn up and excitedly the Prime Minister yelled, 'That's him! That's him to a T!'

The chief inspector groaned. In front of him on the desk he had twelve more Identikit pictures of the man from his interviews with the press people who were present at the time. He looked despairingly at the line of faces in front of him. It looked like the band of Dr Crock and His Crackpots. Each face was different: one wore glasses, another a beard, protruding ears, then ears that were hidden under white, lank hair.

Chief Inspector James was coming to the end of a long and illustrious career and his retirement was inexorably creeping up on him – in eight months to be exact. Pray to God this was not to be his last case. He wanted to go out in a blaze of glory. This was more like a slow canter to the knacker's yard. In a fit of rage he brushed the Identikit pictures to the floor. The only chance of apprehending the pimply faced git was to nab him red-handed actually posting the letters. He wondered where the next location would be and as if to answer his question the phone rang. He picked it up.

'Chief Inspector James,' he rasped. Then he sighed, 'Where's that?' Glancing at a map of the British Isles on the wall, 'Yes, I know it, near Norwich. Yes, OK, send the letters over and do the usual interviews. Thanks.'

He put the phone down, took a blackheaded pin from a box on his desk, then moved towards the map and stuck it in a little town two miles to the north of Norwich. It was the twentieth black pin sticking like fungus to the large map. He stared at it for a moment, then in a sudden fit of anger and frustration tore the whole thing off the wall, punched it into a ball, black pins and all, and slung it into the metal waste bin.

He lifted the telephone receiver and jabbed at the buttons.

'Hello Miss Dawson. Is the governor in yet? This is Chief Inspector James.'

He waited a moment. Miss Dawson's voice was replaced by that of the head of Scotland Yard. James didn't waste time on preliminaries.

'Four more letters from a little town outside Norwich called Hampdown. The local bobbies are sending on any pertinent information. Look sir, can you spare me a few minutes if I come up?' He listened, then he broke in, 'I know that this has become a personal vendetta between the Prime Minister and whoever we are after but quite frankly, we haven't a cat in hell's chance of catching this Joker.' He listened again. 'Yes sir, that is exactly what I'm suggesting, close the file – unsolved, and let's get back to real police work. The local lads have enough on their plates without . . . Hello? . . .'

He jiggled the receiver but the head man had already terminated the interview. He slammed down the receiver and slumped back in his chair. He couldn't blame the governor, he knew that the Prime Minister was breathing down his neck. The latest stroke of genius to come out of 10 Downing Street was that local police keep an all-night surveillance on their mayors' houses. The inspector wondered seriously if the PM knew what was going on. Didn't he realise that the cost to the police bill would be astronomical?

'Sergeant Thompson!' he yelled.

There was a scuffle of footsteps and Sergeant Thompson entered the room.

'Yes sir?'

He stopped in his tracks and stared at the lighter part of the wall behind the chief inspector.

'The map, sir,' he pointed, 'it's gone.'

'It hasn't gone,' said the inspector in a tight voice. 'It's in the waste-paper bin.'

Sergeant Thompson raised his eyebrows.

'You heard me,' he said. 'It's in the bloody bin.' He went on, 'God knows how many people have been shot, strangled, murdered, houses burgled, tons of drugs smuggled into the country, and for the best part of a year all we've done is receive a file full of identical letters, stick pins in a bloody map and polish our fat backsides.'

'Yes sir,' said Sergeant Thompson. 'What else can we do?'

Suddenly the inspector reached for his hat.

'I'll tell you what we're going to do,' he said, 'I'm taking you to the pub and you, sergeant, are going to buy me a pint.'

'Yes sir,' replied Sergeant Thompson and hurried after him.

Two months later, the next little town to be targeted was called Grapplewick, eight miles north of Manchester, and although no one was aware of it at the time, it was destined to be almost the last. Unlike all the other small towns, however, the local dignitaries were not forewarned by letter, they were to receive the ultimate accolade: they were visited instead . . . by an Alien from Outer Space.

PART TWO

GRAPPLEWICK, NEAR MANCHESTER

NINE

E ven in Lancashire Grapplewick was a joke. Every stand-up comedian in the north featured the town in his act. It was generally agreed that Grapplewick folk were thick, but this is rather unkind; to be charitable, the townspeople had better things to do than think.

At the turn of the century Grapplewick flourished with the import of raw cotton, but that was in the golden age of the British Empire. Now the two empty mills which had once so proudly dominated and blackened the town were mute evidence of the slump of the thirties. The Second World War brought a timely reprieve, leaving a legacy of small businesses, component parts for this or that, surviving only because they were cheaper than other more notable rivals. A small influx of Asians added to the life support, and Grapplewick was breathing although, according to other Lancastrians, brain dead.

Some of its past glories remained – the town hall with worn stone steps, brave flaking pillars, and masonry so beloved of Victorian architects; two churches; a synagogue; and now a mosque, shining like a cat's eye in the dark. It certainly did better business than the other denominations. For other forms of escape there were two cinemas, one of which had been a music hall and still bore peeling, faded old bills featuring G. H. Elliot, and Mushy the forest bred lion; numerous pubs, and one or two amusement arcades. Dirty little houses built for the workers in the halcyon days of full employment led off the high street in identical poverty-stricken ranks. It was a tired town, cowering in the folds of the moors as if ashamed of its ugliness.

To be philosophical, however, 'In every dustbin there's a daffodil'. Unfortunately, most of the lowly people who rummage around in these receptacles are neither botanists nor philosophers, but the seed of Grapplewick's flower was planted in a small barber's shop on Coldhurst Street.

The owner was Albert Waterhouse and apart from the plate glass window and a striped pole, it was exactly the same as all the other dwellings that propped each other up on either side of the cobbled thoroughfare. Councillor Albert Waterhouse no longer operated in the shop. He'd had to share his haircutting activities with his civic duties, but now, having been next on the list, he was enjoying his one-year tenure as mayor. Naturally, with his newly exalted status it wasn't fitting that he should be seen in such a dump. Indeed, he even went somewhere else for his short back and sides. The running of the business was left solely in the hands of his nephew, Norman.

Having worked in the shop since leaving school, Norman now had seven years' experience behind him, and to be left in charge of the whole shebang pleased him immensely. He was a good-looking young man, proud of being the best barber in Coldhurst Street. It never once crossed his mind that he was the only barber in Coldhurst Street.

'You can't beat Benidorm,' he shouted into his customer's ear, snip-snipping all the time.

The man looked at himself in the flyspecked mirror.

'Who?' he asked.

'Benidorm,' said Norman, looking at the man's reflection.

Everything had to be shouted to overcome the utter mindless cacophony of pop music that blared from a transistor radio on a shelf by the door from the moment the shop was opened to closing time.

'Topless birds,' he blew away some loose hair, 'never got to the hotel till dawn,' snip, snip. 'Bars open all night, English beer and all.'

There was more dialogue in the same vein – topless, beer, and all-night parties. It's amazing what a week's package tour will do for a young man's education.

On the bench a young lad awaiting his turn tried desperately to follow the conversation. He got the odd words interspersed with 'boom, boom, boom, Ah lurves ya bybee'. He tugged at his mother's sleeve. Mrs Dobson was miles away looking idly towards the window, seeing nothing. A bus stopped outside and some people on the top deck peered down into the shop incuriously. Then the bus moved off and it's doubtful if she even noticed it.

'Mam,' hissed the boy tugging her sleeve more urgently.

'What is it?' she mouthed. She wasn't going to compete with the radio. Her son strained up to her to avoid the off-chance of being overheard by the barber.

'What's topless?' he asked.

'What are you on about?' she replied, puzzled.

'He said "topless birds in Benidorm".'

He nodded towards Norman. The penny dropped and, turning on her son, she clouted the back of his head.

'I told you to bring a comic,' she hissed.

His cap fell off and he bent down to pick it up, thankful for the chance to hide his embarrassment as the tears welled up in his eyes. There was a further distraction as the shop bell tinkled. Nobody actually heard it above the continuous assault from the latest hit single, but they all felt the draught from the open door. All heads turned to see who it was but all that could be seen was a tall dark shape, backlit from the sunlight outside. It stood very still.

Mrs Dobson looked enquiringly at Norman, who smiled weakly at the stranger in the doorway. Men often came in the door, looked around the shop and then went out again, but this man just stood there, neither coming nor going. Mrs Dobson's son peeked fearfully from behind his mother and the customer in the barber's chair gulped noisily, never taking his eyes off the stranger. Everyone in the shop remained motionless. It could have been Madame Tussaud's apart from the noise blasting from the radio, which continued to assault everyone's eardrums. In fact no one had noticed the noise, but they certainly did when the stranger reached out and switched it off. The resulting silence was almost tangible, as if one had run through a raging storm into a church.

The people in the barber's were unaccustomed to the quiet and were now gripped by fear. Mrs Dobson was the first to move. Grabbing her little boy's hand she scurried towards the door, averting her eyes lest she looked into the man's face. She could not explain her feeling of dread; it sprang from a long-buried superstition like throwing salt over your shoulder or crossing your fingers when you pass a squint-eyed woman. She dragged her son through the door into the safety of the street. He turned back for a final furtive look, and she clouted him again.

Mrs Dobson's departure was too much for the man in the barber's chair. He snatched the cloth from his neck, and jamming his cap over his half-finished short back and sides he edged quickly past the stranger to the door. 'I'll not be going in there again' he muttered to himself in the sanctuary of the street, not realising at the time the prophecy of his words.

Norman would have given anything to be able to follow his departed customer but he was stuck in the shop, alone and helpless without the caterwauling of the transistor radio backing him up. The stranger now closed the door and to his relief Norman could see that he was just an ordinary well-dressed man – which in itself was odd, as well-dressed men didn't usually come down Coldhurst Street, and they certainly never stopped off at his shop.

'You're closed.' It was a flat statement and Norman was confused.

'No we're not – we're usually open while eight o'clock!'

The man turned over the 'open/closed' sign on the door and took off his hat. Norman pointed hopelessly to the card. 'I can't close the shop just yet,' he said. 'You see, it's not my shop. It belongs to my uncle and . . .' The man appeared not to have heard and simply went over to one of the barber's chairs and sat in it, his hat in his lap. Norman tried desperately to continue. Moving alongside the chair he started to explain: 'Tuesdays and Wednesdays are our busy times . . . I mean, I can't close now as there'll be an early evening rush and I'm short-handed as it is.' He stopped there, quite proud of his last remark. It gave the shop the status of a *salon* – the type you got in a big city. Suddenly another thought occured to him and he smirked knowingly at the man's reflection.

'Oh, I get it. It's privacy that you want, isn't it? You're wearing a wig, aren't you?'

The man didn't react and so with a degree of confidence Norman leaned towards him. 'I've got another customer who wears a wig; it's so obvious as the glue runs down his forehead but he never lets on and I have to trim the fringe and the bits of his own hair that grow around the edges. He knows I know but he won't let . . .'

The man slowly turned his head to face him and Norman stopped speaking. It hadn't been that important anyway.

'Do you believe in UFOs?' the man asked quietly.

The sudden change of topic bewildered Norman; he had to unscramble his brain from wigs and haircuts and start again from scratch.

'Aaah,' he replied – he hoped in a knowledgeable way. 'Flying saucers and all that, well, I don't know. Some people have seen them – but not round here!' he chuckled. 'If we get an aeroplane over Grapplewick then we know the pilot's lost!' Norman had hoped that the man would laugh or at least smile, anything, in fact, other than that intense stare. He turned away and pretended to tidy away his clippers and the rest of his paraphernalia.

'I'm from another planet.'

Norman froze and his mind suddenly blanked. There weren't too many answers to that and he couldn't think of one of them, so he turned back and smiled tentatively.

'Is this for a bet?' he asked.

'Naturally you are sceptical.'

'No, no, it's not that, it's just that, er . . .' he floundered. He didn't want to upset the man and thought it would be best to keep on the right side of him and keep him talking until someone came into the shop. The door wasn't actually locked and nobody took any notice of the sign anyway, so maybe somebody would come – then he could make a run for it.

'I am from the planet Androm,' the stranger continued, 'and at present am attached to the Inter-Galactic Peacekeeping Force.'

A small worm of recollection began to turn in Norman's memory and he snapped his fingers.

'Wait a minute! Wasn't there a lot about this on the box, oh, er, a few months ago – I remember now – "UFOs are coming Wednesday" or something like that.' Norman was extremely pleased with himself. He never read the newspapers and so all his worldly knowledge came from the TV, yet it enabled him to pontificate on most subjects as he snip-snipped. Only yesterday he had been discussing the plight of lemurs in South America.

'That's right,' he continued, 'then another town got a letter – yes, I remember now, some lads went from here but only got as far as Cheadle because of the traffic. I watched it on the telly – well, we all did – but the flying saucer never came. I think three towns got this letter and then the whole thing fizzled out.'

The man nodded slowly.

'Not quite true, but close enough. Thirty-two towns received letters; they didn't keep quiet about them as we had asked, so now there will be no more correspondence. Instead, I have been despatched with our message.'

By now Norman was terrified. The man was obviously raving mad, and although he seemed quite quiet and controlled at the moment, the slightest wrong move could set him off.

41

'I was just going to make some tea. Would you like a cup?' It was an inspired question. Once in the back room where the kettle was, he'd be through the lavatory window and across the moors like a whippet. It was as if the man had read his thoughts.

'I am neither mad nor am I of this planet. This earthly human form I have assumed enables me to pass freely amongst your kind. To all intents and purposes I look human, except for my eyes.'

Norman's curiosity overcame his fear.

'Your eyes.'

He leaned forward to look more closely, they seemed to be quite ordinary. There was nothing thaaaaaat waaaaaa . . . he felt light-headed and relaxed. The man was slowly dissolving before him; no, not dissolving, changing shape, the face filling out and getting darker. His overcoat was now a brightly coloured poncho and the hat on his lap was now a small brown monkey. The man had gone and in his place was this large, jolly, black African. But no, it wasn't somebody else, it was still the man. His voice hadn't changed.

He spoke. 'Supposing my mission was to some destination in Central Africa, this is the form I would assume.'

Norman gaped, he wasn't mentally equipped to take all this in. It was one thing for some nutter to say he was a spaceman, but this was something else. The monkey regarded him solemnly.

'You like to play with him,' said the man tossing the animal over.

Norman caught the monkey, or rather it grabbed on to him and nestled in the crook of his arm, head jerking up, down and sideways, big, black, round eyes flickering, taking everything in – photos of the models on the wall, the cracks in the ceiling – then bending its head right back to examine itself in the mirror. Norman laughed and the startled monkey shot on to his shoulder and made its way round the back of his neck. He reached for it but it wasn't there, it wasn't on the bench either. He turned a complete circle but there was no sign of it. He looked quickly to the man's lap but no, just a trilby hat. He was about to look under the wash basin when the thought struck him – *a trilby hat!* He peered fearfully over his shoulder at the man sitting there, dressed as before, and the enormity of the last five minutes hit him like a runaway bus. The man had actually changed himself to a black African and back again, and in full view. He hadn't nipped behind a screen or anything. And what about the monkey? Was he a spaceman too?

42

'Are you convinced now that I possess extraordinary powers, or must I subject you to further demonstrations?'

'No, no thanks,' stammered Norman, although if this man could change into anything, he wouldn't have minded a few minutes with Dolly Parton.

The fact that he had been subjected to a sophisticated form of hypnotism never crossed his mind, indeed very few thoughts had ever made the journey and hypnosis was way down the list.

'Good,' said the man. 'Having got this far, questions about why I am here on your planet, and how, will have to be postponed for a further meeting, but everything will be explained to you in due course.'

They were interrupted by the tinkle of the shop doorbell, but Norman had forgotten all his earlier fears, and this was an intrusion. He whirled around.

'I'm sorry, sir, we're closed. What's the matter with you, can't you read?'

He pointed to the sign. It was only then he noticed the man had a white stick and he was staring vaguely at the ceiling.

'Oh, I'm sorry,' said Norman acutely embarrassed.

'That's all right,' said the blind man. 'I'd like two pounds of streaky bacon and a small brown loaf.'

Norman frowned, then smiled kindly. 'You're in the wrong place mister, this is a barber's shop.'

'It's not Smith's then?'

'No, this is Albert Waterhouse's Gents' Hairdressing.'

He didn't realise that he was now talking to the man as if he were not only blind, but four years old and deaf with it.

'Smith's is down by the traffic lights, next door to the tandoori . . .' He could have bitten off his tongue. 'I'm sorry, you won't be able to see it, but you'll be able to smell it,' he added in a sudden flash of brilliance. 'Tell you what, I'll walk you down there,' but before Norman could take the blind man's arm the alien visitor had risen from his chair and stood in front of the man, putting the palms of his hands over the man's eyes.

Norman watched with his mouth hanging open. He had a feeling he knew what was going to happen but he wasn't sure whether he'd believe it. The spaceman took his hands away and walked back a step. For a moment the blind man remained motionless, then he started to blink hard, looking around the room with growing wonder. He staggered back into a chair then bent forwards to look at himself in a mirror. Slowly turning to the spaceman he dropped to his knees, whispering, 'I can see, I can see,' in an increasingly louder voice. He took the spaceman's hand and kissed it. 'Thank you ... thank you' was all that he could say. The spaceman raised him gently to his feet and turned him towards the door.

'Smith's,' he said, 'I believe it's next to the tandoori restaurant.' Norman didn't see the man go; he was too busy staring, awe-struck, at the spaceman. If he had had any remaining doubts about him five minutes ago they had been instantly swept away, and if the spaceman were to tell him to jump off the roof, well, he'd be halfway up the stairs without a second thought.

The man put on his hat and a wave of panic hit Norman. He didn't want him to go; he might never see him again and he wanted to take him home and introduce him to his aunt and uncle. For years his Aunt Florrie had staggered around on bad legs and Norman was convinced that if the spaceman could restore a man's vision, five minutes with him and his aunt would be ready to compete in the Commonwealth Games. Again the man seemed to be reading his thoughts.

'Your uncle is the present mayor of Grapplewick,' he said.

'Yes, sir,' Norman replied with a slight bow.

The man handed him a small business card. 'You will bring him to this address at eight o'clock this evening.'

Norman looked at the neat print on the card. All it said was 'Kershaw's Croft'. He turned the card over, but there was nothing on the other side. Kershaw's Croft ... slowly he remembered – it was a tumble-down old place on Windy Moor. 'Is this the ...' he began, and looked around the shop. The man had gone, the shop door banging shut in the breeze.

Norman dashed into the street, looking up and then down, and although there were one or two people about, there was no sign of the tall, mysterious stranger. He shook his head and slowly walked back into the shop. The first thing he had to do was to contact his uncle. He dialled his number but it wasn't until the phone was ringing that the scale of what he was about to divulge hit him. He slammed the phone down in a panic. What could he say? A spaceman had just dropped in and wanted to see the two of them up at Kershaw's Croft. No; he couldn't come out with the news just like that. His uncle wasn't the most receptive person at the best of times and he seldom took a statement at face value.

44

If you told him it was raining, he would go outside to check for himself. Somehow Norman had to convince his uncle of the incredible, miraculous, fantastic happenings of the last half-hour, but at the same time it occurred to him that he and his uncle had never really had a conversation.

Norman had never known his parents, which is hardly surprising as they abandoned him when he was six months old. His mother, sickened by the vision of dullness and monotony that stretched out in front of her for the rest of her life, decided one morning that it was too great a price to pay for one night of fumbling passion in the churchyard. Tucking little Norman into the bottom drawer of a dresser that served as his cot, she wrote out her abdication letter to her husband and decamped without a backward glance. It wasn't that she was heartless, but she was fed up. Marriage hadn't stopped her husband putting it about with other women and for the past three nights he hadn't been home at all, which in retrospect wasn't surprising as he was halfway to Australia on a ten-pound assisted passage.

Thus baby Norman was left in sole charge of himself, which was an enormous responsibility for one whose only qualification in life was sucking his toe. Fortunately for Norman, just as he was beginning to feel hungry his Uncle Albert called round to see whether his brother had finished varnishing the harmonium, and that was the start of his new life with his adoptive parents. They didn't even have to change his surname, he was well looked after and, possibly because he was adopted, not much was expected of him; indeed his main achievement to date was in getting older, but now Norman felt that things were about to change. He had been hand-picked by an alien and in his bones he knew that, for him, life was just about to begin. Squaring his shoulders he dialled home again, hoping in his heart of hearts that nobody would be in to take the call. 'Hello?' said a fearful voice at the other end. It was his Aunt Florrie, who still mistrusted the telephone.

'Hello, Auntie, it's me, Norman.'

'Norman,' she replied incredulously – he didn't phone very often. 'Are you all right? Nothing's happened, has it?'

'No, everything's fine. Is me uncle there?'

'No, your uncle's not here, you should know that by now. It's Wednesday afternoon so it's his dancing lesson.'

Norman clucked his tongue. Of course, it was Wednesday and his uncle would be at Madame Lesley's. 'I forgot it was Wednesday, Auntie. Have you got Madame Lesley's number?'

'Well, I don't know, Norman. Can't it wait until he gets home?'

'No, I must speak to him now. It's urgent!'

'Well, you know best,' he heard her say as she put the phone down while she rummaged around for the number, and he wondered again what was so special about Madame Lesley's phone number that it couldn't be entered into the little address book on the hall table.

'Hello, Norman. Are you there?'

'Yes, Auntie.' He clicked the top of the pen to take down the number.

'It's Grapplewick . . .' uselessly she waited for him to write that down and, even worse, he did.

'Got that, thanks, Auntie.'

'Grapplewick 0423.'

'0423, thanks, Auntie.'

'Now, are you sure, Norman? Your uncle said he was only to be rung there if it was something very important.'

'Don't worry, Auntie. It is important, believe me.'

'It had better be, because . . . Hello? Hello?' but Norman was already dialling 0423.

Madame Lesley's Dancing Academy was originally built as a tabernacle. It was well constructed and on the outside it didn't look that different from the local library or town baths. Inside, however, it was derelict and worm-eaten and so, with a small legacy and savings scraped from years performing at music halls around the country, Madame Eunice Lesley was able to secure the freehold at a giveaway price. Turning the building into a dancing academy swallowed her remaining capital and so it was with great relief when she opened for business that she found Britain was undergoing a renaissance in ballroom dancing and everybody wanted to take classes. Soon the money would come pouring in and she wouldn't have to pass the bank on the other side of the street.

That was the theory, anyway. In actual fact Grapplewick turned out to be the only place in the country that wasn't interested in the passion of the tango or the exuberance of the quickstep. Sadly she had just one pupil, and that was a small, portly, middle-aged man. He was, however, a town councillor and so would be a useful connection for her. Unfortunately for Madame Eunice Lesley, Albert Waterhouse was the last person on earth she should have relied upon to spread the word about ballroom dancing. No way was he ever going to blab it abroad that he had a dancing lesson every Wednesday afternoon. Secretly it had always been a cherished ambition of his to be able to glide effortlessly over a ballroom floor in top hat and tails with a number on his back, but it was an ambition doomed from the start. Not only was Eunice six inches taller than him, but when they danced he held her in his arms like a guardsman presenting arms, his eyes staring fixedly at her chin as they lumbered around the hall. Eunice suffered bruised toes after every session, and even worse, she developed a rash under her chin from his brillantine.

She did, however, have a flat above the academy and on every Wednesday after the dancing lesson she would invite him upstairs for tea and cakes. Very soon this had become a regular routine and eventually the dancing was dispensed with altogether, Albert Waterhouse coming around on every Wednesday just for his tea. One thing led to another and after a few weeks they would hop into bed first and then have their tea and cakes. As he was now the mayor Albert considered it imperative that no one should find out about this enjoyable liaison. Florrie was certainly unaware of it; every week she wrapped his dancing pumps in brown paper and off he went to his lesson. It never occurred to her that after all these years at Madame Lesley's his pumps were still as good as new. Perhaps he was particularly light on his feet?

On this particular Wednesday the mayor was propped up in the large soft bed, making out his racing selections in the newspaper. Eunice, overflowing her stool, sat at her dressing table, dabbing at her eyes with a mascara brush. 'Big Jessie,' muttered the mayor almost to himself. Eunice didn't seem to hear; fastidiously she selected a chocolate from the box in front of her and popped it in her mouth. 'You what?' she said, although with her mouth crammed full of chocolate it sounded like 'Ott?'

The mayor looked over his half-moon glasses at her. Every week he bought her a half-pound box of chocolates and they never lasted more than twenty minutes. Silently the mayor thanked God that she was a dancer and not a sweet manufacturer, otherwise she'd be bankrupt within a month. Even now, with a fresh hazelnut whip in her mouth she was peering into the box, fingers wriggling, ready to pounce on the next one. 'Big Jessie,' he repeated, louder this time, 'I reckon she's worth a pound each way in the 3.30 tomorrow.' Eunice was now leaning towards her reflection in the mirror, jaws on hold while she concentrated on

47

applying her eye makeup. Satisfied, she leaned back and dabbed the corners of her mouth with a Kleenex.

'Oh, racing,' she said, 'I thought you were still on about that traffic warden.'

The strident ring of the telephone interrupted their pleasant domestic exchange. This was not unusual as people often rang to talk to Eunice, so the mayor just ignored it, turning back to his racing paper. Eunice ambled over to the bedside phone. 'Hello,' she answered uninterestedly, and then stiffened, putting her hand over the mouthpiece. 'It's for you!' she hissed. Albert stared at her with a look of incomprehension in his eyes. 'It's your nephew!'

The mayor's stomach lurched – nobody phoned him here; obviously something was wrong, something had happened to Florrie or there was some trouble at the shop. He nodded to Eunice and she took her hand away from the mouthpiece saying, 'If you want Mr Waterhouse he'll be in the ballroom. Hang on a minute and I'll put you through.' Dropping the receiver on the bed she then hurried over to put a record on to the turntable. By the time she picked up the phone again the room was filled with the sound of *La Cumparsita*. In a very posh voice she then said, 'To whom do you wish to speak to?' She listened for a moment and then replied, 'I'll get him for you.' Holding the phone at arm's length she called out, 'Mr Waterhouse, Mr Waterhouse, telephone. It's your nephew!' Albert waited a couple of seconds and then took the phone.

'Hello, Norman, what's the matter?' He stuck a finger into his ear and tried to listen, but it was hopeless. 'Hang on a minute, lad, I can't hear you – will somebody switch that damn thing off!' he yelled. Eunice, anticipating his reaction, whipped the needle off the record and in a loud voice shouted at the wall, 'Take five, everybody!' Albert winced. It sounded patently false to him, but then again, it was only Norman at the other end of the phone.

'Right, lad, now what are you ringing me here for?' He listened for a bit. 'Tonight.' He glanced over his shoulder at his pocket watch hanging on the headboard. Eunice was back at her dressing table and she seemed to be concentrating on her eyes again, but she wasn't missing a trick.

'Listen, Norman, can't it wait until tomorrow ... what do you mean, no? Who is this Mr High and Mighty? No, don't tell me over the phone. I'll see you at home in about half an hour, all right,' and with that he put the phone down and took his trousers from under the mattress.

48

'Trouble?' asked Eunice as he slipped his arms through his braces and reached under the bed for his boots.

'Now, Eunice lass, you should know better than to ask a question like that.' She shrugged her shoulders. It would have to wait until next Wednesday, but she would find out.

At home Florrie was agonising over her decision to give Norman the telephone number. She understood the need for secrecy; after all, to be taking dancing lessons at Albert's age was ludicrous anyway, but if this knowledge fell into the wrong hands it could be political dynamite. Albert had often stressed that point and Norman was daft enough to ring up just to tell him they were low on shampoo. She wished to God that she'd never given him that phone number. Florrie crossed over to the window and looked up and down the street. She noted that on the other side of the road the coal lorry was still parked at number 26. She sniffed. He must have been over at that house for about two hours now, and they hadn't even got a fireplace. She was about to drop the curtain when the bus pulled up at the stop and Albert got off. Panic fluttered in her breast – in all the years he'd been going to dancing lessons he'd never come back this early. Whatever Norman had said to him it wasn't about shampoo, so taking a deep breath she waddled over to the front door and jerked it open to let him in, but his key was already in the lock, and as it was attached to his braces she ended up hauling him indoors and they crashed down on top of each other. It was the closest they'd been in years.

'What the hell do you think you're playing at?' Albert snarled as he snatched the key out of the lock and examined his trousers to see whether there was any obvious damage.

'Did our Norman contact you?' Florrie said in reply as she picked up his brown paper parcel.

'Give us a chance to get me things off,' he said, hanging his hat and then his overcoat behind the door. It seemed to take him hours to do this and he still had his scarf on. Florrie hovered around impatiently as he took his hat down again and brushed it. The suspense was killing her; she couldn't bear it any longer.

'Well, did he ring you?'

Albert handed her his jacket. 'Yes,' he grunted, making his way straight over to the television set and switching it on. As he flopped into the high-backed chair opposite, Florrie hesitated for a

49

moment, then flounced out into the kitchen. She realised this was the end of the conversation with her husband, but she'd get the full story from Norman when he got in.

Albert stared at the TV screen. An American police car, lights flashing, sirens blaring, gunshots, but Albert wasn't really watching. His mind was elsewhere. Florrie came out of the kitchen, drying a plate.

'He said it was important so I gave him the number. I mean, what else could I do? – he said it was urgent.' She waited for Albert's response but all she could see was the back of his chair. 'I couldn't very well say no, could I?' More sirens, screeching tyres and the splintering of glass. Suddenly the chair back spoke: 'And we pay good licence money for this rubbish!'

'Well, you don't have to watch it, do you?' Florrie replied, still wiping the same plate – it was a wonder there was any pattern still left on it. 'Any road, I've got more things to do than to wait on you hand and foot and I'm going down to our Emmie's before I . . .' Her voice faded as she went back into the kitchen but Albert had every confidence that she was still talking to him. He leaned forward and changed the channel. A burst of inane studio laughter filled the room as some idiot staggered through a yard balancing a bucket on his head. Albert clucked his tongue in disgust. Outside the 6.30 pm train thundered past. Albert didn't hear it; he could feel the vibrations through his chair. Automatically he pulled out his watch and looked at it. At the same time a cold draught swept through the room followed by the sound of the front door slamming, and Norman hurried in. Again Albert lugged out his watch.

'Who's looking after the shop then?' He tapped the timepiece, mute testimony to the fact that there was still an hour and a half to go before closing time.

'Something cropped up, Uncle,' Norman said, addressing the back of the chair, although his eyes were straying sideways to the TV set. A shriek of laughter greeted him and he smiled.

'It had better be important or I'll be advertising for a new apprentice hairdresser tomorrow.'

Norman didn't hear this as he was too busy looking at the man with the bucket on his head staggering towards a large hole in the road. The mayor exploded. 'Never mind all that rubbish,' he bellowed, indicating the TV set. 'What was that phone call about?'

'Phone call?' echoed Norman vaguely. His uncle shook his head in despair.

50

'You rang me at Madame Lesley's.'

'Ah yes,' said Norman, television instantly forgotten. 'There's been a visitor at the shop.' Albert looked at him quizzically.

'It wasn't the health department again, was it?'

'Er, no, Uncle, he, well, he wasn't an ordinary visitor, he, er . . .' Norman was floundering so the mayor waited a second or two before losing his patience.

'Well come on, lad, you said it was important. Who was it?'

'He was a spaceman!' Norman blurted, blushing like a Barbara Cartland virgin. His uncle looked at him directly for a moment and then crouched forward to turn the sound up on the television. Whatever Norman was about to divulge wasn't going to be for Florrie's ears.

'What did you say?' he asked incredulously.

Norman gulped. 'He said he was from another planet.' This time the mayor put on his glasses and peered at Norman closely.

'Have you been at the conditioner again?' he asked quietly.

'It's true, Uncle, honestly!'

The lad was tremendously sincere but that didn't necessarily mean he was tremendously sane. He wondered whether there was any history of lunacy on the lad's mother's side of the family. He took off his glasses.

'I'm telling you this, Norman, so think on. If that shop isn't open in half an hour then you'll be signing on at the DSS tomorrow morning.'

Norman was desperate. 'It's no joke, Uncle. I'm telling you the truth. I saw him with my own eyes!' The mayor was silent for a moment.

'Was he collecting for anything?'

'No, nothing like that. He told me to bring you to a meeting tonight.'

Albert's eyebrows shot up. 'Oh, he did, did he? This Mr High and Mighty, who does he think he is?' He was gathering steam now. 'I'm the mayor of this town and I don't come running at anybody's beck and call. Number one in Grapplewick, that's me; I'm not a pile of horse droppings, you know.'

Norman tried to placate him. 'He knows you're the mayor, Uncle, that's why he wants to talk to you. Maybe they've been watching you for years.'

Albert was suddenly wary. As far as he could remember he had kept his nose clean, but there was always something that he could be trapped over.

'He wasn't a little fat fellow with glasses, was he?'

'No, Uncle, he's tall and there's something about him; well, you won't believe this but . . .'

'Did he have a briefcase with him?' the mayor broke in sharply.

'He didn't have anything with him – listen, he just came into the shop and sat in the chair, and with me not two feet away from him, he changed into an African Chief.'

'A blackie in my shop?' asked Albert, affronted.

Yes, and he had a –' Norman stopped suddenly. A sudden flash of insight warned him not to mention the monkey; he had just remembered his uncle's aversion to all pets. 'Then he changed back and a blind man came into the shop.'

'How do you know he was blind?'

Norman snorted. 'Because he had a white stick with him.'

It was the mayor's turn to snort. 'Well, that's nothing, is it? You can buy a white stick at a novelty shop; anybody can walk around with a white stick and get people to see 'em across the road.'

'Let me finish, Uncle, *please*!'

His uncle nodded.

'The man got up and put his hands over the blind man's eyes and he could see, I'm telling you, I've never seen anything like it!'

Albert was impressed. 'And this man wants you to bring me to a meeting tonight?'

'Yes, at eight o'clock tonight.'

Albert wasn't entirely convinced by Norman's argument. 'It sounds like a load of old cobblers to me.'

Norman was desperate – he knew he had to persuade his uncle but shifting him was like trying to empty the bath with a sieve. Then for the first time in his life he had a brainwave, and although he didn't realise it at the time, Norman was about to deliver his trump card.

'Look, Uncle,' he said, resting his hands on the arm of the chair, 'has it occurred to you that if this man has the power to bring back a man's sight, he may also have the power to take it away, so don't expect me to see you across the road when he does.' Albert looked at him sharply. 'Well, Uncle, if we upset him there's no telling what he may do.'

The mayor slumped forward with his chin in his hands, his mind racing back to the days when he was a young man working at Hobday's cotton mill. Making his way home one night he'd

52

realised he had left his money in the back pocket of his overalls. Immediately he dashed back to the mill and just made it through the gates before they were closed for the night. He ran past the lodge and along the long passage into the card room, zig-zagging between the cotton skips and machinery, when suddenly all the lights went out. He stood stock-still in the middle of the floor, paralysed. The blackness was almost physical; there hadn't been a chink of light anywhere as, being wartime, the blackout boards had been placed over the windows. For a minute or two he didn't move, panic creeping slowly and insidiously into his mind. He tried to orientate himself but he was hemmed in by the still-warm machinery, so he closed his eyes. When he reopened them it seemed even blacker than before; the darkness was so absolute he wasn't even sure whether his eyes were open or not. He heard his heart thumping and a scuffling noise that could have been mice or rats. He desperately tried to remain calm and logical, and with hands outstretched before him he inched forward only to fall into a skip half-full of cotton waste. Something ran over his hand and that was the point when he started screaming. He yelled and yelled at the top of his voice and then, by the grace of God, the lights came on. Two of the fire-watchers appeared at the far end of the hall to see what all the commotion was about. Albert had almost fainted with relief on seeing the two men; five minutes more and he would have been a total gibbering wreck. But as a result of that incident he had developed a pathological terror of losing his sight.

Albert shuddered at the recollection. 'All right, Norman, best be off; it's after seven now.' As he shrugged on his overcoat some of his old spirit returned. 'If you're wasting my time, I'll have you open all Sunday.' Norman didn't care about Sunday; once he had delivered his uncle to Kershaw's Croft it would be up to the spaceman to decide what would happen next.

'Where is this place then?' asked Albert, winding on his scarf. Norman proffered the business card the alien had left with him. 'Kershaw's Croft? But I know where that is!' he said in disbelief. 'That place has been derelict for years; it's falling down!' Suddenly another thought struck him. 'If this man is so special, why isn't he staying at the Metropole?'

'You won't listen, will you, Uncle? He's not like us!'

'Aye, and if this thing turns out to be a joke, you won't be like us neither!' his uncle retorted, and they let themselves out.

Not two minutes after they had left the house, Florrie came downstairs in her street clothes. With shrieks of canned laughter still blaring from the television, she was unaware that Norman had come in and gone out again with his uncle, leaving the house empty. 'So anyway, I'm just popping down to our Emmie's like I said, and I'll make your supper when I get back ... Oh, and tell Norman where I've gone and tell him I'll not be long – and ring Alec about that pot of paint.' She lumbered over to the front door without looking back, and let herself out. 'Well, ta-ra then,' and she was gone also.

CHAPTER

TEN

Norman and his uncle sat side by side on the otherwise empty bus. Not a word passed between them, and when they arrived at the last stop at Windy Moor they were loath to get off. The Lancashire moors can be forbidding enough during the day, but at night, anyone crossing the moors by foot is extremely uneasy – and those are the stout-hearted ones. The mayor and his nephew could hardly be put into that category. They had, however, come all this distance on a weekday, so they thought they'd best get their ordeal over and done with.

The bus driver jumped out of his cab, taking half a fag out from behind his ear. 'Camping out, are you?' he asked, cupping his hands while he lit what was left of a Woodbine.

The mayor buttoned his overcoat and tightened his scarf. A cold wind was blowing and he didn't like the driver's remark, but equally he was in no hurry to leave the friendly lights of the bus. 'Just paying a social call,' he said.

'Oh, aye. Well, there's nowt between here and Bradford.'

The mayor chuckled grimly. 'It'll be a long walk, then.' He was pleased with this comment as he prided himself on his repartee. 'Come on, Norman, let's make tracks,' and both men strode out towards a tiny pinprick of light in the dark lane. It didn't take them long to reach the streetlight, and Kershaw's Croft was another half mile or so from that point. As they looked back down the lane they saw that the bus had already left for its return journey into town. They were now well and truly marooned on the moors. As Norman turned to walk further down the lane the mayor surreptitiously picked a large stone from the wall and slipped it into his pocket. If there was going to be any trouble up at the croft he wasn't going to abide by Queensberry rules.

There were only a couple of stars twinkling in the wintry sky and when Norman and Albert reached Kershaw's Croft they could only vaguely make out its shape. 'I told you it was derelict,' wheezed Albert. The walk had left him breathless but he wasn't afraid – the stone lying heavily in his pocket gave him courage. Norman knocked hesitantly on the door but there was no response; the low keening of the wind was the only sound to break the night's silence. The noise of the wind was somehow malevolent and both men were feeling increasingly unhappy about being stranded on the moor in the middle of the night. Norman knocked again and they waited.

'I told you you were wasting your time,' said the mayor uneasily and turned to leave.

A well-modulated voice spoke.

'Please enter, gentlemen.'

Norman and Albert stood stock-still, frozen to the spot. It was Norman who recovered first. He cautiously stepped forward and was about to push the door when he noticed that it was already open. Inside, the croft appeared even darker than the moor and Norman hesitated before entering, but his uncle behind him shoved him in. 'Don't be so bloody soft, Norman,' he said. With a clomp, the croft door swung shut behind them. At the same time the place was flooded by brilliant powerful lights, and in front of them appeared a tall man.

Norman immediately recognised the man, but he was not dressed in the earthly gear that he had worn earlier that afternoon. He was now wearing a close-fitting garment made of some silvery metallic substance, the sort Norman would have expected a spaceman to wear. In fact, the man no longer looked human but more like a robot. He sat in what appeared to be a command chair. On each arm rest there were scores of different coloured buttons. Apart from the chair – or throne, to be more precise – the croft was empty and everything was white; the floor, walls and in all probability the ceiling too, only Norman found it impossible to look up into the glare of the bright lights overhead.

The man spoke. It was the same voice that had bade them enter.

'Welcome, gentlemen,' he said, 'welcome aboard Space Vehicle Limbo Two.'

The bright lights restored the mayor's confidence and now he was convinced that this was all one big joke; probably some kind of *Candid Camera* set-up. This man looked like he was part of a carnival, dressed up to look like something out of *Star Trek*.

'Never mind all that,' he started. 'I don't know what your game is, or what it is you hope to gain by it, but I'll have you know . . . have you know . . . haaaaa . . .' His voice trailed off and he stared mutely at the spaceman. Norman looked on in amazement; he'd only seen that expression on his uncle's face once, and that was on the day that Norman had come home from school to tell him he'd passed his O-levels. The spaceman stared calmly back at his uncle for a few moments and then repeated, 'Welcome aboard Space Vehicle Limbo Two.' In return the mayor beamed. He took off his hat.

'Welcome to Earth,' he replied, looking around him, 'and may I say with all humility what a great example of technicalogical gadgetry your spacecraft is.' He moved over to the wall and, bending forward, pointed at nothing, saying, 'Can you get BBC2 on that?' Norman wandered over to see what it was that his uncle was looking at, but his uncle pulled him back. 'Don't touch any of them switches.' Norman couldn't guess what his uncle was on about; to him it just looked like a blank wall. The mayor shook his head vigorously. 'And I thought this place was derelict!'

'Naturally you did,' replied the stranger. 'From the outside it is just a derelict croft, thus avoiding any suspicion that the place is anything else but that. Even you, born and bred in Grapplewick, would not have thought otherwise had you not entered at my invitation. You can see now that a space vehicle can take many different forms.'

The mayor laughed. 'I've passed this place many times. If I'd known then what I know now I would have popped in for a cup of tea!'

'Then you would have been no wiser,' replied the man; 'you would have found the inside as derelict as the exterior. Our space vehicle would have been elsewhere.'

'Of course,' nodded the mayor sagely. Norman looked on, perplexed. He knew the man was different – he'd seen that for himself – and if truth be told he even believed that the man was an alien, but he found it a little hard to swallow that Kershaw's Croft was really a space vehicle. Again, uncannily, the man seemed able to read his thoughts.

'Your face expresses doubts, my young friend.'

'No, no,' protested Norman, 'it's just that, well, they look like bare walls to me,' he finished lamely. He was surprised at his own temerity, but he'd been brought up to be honest and straightforward, and he couldn't understand why his uncle was bowing and scraping to this stranger.

The man smiled. 'I appreciate your scepticism. It's actually one of the reasons you were selected, but I must tell you that we only allow humans to see what is absolutely necessary. I have granted that power to your uncle the mayor in order that he will truly appreciate the reason for my visit. In your case it's superfluous as you have already witnessed demonstrations of my power. However, to convince you further,' he pressed several buttons on the arms of his chair, 'come.' He went over to the wall. 'Do not be alarmed at what you are about to see. You are perfectly safe.' He slid back a small panel and in the blackness beyond it Norman saw a myriad of twinkling lights. He turned to the spaceman for enlightenment. 'Don't you recognise Grapplewick from three thousand feet?' asked the alien as he slid back the panel. 'Have no fear,' he added, 'I will return you to *terra firma* in a moment and once more this ship will become Kershaw's Croft.'

Norman was staggered; he now wouldn't have minded a closer look to see whether he could spot Coldhurst Street, but a new thought pushed all others aside. 'Can you go anywhere in this?' he asked eagerly.

The man spread his arms. 'Where is anywhere? Venus, the outer galaxy, the sixteenth century, tomorrow?' Norman stared at him, aghast, and was suddenly very glad that he hadn't actually mentioned Benidorm.

'Oh, it's nothing,' he said weakly. 'It's just hard to imagine Kershaw's Croft whizzing around the world.'

'Don't be embarrassed, Norman,' said the man kindly, 'a space vehicle can take on many forms, too many for an Earth mind to comprehend. Really, though, it's very simple. Do you remember a TV series called *Doctor Who*? His space vehicle was a blue police box. We thought that was very imaginative – in fact you had us worried for a time!'

A door at the rear of the room opened and a girl stepped through. She was clad in the same material as the spaceman, only there wasn't so much of it. She actually reminded Norman of the principal boy in last year's pantomime, although this pantomime character didn't smile – she just looked straight through the two Earthlings as if they weren't there. She moved behind the spaceman's chair and put her hands on his head. He closed his eyes and a burst of indecipherable radio static filled the room. It stopped as quickly as it had begun, then the man opened his eyes and the girl stepped away from the chair.

'Good news,' he said, 'our forward party is already orbiting the sun.' Norman and the mayor looked suitably impressed. 'That was my assistant Oomi,' continued the spaceman. 'You will be meeting her again over the next few days as she will be acting on my behalf in Grapplewick.'

'Of course,' the mayor replied with a half bow, 'of course.'

The spaceman stood up. 'Now – to business!'

'Grapplewick is at your disposal,' said the mayor and Norman couldn't help but feel that his uncle was overdoing it a bit.

'Mr Mayor,' said the spaceman, ignoring the sycophancy, 'you will convene a meeting at the town hall tomorrow morning at ten o'clock. Those present will form the emergency committee; that is yourself and Councillor Butterworth, the Superintendent of Police, Mr Smith and, of course, your nephew.'

The mayor was slightly disconcerted by the inclusion of Norman; after all he was just the messenger. Why did he have to be present? He cleared his throat. 'It will be as you say, but why him?' He gestured at Norman. 'I mean, he closed early tonight and he'll be up to his eyes tomorrow, what with half term and everything, and then there's the . . .'

The alien cut him short. 'If it is so important then you will be at the shop tomorrow, not Norman. I have specific instructions for him.' The tone was hard, commanding.

'Of course,' said the mayor meekly. 'We can always say we're closed for alterations.'

'Thank you,' said the alien, his voice gentle again. 'I will see you both tomorrow at ten o'clock. In the meantime I have a small gift for you both.' Oomi came in again carrying a silver tray on which were two small round badges. The mayor took one and studied it with reverence. They looked just like ordinary badges to Norman, and on the front of them were embossed the words 'Beautiful Grapplewick'.

'Thank you, sir,' gushed the mayor. 'This town needs something like this.' He nudged Norman, who mumbled his thanks. In fact he would rather have had a spacesuit – or the console.

The alien shook his head, sensing Norman's disappointment. 'You will wear these at all times, for they are not as dull as they appear.' Norman perked up on hearing this. 'They are in fact anti-module badges and will offer you protection should our vehicles contaminate the earth on arrival. This is highly unlikely, I might add, but it's better to err on the side of caution.' Norman and his uncle couldn't get their badges on quickly enough. 'I shall look forward to seeing you tomorrow, when my mission shall be explained to you in full. Then you will learn what is expected of you.'

The mayor was about to make a farewell speech when a gust of wind blew open the door of the croft – how or why was a mystery – and once he and Norman had stepped back into the night, it slammed unaided behind them.

They stood for a moment, looking back at the dark silent shape of the croft and then set off for home, slowly at first, then gradually quickening their pace until they were both running at full speed for the sanctuary of the bus shelter. As they staggered to a stop under its welcoming roof, Norman was bending forward with his hands on his knees, trying to catch his breath. His uncle was in a worse state, hugging the lamp post for support and struggling to breathe. He rasped and retched in a desperate effort to fill his lungs with sweet cold air.

'Are you OK, Uncle?' gasped Norman. The mayor didn't reply; he couldn't, he just waved his hand and pointed to his chest to signify that as soon as he'd sorted out his respiratory system and had recovered enough to stand upright, he'd speak.

'Now do you believe me?' cried Norman, wiping his nose with the back of his hand.

The mayor reached out and patted the boy's shoulder. 'Norman,' he began, 'we've seen some things tonight.' He stopped and gathered his breath for the rest of the sentence. 'We've seen things tonight that are beyond human comprehension.' Norman nodded and looked back fearfully in the direction of the croft, but he could see nothing in the darkness. Anyway, maybe the croft was no longer there – it could be hovering over Grapplewick again, or it may have even gone back to the sixteenth century. He shuddered.

Simultaneously, Norman and the mayor saw the bobbing headlights of the bus as it made its way up the hill and juddered to a halt by the stop. They boarded it in silence.

During the return journey Norman imagined himself in control of Space Vehicle Limbo Two. He'd spend a week or so in Spain and then on the way back he'd press a button for a week ago and nobody would even know that he'd been away. His uncle, meanwhile, pondered on more down-to-earth matters: how was he go-

60

ing to convene a meeting at such short notice? How could he impress upon such cretins as Councillor Butterworth and the unimaginative Police Superintendent the importance of the meeting, and what on earth could he tell them over the phone? In the end he decided that the less that was said, the better. He'd leave it up to the spaceman to explain it all tomorrow. In fact he wouldn't mention the word 'spaceman' at all on the phone; he'd say that a Very Important Person had come a long way with the express purpose of divulging information which could be of benefit to them all – yes, that was it, that was the clincher. If he mentioned the word 'benefit' then wild horses wouldn't keep them away . . . and he was right.

CHAPTER

ELEVEN

Councillor Arnold Butterworth was the leader of the opposition in Grapplewick, staunch Labour, somewhere to the left of Stalin. He believed passionately that all workers were downtrodden and that the sooner they all united and marched forward, the better the world would be – as long as he was in charge. It came, therefore, as a complete surprise to him to receive a phone call from the mayor who, being a right-wing fascist, had never spoken a word to him outside the line of duty. Butterworth's first reaction on being called to the meeting was to tell the mayor to get stuffed but, on reflection, he was intrigued by the fact that the Conservative leader would not be present and that the superintendent would. Perhaps the matter was a criminal one, involving the leader of the council.

Butterworth's mind was working overtime as he dodged in and out of the pedestrians ambling, grey-faced, up and down the high street. Suddenly he paused. Maybe the criminal matter involved himself; what about that free fact-finding mission to Romania? After two weeks living the life of Riley, he had come back eulogising the Romanian regime. Six weeks later they had executed his host together with his wife. No, it couldn't be that. He hadn't signed anything, and Romania was now old news, but all the same he doubled his pace, holding on to his trilby when a strong gust of wind tried to tear it from his head. He bounded up the town hall steps into the quiet sanctuary of the main hall.

'Morning, Councillor Butterworth,' said the town clerk. Grapplewick was an urban parish council and still retained some of the old titles. Butterworth, as he always did, ignored the clerk – another right-wing lackey – but his scowl faded as he spotted Mrs Dobson, one of the council cleaners, on her knees scrubbing the floor. He felt an overwhelming urge to give that ample behind a playful smack – why shouldn't he? Other people did, but he had never really had the courage. In any case, on hearing his footsteps she straightened up and moved her bucket so that he could pass.

'Morning, Mrs Dobson.' He smiled and raised his hat.

'Morning, Mr Butterworth, a right procession passing through here today.'

'Oh, yes,' he replied, a touch smugly. 'Important meetings you know, no rest for the wicked.' He allowed himself a sideways glance at her. Big she might be, but well formed, and although she was married with a young son she still dispensed her favours when her old man was on nights.

Mrs Dobson nodded up the stairs. 'They're in the mayor's office, been there half an hour I reckon!'

'Half an hour!' he repeated, annoyed. Trust them, he thought, the meeting had been called for ten and it was only five to now so they must have come in early to discuss something privately, without him being there. And why was Norman present? Maybe he was an independent witness to whatever it was the council was going to charge him with. He nodded at Mrs Dobson and ran up the marble steps.

The town clerk sauntered over to Mrs Dobson. 'He looks like someone in a hurry,' he said.

Mrs Dobson wrung out her cloth into a bucket. 'He always is,' she said enigmatically and the town clerk felt a twinge of jealousy as he looked at the retreating form of the Labour councillor. He looked again at Mrs Dobson. She couldn't be having it off with him as well, could she? He dismissed the thought instantly. She wasn't that hard up.

Butterworth strode into the mayor's office. 'I'm not late, am I?' he said as he took off his overcoat. Everybody looked at him but no one said a word. 'What's all this about then?' he continued as he took off his hat and scarf. The superintendent was busily writing in his notebook but he broke off long enough to say, 'Not now, we're busy.'

Butterworth was mortified; he was, after all, leader of the opposition and not some snotty-nosed kid from Northmoor Street.

'Go on, lad,' the superintendent was saying to Norman, 'describe him.'

Norman shrugged. 'Well, he was in and out like, and he asked for a pound of streaky bacon, and when we found out he couldn't see, the man put his hands over his face and that was it, he had his sight back.'

The superintendent stared at the ceiling in exasperation. 'Yes, yes, you've told us all that,' he said. 'He was blind, OK, I've got that. Now, what did he look like?'

Norman screwed up his face in concentration. 'Well, he was, er ... I'm sorry, I wasn't paying much attention to him. I was watching the spaceman.'

'Spaceman,' Butterworth interrupted sharply but the superintendent waved at him to keep silent and leaned towards Norman, struggling to keep his temper.

'How tall was he, was he white, short, fat, thin, medium?'

'Yes, I think so,' said Norman unhappily and the superintendent slammed his notebook on to the table, muttering through clenched teeth, 'It's like talking to a cushion!'

'What's all this about a spaceman?' Butterworth persisted.

In response, the mayor began to recount the remarkable events of the previous day, but as he spoke the town hall clock boomed out the hour of ten o'clock and they all moved across to the window overlooking the high street to watch the arrival – all, that is, except Norman whose eyes were fixed firmly on the grey skies. The superintendent spotted this and shook his head in disgust – was the lad really expecting to see Kershaw's Croft circling the town prior to landing in the town hall car park? The others were eagerly craning forward as a bus pulled up, but only two people got off, and unless he'd transformed himself into a geriatric, the spaceman wasn't one of them.

The last stroke of ten passed unnoticed but behind them came a voice: 'Good morning, gentlemen.'

They whirled round and stared at the man, slack jawed. It was uncanny, they hadn't even heard him close the door.

'Good morning,' said the mayor, finding his voice. 'Ha, ha, bang on time.' He nervously 'ha-ha'd' again.

Superintendent Smith pulled himself together and looked at the man with a policeman's eye: about six foot, mid-fifties, white, Caucasian, or perhaps not; a man who would fit into any of the major capitals of the world, but here in Grapplewick he stuck out like a twenty-carat diamond in a Nubian's belly button.

The man spoke as he was taking off his hat and gloves. 'Please be seated, gentlemen.'

They scrabbled for seats. 'Just like musical chairs,' thought the policeman wryly. He remained standing; nobody was going to tell him when to sit down on his own manor. The man regarded him coolly, and the superintendent sat, knowing he'd lost the first round.

'I will be as brief as I can,' said the man. 'Unfortunately, I have a luncheon appointment on the other side of the world – Brazil to be exact.'

The mayor glanced at the superintendent who winked back at him: he could easily check the airports. Norman stared at the man incredulously. He didn't doubt for a moment that the man was having lunch in South America. He was visualising Kershaw's Croft hurtling across the Atlantic. In the distance a train whistled and as the mayor automatically reached for his watch the man spoke again.

'No need for introductions, I know who you are. As for myself, I am at present a member of the Inter-Galactic Peacekeeping Force, representing many planets in the solar system, or to put it crudely in your language, I am a spaceman.'

The superintendent raised an eyebrow and studied the man with that particular policeman's look that would have made George Washington wonder if he really had chopped down a tree. Butterworth, however, not having been fully briefed on the previous day's events, threw down his pencil on his doodle pad and cleared his throat. The man only held up his hand and whatever objections the councillor had been about to raise remained unspoken.

'Yes,' continued the spaceman, 'I am from the planet Androm. This you will believe in due course, but as time is short I'll get straight to the point.' Norman and his uncle leaned forward eagerly but Superintendent Smith lolled back in his chair, waiting to be presented with the evidence.

'I have to warn you, gentlemen, that although your planet Earth is but a speck in the cosmos, it is important in its strategic position.' The mayor nodded wisely as if astronomy was an open book to him. 'Many thousands of years ago you Earth people dabbled with nuclear fission, and with catastrophic results. Your illustrious ancestors succeeded in destroying each other, along with all other life forms on your planet. Not a tree, not a river or ocean remained. You were, in effect, a ball of dust, and may I say, in all modesty, that it was due only to our swift actions that we were able to maintain the rotation of this galaxy.'

'How do you know all this?' quizzed the superintendent.

'I know because I was in charge of that particular operation,' replied the man coolly.

There was stunned silence around the room, broken finally by the superintendent, who now felt he had enough evidence at least to have this nutter certified. 'You must be getting on a bit,' he sniffed.

The man appeared not to notice the sarcasm. 'Our intellect does not wither; we merely change the casing when necessary.' The mayor was impressed; he wouldn't mind a body transplant although he was pretty sure Eunice would get a shock.

'To continue,' said the man, 'it was essential to maintain life forms on earth. A repeat of the fate which befell the planet Mars would have been disastrous. Therefore, after carefully monitoring radiation levels across your world, we were able to drain off the excess and create new life on the planet.'

This was proving to be too much for Councillor Butterworth's socialist philosophy. 'All right then,' he challenged; 'if you recreated humans, why did you make them black, white, yellow, red? Why did you give them different lifestyles, different languages, why did you make a few rich, them that feed off the workers . . .'

The man suddenly slapped his hand on the table and Butterworth stopped in mid-sentence as if someone had cut out his tongue. 'I'm not here to defend our motives,' replied the man curtly, 'but in order to satisfy your curiosity, it was an experiment which unfortunately didn't turn out as we had hoped. It might have gone better had we not, in our generosity, granted you free will.'

'Free will!' spluttered Butterworth. 'Who d'you think you are, God?'

The man smiled for the first time. 'Ah yes, God. He was one of our better ideas.' The gathering around the table stared at him in stunned amazement – even Butterworth, who was a staunch atheist, was taken aback by such blasphemy, especially coming from an alien. The man sighed as if he'd just asked them to add up two plus two.

'Yes, God,' he mused. 'Brilliant in its conception, a God with no shape or form, God, the ultimate deterrent, the guider and provider. Sadly, as with all good ideas, the concept of God was plagiarised by intellectuals in order to assume their dominance over more simple minds. Swayed by the powerful, you created your own gods of the elements and when they proved insufficient you built idols of stone and wood. Even now in some parts of the world there are people who worship beasts. You, in your enlightened state, ridicule these fetishes of backward nations when

66

you yourselves have created new, less worthy gods – the gods of money, possession and pleasure, which in themselves are evil when pursued to the detriment of others!'

There was an uncomfortable silence around the table as they accepted the truth of his words, but equally they hadn't gathered here in the early morning to be lectured; they were busy people and he hadn't told them anything that they couldn't have read in a church magazine. The superintendent cleared his throat.

'Forgive us misguided mortals,' he began, 'but if I read you right, your presence here seems to be of great importance, not just to our small town but to the whole world, so why are you telling us all this, and what do you want from us?'

'I will explain in due course,' said the man, 'but first I must make clear to you all the urgency of our mission. You Earth people have again reached the same dangerously high level of nuclear development. I'm not talking just about the superpowers but the smaller Middle Eastern nations as well. Nuclear arsenals are being stockpiled and unless we intervene, humans may once again unleash a holocaust that even we wouldn't have the resources to repair.'

The superintendent shifted uneasily in his seat. 'With all due respect, Mr ... whatever your name is ... we're not entirely ignorant of the situation. Great Britain, Russia, the USA and others are all monitoring each other's nuclear capabilities as well as those of the Third World nations. What I want to know is why you're not talking to those countries' leaders. Why us here in Grapplewick?' The mayor nodded in agreement and the committee turned as one to face the spaceman.

'We already have,' he replied, 'and not just once but many times. Yes, even with Stalin in his day as well as Churchill, Truman, Kennedy, Thatcher and many others.'

'And they didn't believe you?'

'Oh yes, they believed us and wholeheartedly agreed with us, but then – as is the case now – no one wants to be the first to make a move. Ironically, they trust us but are deeply suspicious of each other.'

Norman felt that it was now time that he spoke. He had never been to a grown-up meeting before, but he didn't want the others to know that. 'Excuse me,' he started, 'but why are you telling us all this?'

'Because,' answered the alien slowly, 'one of our space vehicles will be landing here next Wednesday.'

They were dumbstruck. Four mouths fell open like a choir on television with the sound off. A trickle of saliva rolled down the mayor's chin and he wiped it away with his hand.

'Here?' he gasped.

'Just outside the town on a site you call Sagbottom's Acres.'

Enlightenment dawned on the superintendent's face.

'Wait a minute, aren't you the nutcase who's been sending letters every fortnight to various town councils?'

Butterworth nodded eagerly. 'That's right, UFOs have been threatening to come for about a year now, and always on a Wednesday, too.'

The man studied him for a moment.

'I did not write the letters personally, but yes they were sanctioned by my department. Sadly, on each occasion the letters marked "Strictly Private and Confidential" were leaked to the press and higher authority, resulting in devastating public curiosity. In the circumstances, it was therefore impossible to permit our vehicles to land to a pop star's reception. The success of our mission depends on absolute secrecy.'

Superintendent Smith had heard enough and felt a warm feeling of elation. Any information regarding the letters was to be forwarded immediately to Scotland Yard, and he not only had information, he had the squire responsible, game, set and match. He began to develop his case.

'Let's look at a few facts, shall we?' he said, leaning his hands on the table. 'You sit there and tell us you're a spaceman, no papers or identification. That's just for openers. Secondly, we're expected to believe that a spaceship will be coming here next Wednesday.'

He strolled over to the window and looked out.

'Take yesterday for instance. You walk into a barber's shop and hypnotise *him*,' he turned and pointed dramatically at Norman. 'Just look at him, I ask you, anybody could put him under. He walks around in a trance most of the time anyway.'

Norman blushed. 'Oh yes,' he blurted, 'and what about the blind man then?'

'Oh, the blind man,' retorted the superintendent. 'Well, we've only got your word for that, haven't we?' He turned triumphantly to the man. 'And now, sir, I think you have a bit of explaining to do and I must ask you to accompany . . .'

The mayor interrupted him.

68

'Hang on a minute, Wilfred, why don't we hear what he's got to say first? After all, the other towns only got letters but we've been honoured by a personal visit.'

The superintendent turned and surveyed him with raised eyebrow. The mayor fidgeted uncomfortably.

'All right, all right, so he hypnotised me in Kershaw's Croft . . . I was tired,' he added lamely.

Norman sprang to his defence. 'He didn't hypnotise me, and I saw Grapplewick through the window.'

Superintendent Smith snorted, 'If he'd said it was Father Christmas's workshop you'd have believed him.'

The spaceman was unperturbed. 'Superintendent,' he said softly, 'would you do me the courtesy of going back to the window?'

The policeman stared at him quizzically, then did as he was asked.

'Fifty yards down the high street a woman is looking into a bicycle repair shop window.'

The superintendent searched for a moment. 'I see her, an Indian woman.'

'She is actually from Hyderabad, but no matter.'

The others, unable to contain their curiosity, joined the superintendent at the window.

'You will also notice that she is pregnant.'

'Well gone,' added the mayor, craning his neck over Norman's shoulder.

'Either that or she's been doing a fair bit of shoplifting,' smirked the superintendent. Then a sudden realisation hit him. He whirled around to face the spaceman and confirmed that from where he was sitting there was no way he could see even the rooftops opposite, let alone down into the street.

'Watch her carefully,' said the man. 'She appears to be healthy, but observe now how she staggers and clutches the wall for support. She's now collapsed.'

They stared down, fascinated, as the colourful sari crumpled into a heap on the pavement. A young woman rushed across to help; she was followed by an elderly man and very soon a knot of people had gathered around the fallen woman. Together they carried her into the bicycle shop.

'Call an ambulance,' ordered the superintendent.

'It's not necessary. The people in the shop are already calling the hospital.'

'Is she having the baby?' asked Norman.

'Alas, no,' replied the man quietly. 'In five minutes she will be dead.'

Horrified, they all turned towards him.

'Dead?' repeated Butterworth incredulously.

The man spread his hands. 'You are the judges. Shall she live, or will she die?'

'Us,' whispered Norman through dry lips. 'What can we do?'

'I have the power of life and death,' said the man, 'but her fate depends on your verdict.'

Uncomprehending, they stared at each other.

'You have three minutes left, gentlemen.'

'Live,' shrieked Norman and the others nodded hurriedly in agreement.

'So be it,' said the man. 'Please continue to watch the shop.'

They all turned back to the window. A few seconds later the sari-clad woman walked out of the shop into the street, obviously reassuring the people around her, and a policeman who had now arrived, that she was all right. The policeman spoke into his radio, perhaps to cancel the ambulance. Superintendent Smith made a mental note to quiz the constable later when he returned to the station.

'As you have just witnessed,' said the man, 'the woman is now as healthy as she was before she took that turn, and her son will be born in six weeks' time.'

Totally impressed, the committee returned slowly to the table and sat down again. They were beginning to believe in the awesome power of the man in front of them.

Outside the mayor's office in the body of the town hall there were the usual queues of people, mainly elderly folk enquiring about the rates, disability allowances and old-age pensions but there were also one or two younger people there, worried about housing. Mrs Dobson, along with Cissie, another cleaner, was now scrubbing away at the corridor not too far away from the mayor's office. Anybody watching them would have surely noticed that they had been scrubbing and polishing the same small area of corridor for the past twenty minutes. The town clerk paced the same corridor with a piece of paper in his hand, ostensibly for the mayor. He paused every so often outside the mayor's office door, desperate to know what the meeting was about. He'd tried going into the office next door and putting a glass against the wall but that was a pointless exercise; the Victorians had built their town halls to last and a cheap glass was no match for the thick stone walls holding the rooms up. The investigation as to what was going on in the mayor's office was therefore left to the cleaners.

Cissie leaned over to her friend. 'Are you positive that's the same man?'

Mrs Dobson nodded. 'I am that, it's the same one all right. I'd recognise his shoes anywhere – you won't find another pair like that in Grapplewick.'

Cissie was convinced. Mrs Dobson was something of an expert on footwear as she spent so much of her time on her knees. Scrubbing the floors all day she had the opportunity to study many pairs of shoes as they walked in and out of the town hall.

Mrs Dobson continued, 'I'd know that man anywhere; like I said, I was in the barber's with our Jack when he came in. I never saw his face but I noticed his shoes when I run out!'

'What's he doing in here then?'

Mrs Dobson leaned on her bucket and shrugged, then she looked over to where the town clerk was pretending to pick up his piece of paper outside the mayor's door. She winked at Cissie. 'I'll soon find out,' she promised. Tiptoeing up to the unsuspecting clerk, she quickly goosed him.

'Oh!' he shrieked and immediately clasped his hand over his mouth. Cissie giggled into her bucket as he whirled around to face Mrs Dobson. OK, so he'd been to bed with her a couple of times, but that didn't entitle her to that sort of familiarity, and certainly not in the town hall. He really didn't know what attitude to take. If he smiled and passed it off as a joke then he would be undermining his authority, but on the other hand if he was stern and rebuked her, it could be the end of his carnal pleasures. Before he could decide on which course to take, Mrs Dobson spoke.

'Tom's on nights again,' she said in a little girl voice. The clerk gulped. Under that floral pinny and those thick stockings, she was all woman.

'Same time?' he croaked and she nodded.

'I'll leave the door on the latch. By the way, what are they talking about in there?' she added as an afterthought. 'You're the town clerk. You should be in there with them.'

She was right. As he was virtually the chief executive of this place it was his duty to know what was going on in every meeting and he was dying to know what was going on in this one. 'I can't

71

just barge in,' he said, 'it's a private meeting.' Mrs Dobson sniffed, and the way she sniffed somehow affronted the clerk's manhood and pride. 'Tell you what,' he went on, 'you keep your eyes open and see that nobody comes up the stairs or around that corner. If they do, then cough loudly.'

Mrs Dobson scuttled back to Cissie.

'What's going on in there then?' asked Cissie.

Mrs Dobson leaned over and whispered in her ear. 'I'll tell you tomorrow,' she promised. 'Now take your bucket over there and keep your eyes peeled on the corridor. If anyone comes, cough.'

Cissie gave a practice cough and carrying her cleaning accoutrements she ambled down to the far end of the corridor. Taking up her new position she glanced over at the town clerk, who was standing rather undecidedly outside the mayor's office. She hissed and when he turned to look at her she put her index finger and thumb together and peered through them. He nodded eagerly, taking the hint, and bent down to the keyhole. He couldn't see very much as the man talking had his back to him, so he put his ear to the keyhole instead, and listened.

'When our space vehicle lands on Wednesday, you will be introduced to your teachers.'

Norman immediately visualised a teacher coming down a ramp from the spaceship, wearing a tweed jacket with leather patches at the elbows and smoking a pipe. He blinked rapidly and turned his attention back to what the man was saying.

'Four vehicles will land throughout the world. They won't land in the capital cities of the world but in humble locations such as yours. Once they have landed, the teachers will train the future governments, which will consist of ordinary people selected much as you have been selected.' He paused. 'Is that clear so far?' Everybody nodded in assent, although if truth be told, what the alien was saying was well beyond their comprehension.

The mayor took the opportunity to speak out loud. 'On behalf of Grapplewick Council, may I say how honoured we are by this undoubted faith you place in our stumbling abilities. Please rest assured that we will do all in our power to assist you in your endeavours.' Butterworth patted the table in agreement and the superintendent nodded.

The man continued. 'So far so good. Planet Earth will be divided into four sections, which means that you will be responsible for one quarter of the world and its population.'

A shockwave ran through the room and at the keyhole the town clerk paled.

'One quarter of the world and its population,' repeated the man. They looked at each other in dismay.

'But that's just not possible!' blurted the mayor. 'I mean, we don't mind helping out but, er, with all due respect we haven't got the office space or the staff; we're up to our eyes in administration as it is!'

Butterworth nodded gravely in agreement. 'We've a housing list that's as long as your arm, and that's just here in this small town. We certainly couldn't cope with a few more hundred million homeless.'

The man shook his head slowly. 'Your agitation is natural but you need have no fear. Your positions in the new government will depend entirely on the good sense of your President, who will guide and educate you.'

'You will be our President?' asked the superintendent.

'Alas, no,' replied the man, 'after Wednesday my work here will be done. Your new President, however, is sitting here at this table.'

They gaped at him, each one hoping beyond hope that they were not to be the chosen one, the scale of the responsibility being way beyond even their combined abilities. Grapplewick was one thing but this was a whole new international ball game.

Finally, after surveying them all silently, the man spoke. 'Norman Waterhouse will be our representative here on Earth. I give you . . . your President!'

This announcement was greeted with stunned silence. This lasted just a second and then Butterworth exploded.

'Now I know this is a joke,' he snarled. He was so angry with himself for being taken in by this man. All thoughts of the pregnant Indian woman had vanished from his mind. '*Him*,' he said scornfully. 'President of one quarter of the world, yet he's as thick as two planks. He hasn't even got the brains of a two-year-old!'

Norman shot back without thinking, 'I have!'

The mayor pulled Norman back on to his seat. 'I have to agree with Councillor Butterworth,' he said. 'I've brought Norman up so I know. He's a good lad but he's not really fitted for high office, or even office come to that.'

The man continued as if there had been no interruption. 'All frontiers, all country boundaries will be dismantled. There will be

73

one common language throughout the world, and all the people will be governed by one law!'

The superintendent, whose enthusiasm for the new Jerusalem had slightly waned once he had learned that Norman was to be its President, decided to add his fourpence-worth. 'It's a sensible philosophy, and one – I may add – which would make my job much easier. But there's one thing that bothers me – why him?' He nodded his head at Norman. 'He's only a lad and all he knows is hairdressing, and quite frankly, I wouldn't trust him to mow my lawn.'

Norman was quick to defend himself. 'How would you know? You don't come into my shop any more!'

'Not since I had that rash!' replied the policeman hotly.

The spaceman held up his hands and the argument subsided with ill grace.

'Since the barber's shop seems to have become a bone of contention I shall remove it.' He put his fingers to his temples and closed his eyes. They waited apprehensively but after thirty seconds he relaxed and a collective sigh went around the room. They hadn't realised they had all been holding their breath in anticipation. They waited for an explanation but none was forthcoming. The man simply sat in silence. The mayor made a move to speak but the man shook his head. Again they waited, and then, faintly, from somewhere down the high street, they heard a siren. In a body they rushed to the window just in time to see a fire appliance approaching erratically through the traffic. The noise of the siren reached a crescendo and then receded rapidly as it turned sharp left into a side road.

'It's going up Coldhurst Street!' cried Norman. The mayor nodded sickly in agreement. He had a feeling he knew exactly where it was going.

The superintendent commented drily, 'That wasn't one of our fire tenders. That one was from Manchester.' All heads swivelled as they heard the tinny *clamballang* of a bell getting louder as it fussed past a cyclist before grinding round a corner in the wake of its big brother.

'That's ours,' confirmed the superintendent. He turned to look at the man with a new regard. If the fire was where he thought it was, then this man obviously did possess powers that were beyond the understanding of mere mortals.

The strident ring of the telephone broke the silence and they all jumped as if some puppeteer had jerked all their strings at the same time. They stared at the instrument for a moment, ring ring . . . ring ring. The mayor pulled himself together, walked slowly towards it and lifted the receiver. It could have been Neville Chamberlain expecting a call from Hitler. He nodded a couple of times and then said sadly, 'Gutted . . . you mean gutted completely. Yes, yes, I see. Well, thank you, Mervyn.' He put down the receiver and looked at the man in awe. 'My shop has been gutted,' he said with wonder.

The superintendent put a hand on his shoulder. 'Easy, lad. Come on, Albert, sit down.' The mayor did as he was told in an obvious state of shock.

The man, however, was relentless. 'Your shop is nothing compared to the safety of the solar system, and having to listen to your petty wrangling, my patience is rapidly becoming exhausted. Now, do I continue or do I bestow the fate of your shop upon the whole of Grapplewick? It's of no concern to me to raze this place to the ground and all the people with it.'

They stared at the man, aghast. 'Eighty thousand people,' whispered the mayor.

'As with the lady from Hyderabad, their fate is in your hands. Our space vehicle would encounter no difficulty in landing in the blackened hole that once was Grapplewick.'

They were appalled. The mayor's shop was one thing and the death of the lady from Hyderabad would not have been cataclysmic, but the whole of Grapplewick and its people? What sort of man could do something like this? He was certainly not of this world – they had all witnessed demonstrations of his awesome power – and all lingering doubts had been swept away. Nobody was prepared to speak. There wasn't a coherent thought between the four of them.

The man surveyed them contemptuously. 'Well, gentlemen,' he said, 'do I have your full cooperation?' Nobody moved. They were all shell-shocked. The man sighed. 'Please remember, if it does become necessary to erase Grapplewick, you four will be spared, not out of generosity on our part but so that you can live out the rest of your days with the deaths of eighty thousard people on your consciences.'

By now the committee of four was very afraid, and totally convinced of the spaceman's omnipotence.

'We are your humble servants,' whispered the mayor, looking down on the table top. 'You have only to command.'

The man nodded briefly. 'In order to ease your minds as to Norman's suitability to carry out the presidential tasks ahead of him, I will ask one question. Can any of you tell me the correct definition of "geopotential"?' The mayor, councillor and policeman shrugged their shoulders, utterly baffled. 'Geopotential' was not a word frequently bandied about in Grapplewick, and in any case their minds were still caught up in the events of the past few minutes. They couldn't think straight. The man waited, and when he was satisfied that no answer was forthcoming, he turned to Norman. 'Geopotential?' he asked.

Without hesitation Norman rapidly replied, 'The geopotential is the potential energy of a unit mass with reference to sea level.' He paused to see whether his answer would suffice.

'Go on,' urged the man.

Norman smiled as if further elucidation was unnecessary, then continued. 'Surfaces of constant geopotential, or level surfaces, are fixed in space and may therefore be used as a scale to measure height, and the common unit of measure is the dynamic metre.' Finished, he slowly looked around at his audience.

'By jingo, Norman,' said the mayor, 'you're a bit of a dark horse.'

His nephew smiled shyly. 'By the way, for an average value of the gravitational constant, the dynamic metre is equal to approximately 1.02 metric metres.'

The man spread his hands. 'You have given the correct answer. Alas, I am clumsy, but when the teachers arrive they will educate the extremely fertile mind of this boy.'

Butterworth raised his hand to be allowed to speak. 'Excuse me, sir, but how many years will this education take?'

'One hour,' replied the man calmly. Butterworth whistled silently and they all looked at Norman with a new respect in their eyes. Norman was embarrassed; for the life of him he couldn't understand their change of attitude towards him. They were all staring at him with undisguised admiration. Was it something he had said, or was it something he had done? He couldn't recollect having said anything startling at all.

'You may well be wondering how we will effect these world changes,' said the man, and their attention was turned from Norman back to him. They all nodded, although the thought hadn't occurred to any of them. 'Firstly, on the arrival of our space vehicle, your planet will be bombarded with hypergalactic rays which will immediately suspend all life.'

76

This was greeted by unanimous incomprehension. The man sighed again. 'To make it easier for all of you to understand the new regime, all thoughts will be blotted out and all minds erased, to accommodate the new thinking. Whatever people were before exposure to the rays will be expunged, and incidentally, this time around everybody will be the same colour.'

'Thank heavens for that,' sighed the superintendent, 'I've got used to being white.'

'On the contrary,' said the man. 'You will all be black.'

Again they were fearful.

'Do not be afraid. When the effects of the rays have worn off it will be as if nothing had ever happened. You will not remember that once there were different coloured people, and as I said before, there will also be only one language. In effect, gentlemen, the new history of Earth will begin on Wednesday!' He pushed back his chair and rose. 'For your final instructions, the arrival of the space vehicle will be heralded by two sonic booms. These will alert you on Wednesday evening that the space vehicle's arrival is imminent, and the four of you should make your way to Sagbottom's Acres to greet your teachers. I repeat, only the four of you will assemble. Should there be any more present then I will know at once that secrecy has not been maintained, as I've demanded. Do I have your word, gentlemen, that what has been discussed in this room will remain locked in your hearts?'

They readily agreed, but all they really understood of the meeting was that on Wednesday evening a spacecraft would be landing in Sagbottom's Acres, and that wild horses wouldn't drag this information out of them.

As he stood up to leave, the man turned to Norman. 'I see you are not wearing your badge,' he admonished. Norman smiled and turned over his lapel to show that it was pinned to the underside of his jacket. The mayor showed that he had done likewise. The man shook his head. 'It is necessary to display these badges for all to see as they have no power whilst hidden.' Both Norman and his uncle hurriedly pinned them to the front of their jackets. The man continued, 'And I have badges for the two of you.' He handed them to the superintendent and Councillor Butterworth.

The superintendent took his badge over to the window in order to study it in greater detail. ' "Beautiful Grapplewick," ' he muttered. The mayor joined him by the window and explained the badges' unusual properties. Superintendent Smith was impressed.

77

An hour ago he would have tossed the badge into the bin without a second thought, but not now. Had he been given a pair of flippers he would have put them on over his shoes before flapping his way back to the station.

'Thank you, sir . . .' he turned to say, but the man was no longer there. They looked at one another in amazement. 'I didn't hear him close the door, did you?'

They walked slowly back to the table, totally drained, stripped of reason. If someone had walked in and announced that they were all to be shot immediately, they would have meekly lined up against the wall. Minutes ticked by and still nobody spoke. The superintendent lowered himself into a chair and stared unseeingly at his anti-module badge. Norman, with the resilience of the young, was the first to break the silence. 'Why the secrecy?'

They all stared at him as though he were mad. They didn't want to discuss the matter any further. In fact they didn't even want to leave the room and the security of each other – ever. Still Norman persisted. 'Everything that man said seems logical, although upsetting in its own way, but why keep it a secret? Surely the people of Earth have a right to know what's going to happen; what harm would it do to tell them?'

The superintendent's eyes widened. Could this be the same lad who was fully conversant with the intricacies of geopotential? He rose and placed his hands on the table in order to lean over so that his face was close to Norman's. 'I'll tell you why it has to be a secret, sunshine. If what we've just heard in this room went public, then there would be panic in the streets; mayhem.' He pointed to the window. 'What would happen out there would make the war in Bosnia look like a vicars' picnic; cars overturned, looting and . . . Gordon Bennett . . . it would be no good looking at me to sort things out as I don't have enough men under my command to contain it. By the time the military got here, well . . .' He left the sentence unfinished.

Norman remained unimpressed. 'Well, that's just your opinion, isn't it? Why should people panic? We're not panicking, are we?'

He looked around for support but there was none. The mayor smiled sadly, shaking his head at the naivety of youth. 'We're not panicking, Norman,' he said in a calm, reasonable voice, 'because we're all mature people who can be told these things and as rational human beings we can accept them for what they are.'

Butterworth nodded. 'The mayor's right, Norman. That's why

we're the elders of the town council. We're not your average Herbert walking the streets out there.' He nodded out the window to the great beyond. 'Out there, lad, it's a jungle, or a tinderbox. One spark like this and we're all gone. Oh yes, lad, make no mistake about it. If they had an inkling that civilisation as we know it will be finished on Wednesday, why, there'd be a bloodbath . . . It'd be . . . well . . . Goodnight, Vienna!'

Superintendent Smith moved away from the table. 'So you see now why it's imperative that we keep the secret.'

Norman nodded submissively. This little exchange had expelled from their minds some of the horror of the past hour just as a toffee will pacify a bawling infant. In reality, the man had asked nothing of them other than to keep a secret, and the more they thought about it the more relieved they felt. Really, there was no difficulty in keeping the knowledge to themselves. If the aliens did arrive on Wednesday, then no doubt the alien teachers would congratulate them on having kept the secret safe. If on the other hand it turned out to be some gigantic hoax then nobody would be any the wiser. Oh yes, the sun was definitely out again. Indeed they were well on the way to dismissing the awe-inspiring events of the morning as a bad dream.

Their complacency, however, would have gone straight out of the window had they known that already there was a leak. The town clerk had heard enough at the keyhole to tighten his bowels. He would have stayed for more if he hadn't had to scuttle stiff-legged to the toilet, so unfortunately he didn't see the man leave. Nor did he hear the pledge to total secrecy, and tonight when he kept his assignation with Mrs Dobson, she would also be privy to the startling events of the morning. And apart from her other attributes, she had the biggest mouth in Grapplewick.

CHAPTER

TWELVE

For the purists, town clerks now bear the title of Chief Executive, but there are still some urban parish councils preferring to retain the old values, and town clerk has a grand traditional ring to it. However, chief executives are mainly chartered accountants and here again Grapplewick differed. Sidney not only had difficulty in checking his weekly salary, he hadn't even had to apply for the job. He simply inherited it from his father along with the chauffeur's uniform and all the regalia of the mace-bearer. The yearly balance sheets for the council affairs were drawn up by a distant cousin, a chartered accountant in Manchester, who was competent enough to add authenticity to the yearly figures. So everything in the garden was decidedly rosy. Sidney was content – a job for life, unmarried, and the clout of his position to grant small favours in return for high jinks in the bedrooms and meadows of Grapplewick.

Tonight was Sidney's snooker night, and awaiting his turn at the table he smiled to himself, ashamed of his panic a few hours ago. The mayor and superintendent, in fact all four of them, had left the office together and they didn't seem unduly perturbed. He must have misinterpreted what he'd heard through the keyhole. It could have been something to do with a TV commercial, or better still, they were probably planning a town pageant. That would explain Norman's presence. Being young he would very likely be leading the procession as the spirit of the future or some such nonsense. Yes, that must be it. They'd all been wearing badges when they came out; it must be a pageant of some sort.

In the afternoon, news reached him that the mayor's shop had gone up in flames but he was hardly surprised. Waterhouse's Barber's had always been a fire hazard with a couple of dozen electrical appliances on one adaptor. It could have blown the street up any time. He cleared his mind as he bent forward to smash the white ball into the red triangle; purely by chance one of the reds shot into the corner, and he was left with an easy black. In fact, due to phenomenal luck he fluked his way into the semi-finals. He hadn't bargained for this and it was late when he left the British Legion, too late to catch the last bus, and he had to walk three miles or so to the Dobsons' house.

By the time he let himself in through the Dobsons' front door it was well after one o'clock in the morning. Creeping silently up the stairs, he eased himself softly into the bedroom. In the half light of a street lamp, he could just discern her dark head on the pillow, turned away from him, feigning sleep. With scarcely a rustle he took off his clothes and slipped in beside her.

'Oh!' she said, whipping around to face him. 'I nearly had a heart attack – I were fast asleep!' She wasn't a bad actress and Sidney even half believed her.

'Oh, yes,' he said, fumbling with her nightie and at the same time trying to get his underpants off.

'My God, you're like a block of ice,' she whispered. His hand, flinging off his pants, caught the bedside lamp and it crashed to the floor. She jerked upright into a sitting position, holding her breath while he lay with his face in the pillow. After a moment she relaxed.

'It's a wonder you didn't wake our Jack,' she hissed, lying back.

'I'm sorry,' mumbled Sidney. He started to fondle her breasts and kiss her, but she turned her face away. He knew then something was wrong. Normally by this stage they'd be groping and giggling like teenagers, and she would have got hold of it by now and be saying things like, 'Ooooh, who's a big boy then?' To-night, however, she was lying there like prime beef on a butcher's slab.

'What's to do?' he whispered, sliding his hand down her belly and into the thatch of pubic hair. She grabbed his wrist and moved it back. He struggled up on one elbow. 'What's the matter?' he hissed.

She was silent for a while and then spoke. 'You just dashed past me this morning, not a word, not a gesture!'

Sidney had to cast his mind back. 'Oh that,' he remembered, 'I couldn't help it. I had to go to the toilet and when I'd come out you'd gone.'

'Well, I couldn't hang around on my knees all day, could I now?' She was angry now, and he thought it best to say nothing.

81

Eventually she turned her head to him. 'Well, what did happen in the mayor's office this morning then?'

Sidney relaxed sulkily. He knew he wouldn't get his reward until he'd told her all the facts. He started to put together all the snippets he had heard; something about a woman in the street looking into a shop window, the fire bells and 'Beautiful Grapplewick' badges, but Mrs Dobson wasn't satisfied with his casual descriptions. She questioned him on every point, especially the bits concerning the spaceman – did the man actually say he was a spaceman? What was the reaction of the superintendent and everybody else in the room to his statements and where would the spaceship be landing on Wednesday?

By now all Sidney's desire for her had gone, and as the interrogation progressed he became increasingly uneasy as all his fears and uncertainties of that morning came flooding back to him. He began to remember things that his mind had mercifully blotted out, and he realised that his conclusion that the meeting was just a preparation for a pageant was simply his brain's way of hiding under the sheets.

On the moors outside, a cock observing the coming of day fluttered importantly on to a fence and, checking again that it really was getting lighter, puffed out his chest, crowing loud and long. It was a totally unnecessary reveille. People were programmed to their alarm clocks and no longer relied upon mangy old cockerels, but in the distance Mrs Dobson caught the sound of its final crows and quickly sat up in bed. It was indeed getting light; she could now see articles of bedroom furniture and discarded clothes on the floor. Nosy neighbours with incontinent habits would soon be able to recognise a man other than her husband creeping out the back door.

'Hey,' she hissed; 'it's daylight, you'd best be off before anybody sees you.'

Sidney was out in five minutes. He had a reputation to keep up as well and as it turned out his timing was spot on. He spotted Mr Dobson at the end of the street coming home early from his night shift. Luckily it was a blustery morning and both men passed each other with heads down against the wind, so Mr Dobson did not recognise Sidney, although he did wonder afterwards who was the silly bugger hurrying along in his stockinged feet with a pair of boots under his arm.

However, the secret details of the meeting were well and truly blown. By the time Mrs Dobson arrived at the town hall, the milkman had a potted version of the advent of the men from space and the bus conductor was already regaling his passengers with tales of UFOs. Quicker than radio or television, the jungle drums of Grapplewick were being tuned.

CHAPTER

THIRTEEN

O ver two hundred miles to the south-east of Grapplewick, Chief Inspector James sat in his office at Scotland Yard, morosely surveying a bottle of champagne on the desk before him.

A cargo of high-quality cocaine and lesser drugs had been seized yesterday, drugs with a street value of over £80 million. And, more importantly, several big dealers and pushers had gone in the bag to await trial. It was a good result after months of patient police work – a very satisfactory outcome – and he, Chief Inspector James, had set the whole works in motion. For eight months he'd masterminded the operation and now, though he'd tilled the land and planted the trees, someone else was eating the fruit. He smiled ruefully. It was kind of the lads to send him a bottle of bubbly along with an invitation to join them later on for a bit of a do in the Dog and Partridge. He wouldn't go, though . . . he felt deeply ashamed of his present assignment. The drugs bust was in the Premier League and he was piddling about in the fourth division.

The Drugs Squad had lost a good man in the dawn arrests, and another young detective had been shot through the leg. James shook his head sadly: he should have been with them. On his present job the only injury he might sustain would be if his chair collapsed. His phone rang. He decided to ignore it but then he overrode his decision. It would pass a bit of time.

'Chief Inspector James,' he barked.

He listened uninterestedly, taking up a pencil so he could doodle during the conversation. There was a peremptory knock on the door and Sergeant Thompson poked his head in.

'Oh, sorry,' he blurted and made to withdraw.

But the chief inspector motioned him to stay. He still doodled and listened. Suddenly he became alert, and the point of his pencil snapped. He barked urgently into the phone. He reached across for another pencil, but this time he was scribbling hurried notes, punctuated by 'yes' down the phone. Finally he put the thing on its cradle. There was a new light in his eyes.

Sergeant Thompson watched him curiously and wondered if the chief's retirement had come through, or perhaps he'd been offered the Freedom of the City. He knew better than to ask.

The chief rose quickly.

'Sergeant,' he said crisply, 'arrange for two seats on the Manchester shuttle a.s.a.p. tomorrow morning.'

'Yessir,' replied the sergeant, then added tentatively, 'More letters, sir, from the phantom postman?'

James smiled. 'No letters this time, sergeant. This time I think we have *the man*!'

Sergeant Thompson was flabbergasted. 'You mean the Joker, sir?'

The chief inspector slowly nodded, rubbing his hands together in anticipation. A premonitory shiver ran up the sergeant's back. If they should come face to face with the Joker he hoped fervently that his chief would not jeopardise the end of a glowing career by battering the man to death with his bare hands.

'Get two mugs, sergeant,' ordered the chief inspector. 'We'd best drink this before it goes off.'

He began to untwist the wire from the cork, as if it was somebody's head.

CHAPTER
FOURTEEN

Bernard Whittaker, just turned sixty, was editor of the *Grapplewick Bugle*. Most of his working life had been on newspapers, and he had no regrets that this undistinguished tabloid was where he would end his career. Interspersed with the national news, he desperately tried to fill his paper with fascinating items of interest, but it was an uphill struggle. Very little happened in this backwater and when it did he beefed it up to make it sound exciting. 'Bus swerved on Featherstall Road narrowly missing parking meter' . . . 'Local boy rushed to hospital after falling off bike.' These gems of journalism were always accompanied by a picture – 'Bus driver standing by his vehicle'. ' "It could have been fatal had there been anybody about," said driver Barnshaw' . . . 'Smiling boy holding up bandaged finger.' ' "There should be cycle paths," said his mother.'

The editor did his best but it was like trying to make a ballroom dress with a Meccano set. He looked through the glass partition that separated his office from the main one, and smiled wryly at the frenzied activity of his staff. He shook his head. One week on a real daily and they'd be screaming for a holiday.

The big news of the week had been yesterday when Waterhouse's Barber's caught fire, and he wondered if it was worth carrying over for another splash. It was pathetic. He flung down his pencil and swivelled his chair to face the window. He couldn't see the street from where he was sitting and was, therefore, unable to watch the arrival of Billy Grout, one of his reporters, who was about to hand him the biggest scoop in Grapplewick's history. Better than that, it would be the highlight of his long journalistic career.

This hot potato of news was being rushed to him by bike, Billy's legs going like piston rods as he cycled furiously down the high street. Twenty-three years old, he was one of two reporters on the staff. His colleague, if one had the temerity to call him that, was a grizzled, disillusioned old man. Only the editor appreciated the talent of Aaron Brandwood, a one-time magical name in journalism. Unfortunately, with the occupational hazard of irregular hours, slow booze and fast food, he had descended steadily towards his current position on the *Bugle*. He rarely set foot out of the office, and when he did he could be found slumped over the bar at the Gaping Goose.

So Billy Grout was the leg man. He covered all the outside interviews and, be it a wedding or a death or Saturday at the football ground, he attacked the assignment with keenness and enthusiasm. And now as he hurtled down Churchill Close, he knew he had a winner, his short cut to Fleet Street. He skidded sideways in front of the *Bugle* office, rushing in to take the stairs two at a time. Normally he would have hauled his bike inside, but today he was too excited for caution. He dashed straight through the main office, raincoat tails flying, scattering papers in his wake. Any other time he would have knocked on the editor's door, but today he barged straight in slamming it behind him. For a moment there was an awkward silence, all eyes on the editor's office. They waited, but seeing that Billy was not immediately ejected, they returned to their work. Papers were picked up from the floor and typewriters clacked again. (Modern technology in the form of word processors had not yet reached the *Bugle*.)

A wag in a cod American voice said, 'Hold the front page, scoop's arrived.'

Nobody spoke, and the typewriters were spasmodic and desultory as furtive glances were directed to the glass partition separating them from the big chief. They couldn't hear what was being said but Billy was obviously fired up, throwing his arms about and striding up and down. Whatever the subject it wasn't the usual run-of-the-mill banality. Perhaps this was the big one, or it could be that Billy was just asking for a rise. No, it couldn't be that, he'd be out of the office by now clearing his desk.

'Now calm down, Billy, and stop marching about.'

The editor had listened but he hadn't stopped marking and crossing out bits from the copy in front of him.

Billy stood in front of the desk, flushed, eyes bright as he waited. 'All right,' said the editor finally, 'so the Martians have landed.'

'No, no, Mr Whittaker, I didn't say that,' replied Billy eagerly. 'Just give me the word and I'll check it out.'

The editor flung down his pencil and leaned back.

'A spaceship will be landing next Wednesday, and one of them is already here.' He shook his head. 'If it was Aaron I'd send him back to the Gaping Goose to sober up.'

Billy was embarrassed. He realised now that Aaron, with years of experience behind him, would never have barged into the editor's office without absolute, cast-iron proof, and all he had was tittle tattle. He rallied. It might only be gossip, but quite a few people were discussing it.

'Let me have a word with Mrs Dobson, she actually saw the . . .'

He stopped at the look on the editor's face.

'She *claims* she actually saw the spaceman,' he ended lamely.

The editor smiled sadly and resumed his work, drawing a square around a piece in front of him.

'Mrs Dobson, eh?' he said, almost to himself.

He put the paper into the wire basket and started on another clipping. He quickly perused it then jammed it on to a spike.

'Mrs Dobson,' he repeated. 'And she's going out with a spaceman?'

By now Billy was convinced that he'd made himself look like a right Charlie and was wishing passionately that he'd taken some statements, or asked a few more questions.

'Still here?' asked the editor without looking up. Billy turned dejectedly towards the door. 'Oh, by the way,' the older man called out just as Billy was turning the handle on the office door, 'any news of Spot?'

Billy stopped, mystified. 'Spot?'

Mr Whittaker peered at him over his half-moon glasses. 'The wire-haired terrier that's been missing since Monday.'

Billy shrugged. 'I don't know,' he said miserably.

'Well, find out, dammit. Our job is to sell newspapers and that's the sort of thing our readers like to read.'

'Yes, sir,' mumbled Billy as he walked out of the office, closing the door softly behind him.

As soon as he had gone the editor leaned back in his chair, chewing his pencil thoughtfully. He found it helped him to think. He knew Billy to be honest and open, and he knew the lad hadn't made the story up. There could be something in this, a humorous half-column in the 'Round and About the Town' section of the paper. He reached towards his phone and contacted the switchboard.

'Ah, Doris. Get me the town clerk, will you?'

'Right away, sir.'

He leaned back again, putting into shape the conversation he would have with Sidney, but before his mind had formed more than 'Hello, Sidney, this is Mr Whittaker from the *Bugle*,' his door opened and Billy stuck his head in.

'Excuse me, sir, but there's nothing on file about a missing dog called Spot.'

The editor certainly didn't want Billy overhearing his imminent telephone conversation. 'Well, find a dog called Spot and lose him,' he snarled, waving his hand in dismissal just as the telephone on his desk rang. He waited a second or two to make sure that Billy was well out of earshot before he answered it. 'Mr Whittaker here, the *Bugle* . . . ah yes, Sidney, I'm fine . . . no, no, it's nothing important; it's just something about one of your cleaners – a Mrs Dobson, I believe . . . Hello . . . Sidney, hello? Oh, I thought we'd been cut off . . . No, it's not important but apparently she's been seeing little green men . . . No, it's just that one of my lads came up with something. According to her there's going to be some sort of invasion from outer space . . . Hello? Hello?'

This time the line really was dead. Whittaker slammed the receiver down and flipped the intercom.

'Yes, Mr Whittaker?'

'I've just been cut off, try him again will you, Doris? On second thoughts, get me the mayor.'

Within a minute he was listening to the effusive greetings of Albert Waterhouse. The *Bugle* may have only been a provincial newspaper but still, a call from its editor was important and intriguing, especially as Bernard Whittaker was not given to idle chit-chat. 'And what can I do for you, Bernard?'

'Just doing a bit of checking and ringing round, Albert. According to one of my lads, you had a bit of an unusual visitor yesterday.' He paused, waiting for an answer but instead all he heard was heavy breathing. 'Can you hear me, Albert?'

There was a click and the connection was broken. Whittaker was fast becoming exasperated. Slamming the receiver down, he asked Doris to redial the mayor. As he waited he ran his fingers through his hair, thinking how outrageous it was that British Telecom spent a fortune on advertising immediate communication to all parts of the globe while he couldn't even hold a decent conversation with a subscriber who was only 300 yards away. His phone rang and he snatched the receiver. 'Sorry, Albert, we were cut off,' he started but it was Doris who was on the other end.

'He's not in,' was all she said.

Whittaker was staggered. 'Of course he's in, I was speaking with him ten seconds ago.' He drummed his fingers on the desktop. 'OK, Doris, keep trying.'

Looking thoughtful, he replaced the receiver. First the town clerk and then the mayor . . . it didn't need a great intellect to realise that both men were avoiding him, but why? Perhaps his young reporter wasn't quite as mad as he had thought he was. Opening his office door he yelled out, 'Billy!'

'Just on my way, Mr Whittaker.'

The editor stared at him uncomprehendingly, then after a moment said, 'Never mind the bloody dog, get in here.' Billy did so apprehensively, closing the door behind him.

Whittaker sat back in his chair and steepled his fingers, indicating that he was deep in thought. Billy's anxiety grew; he was sure the editor was trying to find the right words to sack him. After what seemed a lifetime, the great man spoke.

'Billy, I want you to go up to Coldhurst Street and see if you can find out the cause of the fire that destroyed Waterhouse's Barber's the other morning.'

Billy's relief was so immediate that he spoke before his brain had given him the command to do so. 'It's OK, sir, I covered that last night. The fire brigade said that it was probably an electrical fault.'

The editor humphed and shook his head. 'I know that, Billy, I printed the article. Listen, lad, I want you to go up there and ferret around for yourself. You might find a box of matches, you might find a petrol can. You may even find a lost dog called Spot.'

'I'm on my way,' said Billy, once more taking on the role of ace reporter. He hurried to the door, then stopped and turned slowly around, his brow furrowed. 'Spot?'

'Get out!' bawled the editor.

FIFTEEN

The mayor stared ashen faced at the phone in his hand. Norman, standing by the window with his own problems, turned to face his uncle. 'What's up?' he asked, but there was no reply from the hunched, shattered hulk in the chair. Undeterred, Norman moved over to him. 'Who was that on the phone?'

The mayor stirred himself. 'That was Bernard Whittaker,' he said, and slumped back into his torpor. Norman knew who Bernard Whittaker was, but in the past his uncle had always taken pride in their relationship; after all, not everyone in Grapplewick was important enough to be on first-name terms with the editor of the *Bugle*. Norman didn't want to ask what it was all about – that would be presumptuous and he wasn't the President yet; but the expression on his uncle's face was one of absolute shock. Had the call been from Dr Baines he would easily have assumed his uncle had been given three months to live. Perhaps he hadn't insured his shop, but whatever it was, this boded no good. He was fidgeting with the paperclips on the desk when the phone rang again, so sudden and strident he scattered the lot over the floor. Both stared at the instrument as it commanded them to action.

'You answer it, Norman,' hissed the mayor as if the place was bugged, 'and whoever it is I'm not in.'

He scurried to the hat stand and took down his overcoat. Norman looked at him unhappily and the mayor nodded to the phone urgently. Norman picked it up gingerly.

'Hello?' He looked quickly at his uncle who was now ready for off. 'No, I'm sorry, he's gone out. No, I don't know when he'll be back . . . yes, I'll leave a message, 'bye.'

He put down the phone and the mayor looked at him inquiringly.

'That was Superintendent Smith.'

'Good grief,' expostulated the mayor. 'Why did you have to hang up? I wanted to speak to him.'

'I'm sorry, Uncle, but you said . . .'

The mayor waved him to silence.

'I know what I said, but you must learn to use your head, see if there's any life in that grey matter of yours.' He tapped Norman's forehead to emphasise his meaning. 'Now pick up them paperclips and stop larkin' about.'

Norman knelt on the floor, aggrieved by the unfairness of it all. 'Don't worry,' he thought, 'there'll be some changes when I'm in the big chair.'

The mayor was about to lift the phone when the door burst open and Councillor Butterworth stood for a moment taking in the scene, then with a backward glance up and down the corridor he closed the door behind him.

'Hello, Arnold,' said the mayor automatically.

'Never mind all that, somebody's been talking.'

Norman scrambled to his feet from behind the desk with a handful of paperclips.

'Oh, you're here as well, are you?' sneered the councillor. 'And who have you been blabbin' to? Been flashin' your badge in the Amusement Arcade, have you?'

Norman looked at his uncle, puzzled.

'Oh, don't come the lily white innocent with me,' Butterworth went on. 'It'll be "Beautiful Grapplewick" all right if it's a great black smoking hole on the moors, won't it?'

The mayor rose out of his chair.

'Now hold on a minute, Arnold. Don't go casting aspersions like that. Norman hasn't been out of my sight since the meeting.'

The councillor calmed down somewhat, but he wasn't actually convinced.

'Well, somebody's let the cat out of the bag. Everybody's been asking me questions – what's the badge for, and does it turn blue if there's acid rain, and is it true about a spaceship? A spaceship – I ask you, how did they get on to that?'

The mayor shrugged and spread his hands. 'Don't ask me. The editor of the *Bugle* was on to me five minutes ago, but I didn't say anything, did I?'

He looked to Norman for back-up. Arnold thew up his hands and looked at the ceiling.

'Well, that's it then, isn't it? If all this gets printed in the paper, we're finished. There's no telling what he might do.'

'Oh, Bernie's all right, he won't print any . . .'

'I'm not talking about him,' broke in Butterworth, 'I'm talking about that other feller, the one who was in here yesterday.' Even now, he couldn't bring himself to say the word 'spaceman'. In fact he had begun to wonder whether the previous day had all been a bad dream, but his little badge pinned on to the lapel of his jacket told a different story. 'Any road, if you want me, I'll be back at my house. I have a lot of things to attend to,' and with that he was gone.

Norman looked at his uncle apprehensively. His uncle stared back at him with the same expression. They would have been even more uneasy if they had known what things Councillor Butterworth found so urgent. They involved timetables, planes to distant places, cross-Channel ferries, even a couple of weeks at his sister's in Bradford, anything to get him out of the area until after next Wednesday. Wrapped up in their own miserable thoughts Norman and his uncle remained silent. The atmosphere in the mayor's office strongly resembled a pre-war dentist's waiting room, until at last Norman spoke.

'Well, we haven't spoken with anyone, and Councillor Butterworth hasn't either, so it must be Superintendent Smith!'

The mayor had reached the same conclusion himself but was loath to accept it. 'No, not him. I can't believe that. I've known him for years and he wouldn't let on.'

'What's going to happen, then?' asked Norman.

The mayor shook his head. 'Your guess is as good as mine; in any case, why are you asking me? You're supposed to be the genius, the chosen one, President of quarter of the world. I'm just the simple alderman.' For a second the mayor's spirits rose as he thought this simple truth might extricate him from the trouble which lay ahead, but in his heart of hearts he knew that this was a delusion. All of them were implicated; all of them had solemnly sworn to keep the secret, yet now it might just as well be broadcast on the six o'clock news. So immersed were they in shared misery and despair that they didn't hear the timid knock on the door. It was repeated a second time, only louder.

'Who is it?' shouted the mayor. His secretary, a mousy fifty-year-old spinster, poked her head in. 'It's a lady to see you, Mr Mayor.'

'A lady?' he repeated, puzzled. He was about to say he didn't know any ladies, but just stopped himself in time.

'Yes,' she simpered. 'She wouldn't give her name, but – ' She stopped, flustered, as Oomi walked around her into the room. For a moment they didn't recognise her, but then Norman remembered where he had seen her last.

'It's Oomi, isn't it?' He turned eagerly to his uncle. 'We met last night at Kershaw's . . .'

'Shut up, Norman!' hissed the mayor, and putting on his nice, public face he turned to his secretary. 'That's all right, Edna. This lady is a friend of . . . of Norman's.'

The secretary smiled as if she were sucking a lemon, and let herself out. Norman was busy staring at the girl. He hadn't given her a moment's thought since leaving Kershaw's Croft, but now that he was looking at her in more familiar surroundings he could see that she was beautiful, with long blonde hair and very little makeup. He had already seen her in the spacesuit, but he far preferred her in what she was wearing now – a smart two-piece navy costume under a camel overcoat worn casually over her shoulders.

Norman gazed at the girl with open-mouthed admiration. He'd never come across anybody like her in real life before, and certainly not in Grapplewick. The mayor looked at him with annoyance; for heaven's sake, hadn't he ever seen a woman before? He turned to Oomi.

'Good morning, my dear. Won't you have a seat?' He gestured at the armchair but she ignored him and remained standing, cold and aloof.

The Master is displeased,' she began, speaking without expression.

'Displeased?' smiled the mayor, all raised eyebrows and total innocence. 'With us?' he said, indicating Norman.

'The Master is concerned by the lack of security and has instructed me to impress upon you the importance of our mission. He is angry that the secret arrival of the teachers is already being discussed in the streets of your town.'

'How can this be?' asked the mayor, turning to Norman in surprise. 'If I may say so, I think your Master has been misinformed. I can assure you that no one apart from those present at the meeting has any inkling of what will happen next Wednesday. Wouldn't you say so, Norman?' Norman was about to reply, but the mayor hurried on. 'Believe me, young lady, your Master's secret is safe with us.'

Norman frowned. How could the secret be safe if half of Grapplewick had already ditched the subject of last night's television in favour of the arrival of UFOs next week? Too green to recognise the dubious skill of the successful politician, he was about to speak when Oomi took a step back, and closing her eyes she stood rigidly to attention. Puzzled, Norman looked at his uncle who put a finger to his lips, shaking his head quickly in the universal 'do not disturb' sign. Norman took advantage of her closed eyes to give her the once-over, then the twice-over. She really was quite perfect. His heart sank a little when he remembered who she really was, an alien from outer space – the body was from 'wardrobe'. Well, he thought, if she had been trying to pass herself off as an ordinary young woman then she'd overdone it. No woman in Grapplewick looked like that. Norman was just admiring her shoes when they moved. Slowly, Oomi came out of her trance.

'Feeling better, love?' asked the mayor.

'The Master is angry with your lies and deceit. He instructs me to say that you are fully aware that the landing at Sagbottom's Acres is common knowledge, and he informs you that your fate now lies in the hands of the Overlords of Androm.'

The mayor paled. A smile was etched on to his face but it could have been an attack of wind. 'Forgive me, young lady, the man, er, Master, is quite correct in his assumptions. I admit that there are one or two people who may have stumbled upon the truth – inadvertently, I hasten to add.' By now the mayor was wringing his hands and forgetting to smile. 'I can assure you that by now the gossip and rumours will have died down. I know my Grapplewick. You only have to get three of its leading citizens in a room together and the balloon goes up. Suddenly the pound is being devalued. They're like little children, but there's no malice in them. Tell your Master to rest assured.'

Oomi remained unmoved. 'The Master hears what you are saying.'

The mayor looked up at the ceiling. 'Thank you, Master. Look kindly upon your humble servant. Knowing all things you will be aware that my nephew and I have honoured our pledge of secrecy.' He bowed his head and Norman half-expected him to say 'Amen.'

At that moment they became aware of a commotion outside in the corridor; angry voices were being raised and they were getting louder.

'What the dickens is going on out there?' the mayor asked. He stepped forward but just as he reached the door it burst open and the town clerk stumbled in, hustled by an angry mob. The mayor scurried behind his desk for safety while Sidney, now arched over the front of it, turned his head. 'I'm sorry, I couldn't hold them back. They're all over the town hall!'

The noise of the crowd was subsiding now that they'd reached their objective, but there was still a fair amount of babble from those outside in the corridor and on the staircase. The mayor banged on his desk for silence. Following the events of the last couple of days, this rabble was easy to handle. They were, after all, only human.

'All right, all right!' he shouted. 'Calm down. You've had your fun.' He waited until all the muttering had died away. 'That's more like it. Now, what's this all about then?' The people at the front of the crowd avoided his eyes, glancing instead at one another and waiting for someone else to speak.

'Well, come on,' said the mayor. 'You haven't all come up here on a mystery tour.'

'Where's ours, then?' piped up a voice from the crowd. Norman thought he recognised the voice, and being taller than his uncle he spotted the man near the door. He knew the face too but couldn't bring the name to mind. Most probably he'd been a customer of his in the shop.

'Who said that?' asked the mayor, on tiptoe now to look over the crowd. A burly man with two days' growth of stubble suddenly leaned over the desk and grabbed hold of the mayor's tie so that their faces were only inches apart.

'Never mind who said that,' he snarled. 'Where's ours?'

The mayor snatched back his tie and tucked it back into the top of his waistcoat. 'What are you talking about?' he squeaked as he eased the knot in the tie, which was now choking him. 'What do you want?' he asked in a more normal tone of voice.

The man jabbed his finger at the badge on the mayor's lapel. 'That's what we're talking about, them badges. Where's ours then?' He turned to the people behind him. ' "Beautiful Grapplewick",' he said in a poncy voice.

'Oh, that,' said the mayor uneasily. 'But that's just a badge, you know, like the ones that say "I'm Backing Britain".'

A big ugly woman suddenly spoke up from the back of the crowd. 'Aye, and I'm Madonna.'

'Why have only a few of the high-ups got them, then?' growled another.

'I'll tell you why,' said the tie-grabber. 'When the saucer lands we're likely to be incinerated while they hand out bunches of flowers to them aliens.'

That got the crowd going again. 'Where's ours, then?', 'What about the children?' and 'One law for the rich' were favourite chants. The mayor had to bluff it out, play for time; after all, he reckoned, somebody in the town hall must have called the police by now. Norman was mortified that Oomi should have witnessed this. He turned to say something to her but just caught a glimpse of her as she pushed her way through the crowd. He tried to follow but the mob surged forward, flattening him against a wall. Through the jostling figures he saw his uncle flailing about with a wooden ruler, but there was no doubt that he was vastly outnumbered. Oh God, thought Norman as he struggled to help, they're going to kill him.

Suddenly a piercing whistle shrilled. All action was suspended and everybody froze as if the film had broken down. Really, apart from a few hotheads at the front of the crowd, they were all normal law-abiding citizens who had turned up at the town hall to voice a legitimate grievance. Most of them had only the vaguest idea of what it was all about, while almost none of them had anticipated the violence the demonstration would entail. The arrival of a posse of police was just the last straw. They struggled to get back to the anonymity of the street, but it was impossible in the crush. Heads turned fearfully towards the door, expecting to see the plastic shields and stout batons of the riot squad. When, after a few moments, nothing had happened, fear turned to curiosity. There were no cries of pain, no panic-stricken wailing, thuds or the sound of heavy boots on the marble stairs, which wasn't really surprising as the police were nowhere in sight. Instead, a wiry little man with a William Powell moustache and heavily Brylcreemed hair was pushing his way towards the office blowing a whistle. The crowd parted like the Red Sea as he made his way towards the mayor. He was obviously someone in authority – why else would he have a whistle? 'Gangway please, make way,' he called, and the crowd did as he asked, squeezing up against each other to allow him passage to the desk.

Norman gaped in astonishment. It was Jimmy Jackson, who owned Sutton's Iron Foundry. He was a local villain, known to the authorities as Oily Jack, but at that moment Norman didn't particularly care. As far as he was concerned, this man had saved his uncle from a very nasty going-over; possibly he had even saved him from being killed.

Jackson edged his way around the desk, took the mayor's limp hand and shook it. 'Got your message, governor, and I came as quick as I could.'

The mayor stared at him through one puffy eye. He was in no fit state to comprehend what was going on – his hair was all over the place and there was a large cut on his cheek.

'You phoned me about half an hour back about badges for all,' Jackson continued, pointing at the mayor's badge, which surprisingly was still in place, although his lapel wasn't. The mayor didn't answer. He had suddenly realised that his dentures were on the floor. He hoped no one would step on them, but he was in luck. Norman spotted them under his desk, picked them up and slipped them discreetly into his hand.

Jackson spoke out for the benefit of the now-silent audience. 'Now, just sit down and relax while I attend to these nice people here.' The mayor nodded and, under the pretext of blowing his nose, popped his dentures back in.

Jackson now faced the crowd. There were still some sullen, angry faces there but most of them were ashamed of themselves and extremely grateful that it was he who had been blowing the whistle, and not the police.

'Now listen, the lot of you,' he started in a voice that carried to the bus stop outside. 'Half an hour ago, his Worship the Mayor phoned me with a specific order that "Beautiful Grapplewick" badges should be made available to you all. He knew you'd all be worried and that's why he rang me.' A slight murmur ran through the crowd, who now felt even more ashamed of themselves.

'So all them as wants badges, call in at Sutton's Iron Foundry on Waterloo Street and place your order. The badges will be ready in a day or two, OK?'

The crowd nodded, some said thank you, and they turned and shuffled in orderly fashion out of the office, slowly at first, then with more urgency until there was a mad stampede out of the main door and up towards Waterloo Street and Sutton's Iron Foundry.

Norman was looking at Jimmy with undisguised admiration at the way he'd handled the mob. 'There's a job for him in my future administration,' he thought. But he was puzzled too: the mayor hadn't phoned anybody that morning, and somebody like Jimmy

98

Jackson was definitely not on his calling list. Not only that, how could he possibly supply the badges? They weren't your everday trash, they'd been forged in the outer Galaxy.

Jimmy had taken the mayor's badge and he was measuring it carefully, making notes in a little black notebook. Norman approached him.

'Where are you going to get the badges from?' he asked.

Jimmy gave him a knowing look and returned to his notes. Norman pointed to his own badge, then to the one Jimmy was examining.

'These aren't just ordinary badges, you know, they're specially treated.'

Jimmy snapped his notebook shut and winked. 'Don't worry son, I'll treat 'em special.' And he strode out whistling.

Their troubles, however, were far from over. As Norman closed the door he became aware of someone leaning casually against the wall. 'Oh no, not him,' he thought. The last person they wanted to meet at that moment was Mr Whittaker, editor of the *Bugle*, the eyes and ears of Grapplewick.

'Hello, Norman,' he said. 'Quite a morning.'

He strolled over to the desk and stubbed out the soggy end of his cigarette. He nodded to the mayor. 'Your cheek's bleeding again.'

The mayor whipped out his already soiled hankie and attended to it.

'Thanks, Bernie,' he said. 'Saw all that, did you?'

The editor didn't reply. He walked over to Norman and bent slightly forward so he could read the lettering on his badge.

' "Beautiful Grapplewick",' he muttered, cocking his head to one side in appreciation.

'It's just a badge,' explained the mayor. 'I don't know what all the fuss is about.'

Again the editor ignored him, addressing himself to Norman. 'Well, well,' he said, 'I hope you know what you're doing.'

Norman was baffled. He looked to his uncle who shrugged helplessly.

'You *are* taking over the whole administration, aren't you?'

Norman opened his mouth to reply but his uncle pulled him hastily to one side.

'No comment,' he blurted.

He recognised the ploy, snip away at the weak link in the chain,

Norman being the dodgy one in this case. The editor surveyed them both for a moment, then nodded as if it was of no consequence and turned away. Quickly the mayor flashed a 'leave it to me' sign to his nephew, and watched the editor warily as he strolled round the desk. Norman took half a pace forward and the mayor dug him in the ribs with his elbow, shaking his head vigorously. The editor seemed unaware of all this and picked up a framed photo of the mayor with his arm around Florrie at Blackpool Tower. With his eyes fastened on the photo he said softly, 'Do you really believe in all this visitors-from-outer-space crap?'

The mayor cleared his throat, but he wasn't about to speak. He'd been in local government long enough to recognise a loaded question, and this one was a floating blockbuster. A straight yes or no either way would have enormous repercussions. The walls wouldn't just be splattered, the fan would get clogged as well. Whittaker appeared to be in no hurry for an answer; in fact he looked as if he might have forgotton the question, but the mayor wasn't fooled. Political clichés and evasions clattered through his brain like a changing destination board at Waterloo Station until finally he decided that the best course of action was to draw a cheque on a long-standing friendship. He worked his face into an ingratiating smile. 'Look, Bernie, we've known each other a long time. I can trust you and I know that anything that is said within these four walls is strictly off the record, so I'll say this . . .' He leaned forward over the desk and lowered his voice. 'Me and Norman have seen and heard things in the past twenty-four hours that are beyond the comprehension of the human mind.'

The editor's eyebrows rose and he put down the framed photo. After a moment he nodded. 'I believe you. Has this anything to do with your shop catching fire?'

'No comment.'

'I see.' The editor stared at Norman. 'And Sagbottom's Acres is to be terminal three for interplanetary flights, with little green men checking the tickets?'

The mayor snorted and waved his hand derisively, mainly to prevent Norman from speaking, but he was too late. 'He's not green; he's just like us, and Oomi is . . .' He stopped suddenly, realising that he had already said too much. His uncle clucked and looked away in disgust.

'And they're landing on Monday?' continued the editor.

'No, Wednesday,' Norman replied again, without thinking. This time his uncle rounded on him.

'You know, Norman, just when I think you're the biggest idiot in Grapplewick, you go one better.'

The editor took pity on him. 'Don't let it worry you, lad. You haven't told me anything I didn't already know. It seems as if the whole town's talking about the spacemen and Kershaw's Croft, and the landing next Wednesday.' He moved towards the office door but the mayor headed him off.

'Listen, Bernard,' he gushed, 'we go back a long time, you and me, and we've done each other some favours.' By now he was dry-washing his hands. 'I've never refused you an interview, have I?' Whittaker looked at him sharply – as far as he could remember he'd never asked the mayor for one.

'What I'm trying to say, Bernard, is that, well, as a friend . . . You won't print any of that in your paper, will you?'

Whittaker smiled and patted his shoulder. 'No need to worry, Albert, there'll be nothing in the paper. Good grief, if I printed all that, they'd have me certified.' The mayor nodded, vastly relieved. 'Mind you,' he went on, 'a year ago the story of UFOs coming on a Wednesday was big news, but now it's a dead duck. It's not even a good joke any more.' Again he turned for the door but still the mayor wasn't fully satisfied. He darted around and pressed himself against the door to prevent Whittaker from going.

'The, er, slight disturbance you witnessed earlier this morning. You can, er, ignore that, can't you?'

Whittaker buttoned his raincoat. 'Oh, that'll have to go in the paper. I've got a photographer downstairs taking pictures, but don't worry. I'll steer clear of science fiction.'

The mayor nodded gratefully. 'Thanks, Bernie. I owe you one,' he said and ushered him out. He almost closed the door but his secretary was quicker, poking her head in the opening. She was about to speak, but changed her mind when she saw his dishevelled appearance.

'Well, what is it now?' he snapped peevishly.

She glared at him through her thick spectacles. 'Just to let you know the police are on their way.'

The mayor sighed and looked at his nephew. 'Well, that's a relief. Thank you very much, Edna,' he grated sarcastically. 'It's nice to know that help is at hand.'

She was about to withdraw when he called her back. 'Oh, and

Edna, you can deal with them when they get here. Tell them the problem's all been taken care of; you know, it was a storm in a teacup. Something about school meals . . . you know.' He flapped his hands and dismissed her.

SIXTEEN

There seemed to be more traffic in the high street than was usual at that time of day, thought Bernard Whittaker as he made his way back to the *Bugle* office. Even more unusual was the knot of people gathered outside the town hall, looking up at the building as if the mayor was on the roof threatening to jump off. Whittaker looked up to check, but there was nothing to be seen; the only signs of life up there were the pigeons, strutting importantly up and down the ledges and window sills. He entered his office deep in thought and slumped behind his desk, not even bothering to take off his hat and coat. He felt a stirring in his bowels and recognised the signs. There was more to this story. Whittaker knew it wasn't a mere hoax.

In all the other towns, letters had been delivered to the mayors, top policemen and other big-wigs, informing them that UFOs would be coming Wednesday, but here in Grapplewick the message had been conveyed in person, by a man claiming to be an alien from outer space. He drummed his fingers on the desk. Deep in his bones he felt that something quite extraordinary would happen next Wednesday, but he was equally certain that whatever it was, it would have very little to do with flying saucers. Frustrated, he banged the arms of his chair and rose to walk over to the window. Whoever this man was, he wasn't to be underestimated. Obviously he was clever; he had managed to scare the living daylights out of three of the town's leading citizens and had convinced them that they were dealing with an eighteen-carat, genuine alien from a distant planet.

Whittaker snorted derisively. Why then were these leading citizens pathetically trying to hold on to the secret when throughout the town it was common gossip ... The phone rang and he snatched it up impatiently.

'Yes ... a bus conductor? What's he want? No, no, put him on, will you?' He nodded and grunted as he listened. 'I see, and after you dropped them they just set off walking?' There was another pause. 'And what makes you so sure they were going to Kershaw's Croft?' Again he listened and nodded. 'Well, thanks for telling me ... yes, if I do print anything I'll be sure to mention your name.'

In the main press room uneasy glances were thrown at the glass partition. Furtively they watched the editor thoughtfully replacing the phone. Billy was busy one-finger typing a negative report on his fruitless investigation of the charred remains of Waterhouse's Barber's Shop. Search as he might, he hadn't uncovered any signs of arson. In any case, what *were* the signs? Heads came up as the editor's door jerked open and he swept through the office.

'Billy,' he barked, 'come with me.'

'Yessir,' squeaked the lad, scrabbling hastily out of the chair to catch up with his boss.

As soon as the door closed, typewriters ceased their frenetic clattering and telephone bells were ignored as the staff eagerly congregated to discuss the unsettling events of the last two days, and in particular next Wednesday. Aaron was the exception: he didn't join the excited jabberings of his colleagues, but put on his coat and decided to go home. No point in going to the Gaping Goose, the topic of conversation would be the same.

Billy eased himself into the passenger seat of the editor's decrepit old Ford. He didn't strap himself in; there weren't any straps. Gingerly he eased the door shut, trying to be gentle in case it fell off, but the editor leaned across him and slammed it fiercely. There was a tinkle on the pavement which could have been the door handle, but Mr Whittaker seemed unperturbed. He switched on the engine and after three protesting screeches from the gear box, he managed to find first, and they were mobile.

'We're just going to have a look at Kershaw's Croft.' The editor had to shout to combat the noise of the engine.

'Oh, Kershaw's Croft,' replied Billy.

He hadn't the foggiest idea why they should want to visit that place, and thinking of the hill up to Windy Ridge, he wasn't sure the car would make it. A few minutes later they turned left down Linney Lane and from there on to the moors. Once they were out of the traffic and free to clank and judder laboriously between the dry stone walls, the editor seemed to relax. With a series of jerks and squeaks he wound his window down. Immediately this doubled the racket of the straining engine, discouraging any further conversation, but worse, a gust of wind joyously rushed in, frolicking with some papers on the back seat. Billy snuggled down and pointedly turned up the collar of his coat. He's enjoying this, he thought, but he didn't know his boss. The editor screwed up his eyes against the cold, but it helped him to think. The icy blasts cleansed his mind, which was cluttered with an endless stream of unanswered questions. For instance, the fire at the barber's. Fortuitously the place was empty, but then why had Norman been given the day off? Normally his uncle worked him from nine to eight, six days a week, with a fortnight's annual holiday and Christmas. And even stranger, why was he invited to attend the meeting at the town hall?

He shook his head trying to put his thoughts into some sort of sequence. Firstly, the bus conductor had taken Norman and the mayor to Windy Ridge on Wednesday night and they had set off walking in the direction of Kershaw's Croft, so the first encounter had to be there. It was the only building within a five-mile range; it couldn't be anywhere else unless they all met under the lamp. More importantly, whatever had transpired between them was shattering enough to induce Norman to change from wearing his usual pair of old jeans to a collar and tie, and shocking enough to turn the mayor into a frightened old man. He remembered a phone call to the police station earlier. As soon as he announced his name he was greeted with a terse 'No comment' and a dead line. As for Councillor Butterworth, he'd vanished altogether. So what the hell was going on?

That angry mob at the town hall this morning rampaging into the mayor's office, that was definitely out of character for the slow-thinking people of Grapplewick. It certainly wasn't spontaneous, so who was behind this carefully orchestrated disturbance? Not Jimmy Jackson, that was for sure. He was too thick, but bright enough to climb on the bandwagon when he saw the opportunity to make a few bob out of the badges. And, incidentally, what about those badges? What was all the fuss about a small piece of enamel with 'Beautiful Grapplewick' stamped on it? Billy interrupted his train of thought.

'I think you've passed the turning, Mr Whittaker!' he yelled.

'What? . . . Oh yes.'

He stopped and, looking over his shoulder, began the erratic process of reversing until they were level with the lane. He shook his head ruefully. If Billy hadn't been with him he might well have ended up in Huddersfield.

A few minutes later they arrived at Kershaw's Croft. Billy eased himself out of the car, thankful he hadn't had to push it. He stretched luxuriously – the journey back would be a doddle, it was mainly downhill. His euphoria evaporated when he turned to look at Kershaw's Croft. Without the noise of the engine, the keening of the wind was more pronounced and malevolent. A cloud passed over the sun and the derelict hulk was thrown into deep shadow. He shuddered and was glad the editor hadn't sent him on his own. Gently Mr Whittaker pushed the heavy wooden door open. He paused, head cocked to one side.

'Did you hear that?' he asked in a quiet voice.

'No, Mr Whittaker, I didn't hear a thing.'

'Exactly . . . these hinges have been oiled,' the editor replied, and carefully he went inside.

Billy followed him, at first fearful and then relaxed. It wasn't as dark as he'd imagined. Two dirt-encrusted windows on opposite walls gave the room light which dramatically brightened as the sun came out. He smiled at his earlier forebodings; it was only a pathetic little one-roomed cottage. Confidence restored, he strolled over to the window and bent forward to peer out. As he did so something glinted between his feet. He stooped and picked it up.

'What have you got there, Billy?' asked the editor, joining him. Billy held it in the palm of his hand.

'It looks like a sequin,' he said. Mr Whittaker took it from him.

'You're right, Billy lad, it is a sequin.'

'Hang on,' said Billy quickly, 'here's another one,' and he handed it over.

The editor looked at the two sequins for a moment, then gazed out of the window for quite a time. Finally he turned to Billy.

'Odd place to find 'em, wouldn't you say?'

Billy shrugged. He hadn't a thought in his head, but he was fascinated when the editor popped the two sequins in an envelope, sealed it and slid it into his inside pocket. Taking his cue from this, Billy scanned the floor eagerly for more. Perhaps Mr Whittaker was just a sequin-collector, but whatever the reason, he was pleased with his discoveries, and at least they wouldn't come away empty-handed.

'Never mind that, lad, nip out the back and see what you can come up with.'

Billy was about to go when he turned, a puzzled look on his face.

'What am I looking for, Mr Whittaker?'

The editor looked at him in surprise.

'How should I know . . . anything unusual. If there's a dustbin, tip it out and sift through it.'

Billy nodded and went into the overgrown yard. The editor called after him.

'And if it barks, you've found Spot.'

Billy nodded again and looked helplessly round the great piles of knee-high rubbish, wondering where to start. He wasn't too despondent, however. The yard was sheltered from the wind and quite pleasant in the sun. Unfortunately myriads of flies thought so too, and they weren't particularly happy about being disturbed. A mass of them rose to investigate the bandit at twelve o'clock high. Billy flailed his arms to ward them off but it was hopeless. He lost his footing amongst the rotting debris and fell back, disturbing more flies. It was too much for him, Spot couldn't have been here, they'd have had him for breakfast. He struggled to his feet and scrabbled to the wall wiping his hands on the sides of his raincoat. What a mess! He tied his handkerchief round his mouth and looked round for a stick with which to sift through the stinking piles of garbage, and then his eye lit on something odd, something definitely out of place here. It was the smashed remains of a light bulb, but not your ordinary 60-watt domestic type. This was much larger: the bulb holder was as thick as his wrist. He picked it up gingerly and took it inside.

The editor was on one knee trying to prise something from between the floorboards. He looked up when Billy entered.

'Good lad,' he said after examining the shattered light bulb. 'We might be able to trace where this came from. It hasn't been outside long either . . . it'd be rusted.'

Billy took the handkerchief from his face. Some of the flies had come in with him but they soon left to get back to their breeding ground.

'See if you can get this out, Billy.'

The editor pointed to a small object wedged in a crack on the floor. Billy took out his penknife, and after a short struggle flipped something out. It was a round, plastic badge bearing the words 'Beautiful Grapplewick'.

'That's it, Billy,' said the editor triumphantly. 'That's what I've been looking for.' His smile faded as he caught the pitying look on his young reporter's face. 'Something the matter, lad?' he asked.

Billy pointed at the badge. 'I could have saved you a journey if I'd known.'

'Known what?'

Billy shrugged. 'Just before you came in this morning Jimmy Jackson phoned for an ad to be put in tonight's edition. He's manufacturing these at the foundry. You could have ordered one from him.'

'Is that so?' asked Whittaker, feigning ignorance. 'Has he put a price on 'em?'

'Five pounds ninety-nine,' replied Billy promptly.

Whittaker stared at him aghast. 'Each?' he asked incredulously.

Billy nodded. 'Bit steep, isn't it?'

'I should say so,' chuckled Whittaker. 'Now you know why we came up here.' He stuffed the badge into his pocket and looked around the room. 'You know, Billy,' he said, 'over the years many people have used this croft . . . tramps, courting couples, hikers seeking shelter from the rain . . . they've all been here.'

Billy nodded thoughtfully. 'Gypsies too, I'll bet!'

Whittaker eyed him thoughtfully. 'Well, doesn't it strike you as odd?'

'Doesn't what?' asked Billy, blinking hard in concentration.

'Where's all the muck, the beer cans, plastic bags, newspapers, rags?' The editor spread his arms and turned a full circle. Billy turned around too but didn't have a clue as to what his boss was getting at.

'No dust on the floors, no cobwebs on the ceiling . . . what does that suggest to you, Billy?'

Realisation suddenly dawned and Billy's eyes lit up. 'Somebody's cleaned it out – and if there's no dust around that suggests that it must have been done recently!'

Whittaker smiled benignly. 'That's what I wanted to hear!' he said. 'You know, Billy, there's more to you than meets the eye,' and he slapped him on the back. Billy glowed with pride. 'Now here's what I want you to do. I want you to go round to all the pubs and hotels in the Grapplewick area and ask if they've had a man and a girl booked in within the last week.'

Billy took out his notepad and pencil. 'What do they look like?'

Whittaker sighed. 'That's what I want you to find out, lad. It's

108

not likely there's going to be too many strangers booked in – Grapplewick's hardly a tourist trap.'

'Right,' said Billy, putting his notebook away. 'I'll do the hotels first.'

'Good idea. There's only three. If you had started with the pubs you'd still be making enquiries by Christmas.'

Billy set off along the lane but Whittaker called out after him. 'Hang on, Billy, I'll give you a lift!'

It was always best to have a passenger in case the damned car decided to call it a day.

SEVENTEEN

By Saturday nearly everyone was aware of the facts: a spacecraft would be arriving on Wednesday. Those who didn't know were either very young or very senile. Very few people actually believed that a spaceship would be arriving at Sagbottom's Acres, but no one was brave enough to come right out and say so as there was now a sort of buoyancy in the town. You'd have to be exceedingly unfeeling to tell little children looking forward to Christmas that there's no Santa Claus. People still gathered in groups but no one was fearful now; instead they discussed arrangements for Wednesday night and how they were going to get up to Sagbottom's Acres. They were excited and happy, as if the following week was an unexpected national holiday and the landing of aliens an extravaganza dreamt up by the Leisure and Pleasure Committee.

This was all well and good for the ordinary folk, but the more enthusiastic they became, the deeper grew the pit of despondency and gloom for the mayor. Normally his greatest skill was to be able to sleep, but he hadn't had much of that since Thursday. Breakfast had always been a high spot of his day, but today he just toyed listlessly with half a fried egg and a sausage congealing on the plate in front of him.

'Would you like another cup of tea?' asked Florrie helpfully. In reply the mayor threw down his knife.

'It's supposed to be a secret and yet everybody knows; they know about me and Nigel Smith and Norman!'

'And Arnold Butterworth,' his wife added.

'Aye, and where's he now? If I know him he'll be on a banana boat to South America, leaving us to hold the baby.'

Florrie hovered around behind him with an empty teapot in her hand. Casually she asked, 'Well, what did the man actually say to you?'

The mayor stared hard at her. 'You know I can't tell you that. I've sworn an oath of secrecy!'

'Yes, but everybody . . .'

He cut her off angrily. 'They don't know it all; they think they do, but they wouldn't be so jolly if they knew all the facts . . .' He became silent.

Florrie tried again. 'Our Emmie says . . .'

He silenced her with a look of contempt. 'Your sister is a big mouth, and always has been. My gallstones were all over Grapplewick before even the doctor knew what it was!'

With a sigh Florrie rose to put the kettle on, speaking as she went. 'I was just going to say that our Emmie wanted to know if we were going in the official party on Wednesday, and if not we could go with them.'

The mayor slapped the table in exasperation. 'This is serious!' he shouted over his shoulder. 'It's not the Grapplewick annual gala!' He was about to follow Florrie into the kitchen when Norman came down the stairs, engrossed in a dog-eared atlas. Oblivious of his uncle, he sat down and flipped over a page.

'Well, don't say good morning, will you?' snapped his uncle.

Norman looked up, frowning a little at his uncle as though trying to place him in a foggy memory. 'Sorry, I was miles away,' he offered as an explanation and returned to his studying of one quarter of the world. The mayor was about to make a comment but it died on his lips when he saw the atlas. He moved around to Norman's back and peered over his shoulder.

'Where did you get that?'

'Eh?' grunted Norman, reluctant to be disturbed.

'That's my old school atlas,' continued the mayor, straightening up. 'I didn't know you were interested in geography.'

'I wasn't until I met the spaceman,' replied Norman with all the reverence of a born-again idiot. The mayor snorted and Norman swivelled around in his chair 'You don't believe him, do you?' he said hotly. 'You don't believe that the teachers will arrive on Wednesday. You think this is all a big joke, don't you?'

His uncle backed away, hands half raised in surrender. 'I don't think it's a joke, Norman. If I did I'd be laughing, but quite seriously, lad, I don't think you should put too much faith in all this.'

'In all what, uncle? You've met the man; you've seen what he can do.' The mayor sighed and made to turn away, but Norman

111

grabbed his sleeve. 'And what about Kershaw's Croft? He might have hypnotised you but I had all my faculties and I know I was looking down on Grapplewick from the air. I know I didn't imagine that.'

The mayor shook his head sadly. 'All I'm saying, Norman, is this: if the spaceship lands on Wednesday, then all's well and good – you'll be quids in and President from here to ...' – he leaned over to look at the atlas – 'from here to Persia, but if it doesn't land, what happens then?'

Norman stared uncomprehendingly at his uncle while the mayor looked at the atlas again. 'Incidentally, lad, I shouldn't rely too much on this if I were you. Persia's gone and you won't find Rhodesia any more, nor Tanganyika, nor British West Africa. It's all a different world now.'

Florrie lumbered in. 'Hark at David Attenborough; you're not so bright yourself, Albert Waterhouse. Do you remember when I told you about the Toxteth riots? You said it would never happen in England.' She picked up the remains of breakfast and lumbered back into the kitchen, full of self-importance.

'I hadn't seen the telly, had I!' yelled Albert to her retreating back, and then, more quietly, 'Bloody women. Always have to put their fourpence worth in.' He looked at Norman. 'Where was I? Oh yes. Suppose all this is some sort of joke; just suppose a spaceship doesn't come. What then?'

Norman was incredulous. 'You don't think it's going to happen, do you?'

'No, no, I didn't say that, but let's suppose that everyone in Grapplewick goes up to Sagbottom's Acres on Wednesday and nothing happens. What then?'

'They *will* land,' insisted Norman fervently.

'Yes, but if they don't, what do you reckon the feeling will be?' Norman shrugged. 'Well, I'll tell you what it'll be. Your life, and mine, and the superintendent's, won't be worth that much.' He clicked his fingers.

Norman stared at him. 'Why?' he asked innocently.

'Because,' said the mayor, tapping his fingers on the table, 'we will be held responsible, that's why!'

Norman digested this slowly, then shrugged again. 'So what? They can't do anything.'

'Oh, can't they?' sneered his uncle. 'Why do you think Superintendent Smith is keeping such a low profile, and where's

112

Councillor Butterworth? We won't see him until all of this has blown over – I'll tell you that for nothing.' He slumped dejectedly back into his chair. 'I wish to God I'd never clapped eyes on your spaceman.'

Norman didn't pick up on the subtle shift in responsibility; he was more concerned with his uncle's heresy. 'Be careful what you say, uncle, he knows what you're thinking.'

The mayor, however, was unrepentant. 'We should have reported this to a higher authority straight away!' He blew his nose vigorously into a red and white spotted handkerchief. 'I blame Superintendent Smith. He should have detained him while he had the chance!' Before Norman could reply, Florrie came through carrying a basket and tying a scarf around her head. She put on her coat and took in the two silent men in front of her.

'Somebody died or what?' There was no reply. 'Oh, well,' she muttered, 'I'm just going to do some shopping. I won't be long.' Norman and the mayor waited for the door to slam, but instead she came running back into the room. 'Quick, come to the window. Have a look at this!'

Norman hurried after her and the mayor followed, curious to know what was important enough to cause his wife to rush around forgetting her bad legs. Before he got to the door he could hear the shrill chanting of young voices, shouting, 'Nor-man! Nor-man!' Outside, a small group of children was bunched around the front gate, some even with their mothers, and all clapping their hands in time to their piping cries of, 'Nor-man! Nor-man!'

Florrie beamed with pride and tried to usher Norman outside to meet his fans, but he wouldn't budge. Red with embarrassment he slunk away from the window, and the chanting tailed off in disappointment. The mayor, however, stuck his head out of the window to tell them to bugger off, but remembered just in time that he was the mayor and their mothers and fathers had votes. Instead he smiled benignly at them and waved as they drifted off down the street. He was about to go back into the house when he noticed that some of the kids were wearing yellow oilskin sou'westers. He looked at the sky but it wasn't raining and neither had it been.

'Must be a club or something,' he muttered to Florrie.

'What?'

'Them sou'wester hats, look.' He pointed down the road.

113

'Them waterproof fishing hats. Look, there's people across the road wearing them too!'

'Anti-fall-out hats,' Florrie replied, still waving.

'Anti-fall-out hats,' he repeated stupidly.

'In case of radiation next Wednesday.'

He frowned. 'What are you talking about?'

Florrie turned to him, wondering if he was having her on. 'For protection,' she said. 'You know, anti-fall-out.' She smiled at another passer-by. 'There's a queue at Bottomley's, everyone's buying them.'

He pondered for a moment, jingling some loose coins in his pocket. 'Well, where are ours?' he eventually said.

'They're not cheap, you know. Any road, I thought you might be able to wangle us some free ones; I mean, you are in with him, aren't you?'

'In with who?' he asked.

Florrie nudged him. 'You know . . . the man,' and she moved away from the window, leaving him to wonder about the headgear.

An old man shuffled past him. 'Morning, Mr Mayor.'

Albert beamed. 'And good morning to you. It's a nice day, isn't it?' His shoulders went back as he watched the old man make his way up the street. Oh yes, he thought, there's still some respect about, some folk know who's number one. Full of self importance, he was about to go in when a new rag-tag of kids dashed breathlessly up to the gate. The smallest of them, with an enormous yellow hat almost covering his eyes, gasped, 'Hey mister, does Norman live here?'

'Bugger off,' said the mayor and slammed the door.

114

EIGHTEEN

Superintendent Smith wasn't particularly imaginative. He'd risen to his present position by his ability to keep his nose clean, proceeding through his chosen career strictly by the book, and his ability to lead men. This was the official appraisal. In reality he'd 'yes sirred' and 'no sirred' through the ranks, a smart policeman covering up the blunders of his superiors by laying the blame on lesser mortals and modestly taking the credit where it should have been apportioned to others. The major breakthrough, however, came during a particularly vicious strike when his bloodstained features took up most of the front pages of the national dailies. One of the headlines read THE BRAVE FACE OF THE THIN BLUE LINE. They were all in similar vein. The sad truth, however, was that Sergeant Smith, as he then was, had been panic-stricken and desperately trying to get out of the way when he ran face first into a wall. But from then on his rapid promotion was assured.

Today he was off duty, an imposing figure in brown tweed jacket and flannels. The queue outside the sport shop waiting patiently to buy their fishing hats amused him, and the sprinkling of 'Beautiful Grapplewick' badges caused him to shake his head ruefully. Everybody knew about next Wednesday, but they weren't panicking in the streets, the man was wrong about that. On the contrary, it was probably the happiest little town in Britain. And again, although the man, whoever he was, must be well aware by now that the secret was blown, he had not carried out his threat. Grapplewick had not shrivelled in a searing ball of flame.

The superintendent shook his head again at the ease with which they'd all been manipulated at the meeting, for he was sure now that it could only be a confidence trick. After hours of careful consideration, he'd dismissed from his mind the extraordinary happenings two days ago – the Indian woman and the barber's shop. They weren't logical and therefore they didn't exist. There were one or two kids hanging about outside the mayor's house and they drew back to let him through. He pressed the door bell and they regarded him seriously while he waited. A curtain twitched aside as the mayor looked to see who it was, and a few moments later the superintendent was ushered into the front room.

'I've been trying to get you on the phone,' started the mayor without the usual formalities.

'I've been out,' said the superintendent, settling himself into a chair.

The mayor was still on his feet. 'You don't seem bothered at all.'

'Why should I be bothered?' asked the superintendent.

The mayor turned a full circle looking up at the ceiling.

'Good grief, you've been out, you've seen 'em, they're treating it like wakes week. They'll be up at Sagbottom's on Wednesday.'

'There's no harm in it, Albert.'

The mayor leaned forward and rested his hands on the arms of the superintendent's chair. 'Not now, there isn't, but what about next Thursday when they're still up there, waiting, eh?' There was no reply from the chair. The mayor nodded and eased himself upright. 'What happens when the spaceship or whatever it is doesn't come. What'll we say? "Sorry, folks, that's all. Hope you enjoyed it"?'

'Why should we say anything?' asked the superintendent coolly.

'Because,' replied the mayor, 'everybody knows about the meeting and they'll think we've led them up the garden path.'

'Oh, come on, Albert, they'll take it in good part. They'll have had a good week and this will be the culmination. Why don't you put on a show for them; arrange a few fireworks or something.' He smiled. 'They're not kids. They don't really believe that flying saucers are going to let down at Sagbottom's Acres.'

The mayor snorted. 'Oh no? Then what about the mad rush to buy those badges and the fishing hats? That's nearly a week's wages for some of these folk.'

He was interrupted by a timid knock at the front door and he moved irritably over to the window, convinced that it was the kids again. He waved his hand angrily to disperse them and turned from the window. He suddenly stopped in his tracks, and turned to look again. 'Come here,' he beckoned to the superin-

116

tendent to join him. 'See that? Those kids are wearing T-shirts with "Norman" on the front.'

'Aye, I believe your nephew's becoming a bit of a cult figure around here.'

'And how much has that set them back? I bet those T-shirts cost more than a dress shirt in Manchester!'

'Oh, I admit there's a bit of profiteering going on. I stopped for a pint at the Feathers on my way here and they've got a new drink out called Space Alien. It's only lager with a drop of whisky in it, but the kids are lapping it up.'

The mayor was quick to take the advantage. 'That's my point. They wouldn't be chucking their brass around if they didn't believe.'

The superintendent surveyed him for a moment and then indicated a chair. 'Sit down, Albert, I want to talk to you.' He waited until the mayor was settled and then leaned towards him, elbows on his knees. 'Albert, you have to understand that we're not living in a perfect world. A lot of flash Harrys in Grapplewick have been smart enough to see that there's a lot of honey in the pot, and this space thing's an ideal opportunity to get at it. Many will come out of it a darn sight richer than they were last week. Jimmy Jackson was the first but he won't be the last; not by a long chalk.'

The mayor frowned in concentration. 'What are you getting at?' he asked, feeling in the back of his mind that there was more.

'What I'm getting at is this: you and I – forget Butterworth – you and I have created the scenario for people like Jimmy Jackson to rake it in. They'll be laughing all the way to the bank, and what do we get in return?' The mayor shook his head. 'Well, Albert, you have just put your finger on it. All we can look forward to is a very angry mob who'll want revenge for all the money they've laid out.' He sat back and regarded the mayor.

The mayor was at a loss as to where the conversation was leading. 'Well,' he finally said, 'what do you propose to do about it?'

Superintendent Smith leaned forward again. 'Sagbottom's Acres,' he began. 'The whole of Grapplewick will be there on Wednesday night, there'll be sideshows, cars, beer stalls, hot dog stands. None of these concessions will be cheap, so whoever owns Sagbottom's Acres is sitting on a gold mine.'

The mayor digested this information, but he wasn't at his best in the mornings. 'Old deaf Crumpshaw owns Sagbottom's,' he said lamely.

The superintendent leaned back and casually examined his nails. 'Not any more, he doesn't.'

Still the penny hadn't dropped and the superintendent sighed. 'I bought it last night.'

This thunderbolt scattered the mayor's wits over a large area. His jaw fell open and he found that he was breathing extremely heavily. 'Just in the nick of time too,' went on the policeman, undeterred. 'Apparently he was earlier approached by somebody else but he said no because he was a stranger and Crump didn't like the look of him. However, when I offered him ten grand he jumped at it.'

'I'm not surprised.' The mayor had found his voice again. 'He must need the cash. He hasn't done a hand's turn at the farm since his brother died.' He thought for a moment. 'He must be the only person in Grapplewick who hasn't heard about the UFO landing.'

The superintendent shrugged. 'Not surprising really. He never comes into town; can't abide it. He has all the groceries and stuff delivered.'

The mayor nodded. Then, in a blinding flash of inspiration, he slapped his forehead. 'Wait a minute! The spaceman – could he be the man who was trying to buy the land in the first place?'

'The spaceman?' asked the superintendent slowly.

'Yes, the main reason we all believed him was that he didn't ask for anything. He was getting nothing out of all this, but if he owned Sagbottom's Acres then that would explain it all.'

The superintendent pondered for a moment. 'You could be right,' he finally conceded, 'but if that was his intention then he's missed the boat.'

The mayor smiled. All his fears dropped from him as he became confident with his appraisal of the situation. The man, for all his clever tricks, was mortal after all, and even more important, he'd met his match in Grapplewick. Oh yes, they weren't the hayseeds that people thought they were. 'I'll just put the kettle on,' he said.

'Wait a minute before you go, Albert. I don't want you thinking I'm just a cheap hustler like the rest of them.' The mayor opened his mouth to protest but the superintendent held up his hand for silence. 'Knowing that you and I are going to carry the can for the whole scam, I can see no reason why we shouldn't make a few bob out of this for ourselves, to heal the wounds, as it were.'

'We?' asked the mayor curiously.

'I'm going to cut you in for half.'

The mayor's wits let him down again. 'Half?' he repeated.

'For five thousand quid we can be the joint owners of Sagbottom's Acres.'

The mayor sprang to his feet. There were a lot of things to think about here. Firstly, £5000 from him would just about drain his bank balance, and secondly, there were ethical considerations to weigh up. After all, he was the mayor and beyond reproach. To enter a questionable deal like the one which was being put forward to him might not exactly be illegal, but it wasn't exactly kosher. The superintendent walked over to the window. 'Car parking alone would be worth, oh, let me see, private cars, buses, coaches at a fiver a time, say seventy-five grand, and that's not counting the concessions, then there's . . .'

'Hang on a minute, I'll get me chequebook.' The mayor hurried over and took it out of a vase on the mantelpiece. 'Who shall I make it out to?'

'Best make it out to cash, don't want the tax people ferreting around, do we?'

The mayor hesitated for a moment, and then the sum of £75,000 flashed in front of his eyes again. He made the cheque out with a flourish and handed it over to the superintendent, and they shook hands, as two honourable gentlemen should. The superintendent then took his leave.

No sooner had the door closed than the mayor gave an exuberant little skip. Not only had he exorcised his fear of the spaceman, he was now a man of means. By next Thursday, come what may, he would have twenty, even thirty thousand pounds. He rubbed his hands together in sheer, breathtaking, intoxicating excitement. It was an invigorating feeling. He wouldn't tell Florrie; he'd just watch her face when the workmen arrived to put in a new bathroom, white tiles and a carpet, with a shower and all. Then perhaps they could go to Scarborough for a week. He raised his arms and pirouetted on one leg. For the first time in his life he was a really happy man.

Superintendent Smith, striding along the high street, didn't feel too bad either. Already some of his policemen were setting up cones and car parking signs around Sagbottom's Acres – all in the line of duty, of course. As superintendent he had impressed upon them all the need for clear signposting to ensure a trouble-free and orderly event. After all, well over 50,000 people were expected to attend and it had to be organised properly. Oh yes, he thought, whatever happened on Wednesday, he didn't plan to come out of this at the bottom of the heap. Perhaps old deaf Crumpshaw had already forgotten that Sagbottom's Acres didn't belong to him any more, or the price that he had been paid. Five thousand pounds. The superintendent shrugged. He hadn't exactly been honest with the mayor but so what? He'd just been taking out insurance; the cheque would cover him in case they were rained off.

CHAPTER

NINETEEN

The bells of St Mary's parish church crashed upon an unsuspecting Grapplewick. Those who treated Sunday as a lie-in sat up in bed wondering if the spaceships had landed ahead of schedule, mindful of the old tradition of ringing the church bell as a warning of invasion. Normally the Sunday morning silence was scarcely broken by the mournful tone of a single tenor bell, and that didn't last long, but this Sunday was different. All the bell ringers had surprised each other by turning up for duty and the *clash-clamballang* of the peal embarrassed even them. They were glad when the conductor finally called stand.

Inside the church itself, the congregation whispered and rustled. There was an air of dankness, of mothballs and bad breath. During the bells, the fluting notes of the organ were puny in comparison, but with no competition from the belfry, the organist was inspired, bobbing and weaving, pulling out stops, fingers darting over keys. It was understandable. He'd never had an audience of this magnitude before – usually the choir outnumbered the congregation. Today, however, there was a full house and he was making the most of his recital. It might have been a Bach cantata, or a Bach fugue, the vicar couldn't be sure, but he couldn't help thinking that it was a good job Johann Sebastian died when he did. Mercifully, the organist played a long chord to signify that he had finished and the whispering died down in anticipation, emphasising the squeaks and clacks of shoes as latecomers entered the church.

The congregation rose during the introduction to Hymn 289 and the vicar surveyed the aisles and pews as 'Praise My Soul the King Of Heaven' was joyously bellowed out. He was proud and humbled by the enormous turn-out. 'Praise Him, Praise Him . . .' It was rousing, stirring stuff and he imagined that somewhere in the vast firmament above, beings from another galaxy were looking down on this solid, devout display of worship and congratulating themselves on choosing Grapplewick as a landing site. Their judgement had not been at fault – these were decent and deserving people.

Ninety per cent of the congregation were first-timers, if you don't count christenings, and not all were from Grapplewick. Two tall men at the back of the church were definitely out of place. They were different, big and brawny like rugby players . . . or off-duty policemen. Policemen, in fact, is exactly what they were, but they were far from off duty.

In the front pew, the mayor fidgeted. He wasn't a regular church-goer and he was nervous. He was about to step up to the lectern to read the lesson. Yesterday he had been flattered when the Reverend Copthorne had invited him to participate in the service, but now it didn't seem like such a good idea. The congregation settled down and the vicar smiled at him encouragingly. He stood up and put on his half-moon glasses, glancing around the mass of faces in the church. He swallowed hard when he saw that nearly everyone was wearing badges. The church looked like a huge dark cotton field. Pulling himself together he began to read from the massive old Bible. 'The Gospel According to St Luke' – he wasn't a bad speaker and the congregation was suitably impressed, but the two tall men at the back hadn't come for the purification of their souls. They just wanted to check out the mayor and long before the end of the lesson they were outside lighting cigarettes in the churchyard.

Later that afternoon, the mayor, as was his custom on Sundays, was snoring gently in his favourite armchair. The *News of the World* slid gently from his lap when his eyes closed and from the kitchen came the clack of plates as Florrie washed up after lunch. This scene of domestic tranquillity was suddenly shattered by the imperative ring of the doorbell. Albert jerked upright out of his sleep, glancing this way and that to establish his whereabouts while Florrie looked in from the kitchen with a frown.

'I wonder who that can be?' she said.

'I don't know, do I?' he snapped. Hastily he stuffed the *News of the World* under a cushion and the doorbell rang again, this time more insistently.

'Well, go and see who it is,' he hissed, smoothing his thinning hair. 'Whoever it is, try and get rid of them.'

But she couldn't have heard him. When she came back into the room she was followed by two large men.

'These gentlemen would like to talk to you, Albert. They're from, er . . .'

'Special Branch, madam.'

The bigger of the visitors proffered his credentials to the mayor. 'I'm Chief Inspector James and this is Detective Sergeant Thompson.'

'Would you like a cup of tea?' asked Florrie.

'That would be nice, thank you,' said one of them.

She looked worriedly at her husband.

'Would you like a fresh pot, Albert?'

He shook his head, he hoped this wouldn't last long and he'd have one later.

'Sit down, will you.'

He motioned to the chairs and they sat. Both held their hats on their knees and the sergeant took out a notebook.

'Sorry to bother you on a Sunday afternoon, but I'm afraid the matter is urgent.'

'That's all right,' said Albert. 'How can I help you?'

The one with the notebook was obviously the spokesman.

'Your nephew Norman lives here, I believe.'

'Yes, he's upstairs. I'll get him.'

'Thank you, sir, it'll save time.'

Albert struggled out of the chair, but Florrie came out of the kitchen.

'I'll get him, you get on with it,' and she began her laborious ascent up the stairs. Any other time she would have stood at the bottom and bellowed 'Normaaaan!' but not when they had company. The mayor slumped back in his chair.

'Been up here long?' he asked.

'A few hours.'

The mayor nodded. 'Well, you won't have had a chance to see much of Grapplewick, then?'

There was no reply. The sergeant was tapping his pencil on his notebook. There was a long, silent pause broken only by the ticking of the clock on the mantelpiece.

'Good grief,' the mayor thought, 'she's no athlete but she should have reached the summit by now.'

'Just got back from church.' He said it as if he was a regular.

He was saved further embarrassment when Norman entered the room, hair brushed and a jacket on. Florrie must have briefed him.

'Ah, this is my nephew Norman. Norman, these gentlemen are from Special Branch.'

Norman nodded and took a chair from the table. He guessed what their business was about and was frightened. These weren't locals, they represented authority with a capital 'A'. He gulped when the bigger one spoke.

'We hope this won't take too long so I'll get straight to the point. You two people, I believe, were the first to make contact with the so-called spaceman.'

The mayor wriggled. 'Well, Norman was the first, and he telephoned me to . . .'

The big man cut him off. 'Yes, I understand, and consequently you two, Superintendent Smith and a Councillor, er . . .' he looked to his colleague.

'Butterworth, sir.'

'Yes, Butterworth, had a meeting with this man in the town hall.'

'That's correct,' said the mayor.

'In this meeting he led you to believe he was an alien from outer space.'

'He's from the planet Androm,' blurted Norman.

There was silence while the big man regarded him. 'Yes, well, be that as it may,' he said.

Norman regretted his outburst, it was childish rather than presidential.

'Now, sir,' the big man addressed the mayor, 'this man had an accomplice, a young lady, I believe.'

'That's right, Oomi she was called.'

He was beginning to relax. It wasn't about the purchase of Sag-bottom's after all, and giving away information like this did not constitute a violation of his oath of secrecy. His composure was shattered by the next question.

'Can you describe exactly what happened at that meeting?'

Florrie lumbered in with a large tea tray of cups and saucers, teapot, sugar and milk, and the mayor sighed with relief.

'Thanks, Florrie,' he said fervently. 'Will you be mother?' The longer she was in the room the more time he'd have to think up an answer.

'D'you take milk?' she asked one of them.

The other looked at his watch, and then pointedly at his colleague.

124

'Yes, thanks, ma'am.'

She poured in the milk and handed over the cup; everyone had to be attended to. The man again looked at his watch.

'Would anybody like a bit of shortbread with that?' she asked, but they all declined and she made her way into the kitchen.

The spokesman was about to continue his questioning when she came into the room again with a plateful of chocolate biscuits.

'One of them won't do you no harm,' she said.

Then the telephone rang and she hauled her aching legs over to see who it was. 'Hello,' she said. 'Oh, hello, Emmie, I was just going to ring you, yes . . . oh did he? . . . Yes, well they don't, do they . . . mmm . . . yes, . . . mmm.'

The big man put his tea cup on the table. He guessed that the phone conversation would go on for some time.

'I think it might be better to continue our discussion on the way to the station.'

Albert spluttered a mouthful of tea across the table and his teeth went with it. Sergeant Thompson looked away in disgust but his superior leaned over and slapped the mayor on the back until he'd put himself together again.

'The police station?' croaked the mayor.

'Just a formality, sir. We've arranged for a police artist to be present, we'd like an Identikit picture of the two.'

'An Identikit picture?' asked the mayor.

'Well, you two must have a pretty accurate idea of what they look like. Also we think it highly unlikely they'll have a police record so it'll be a waste of time for you to sift through the rogues gallery.'

The sergeant snapped his notebook shut and stuffed it in his inside pocket.

'It'll be a great help to us, sir.' He rose to his feet.

'We've asked that Superintendent Smith be present. Between you, you should be able to come up with something resembling the two of 'em.'

The mayor looked across to where his wife was still umming and arring. They might as well have a ride down to the police station, they should be back before she'd finished. In fact, she didn't even see them leave.

The superintendent, however, was not at the police station when they arrived. He had more important things to do. In fact he was up at Sagbottom's Acres supervising crowd control arrangements. Three large fields were being marked off as vehicle parking spaces and there were primitive toilets – 'Elsans' for the ladies and long disinfected trenches for the men – shielded from prying eyes by canvas screens. There weren't too many such facilities, either for the ladies or the gents – they cost money. The superintendent wasn't bothered about that, though. If there was an outbreak of dysentery there was always the moors.

The whole extent of Sagbottom's Acres was quite considerable and at the centre of it all was a natural amphitheatre surrounding a fairly flat circle about the size of half a dozen football pitches. Purple heather and yellow spotted gorse concealed the slight humps and hollows. There wasn't much grass for a landing strip, but good grief, they were expecting a flying saucer, not a Tiger Moth. Presumably it would plonk straight down, not taxi in. As far as the superintendent was concerned, this was the ideal landing site and in order to keep the place clear of inquisitive spectators, he'd had the whole area roped off. As an added deterrent, signs were erected at fifty-yard intervals warning people to keep clear as this area was likely to be contaminated with radioactive particles.

There were enough vantage points on the surrounding hills anyway, so everybody should get a good view of anything that might happen. Workmen were erecting a platform for the dignitaries and the welcoming committee. He watched them hammering and sawing with unaccustomed haste. There wasn't much time. The bunting had to be rigged, and the microphones. He smiled to himself as he thought of Wednesday night. There would be an almighty rush for the toilets if a spacecraft actually did land. With that thought in mind, he called over a sergeant and instructed him to erect one directly behind the platform. The sergeant saluted and was about to carry out the order when the superintendent added, 'Oh, and mark it Decontamination Centre – that should keep the Herberts out.'

He stood there surveying his domain, a commanding figure in his uniform and gumboots. His posse of police was similarly shod. This didn't pass unnoticed by some of the secret watchers from the town; by Monday afternoon, anti-radioactive gumboots would be selling like ice cream in the desert. He gazed around at the frenzied activity and in the distance he took in the tumbledown stone dwelling of Farmer Crumpshaw. Thank God it wasn't built on the landing site or he'd have had to buy that as well. He was about to turn away when he spotted movement. The faraway figure of deaf Crumpshaw had emerged and he was heading in this direction. With a curt 'Carry on, sergeant,' he hurried to his car. He didn't particularly want to meet the farmer at that moment – or at any moment – and in any case, he was already late for a meeting at the police station.

TWENTY

Old deaf Crumpshaw was a recluse, and as his nickname implied, he was totally and utterly deaf. If a land mine exploded in front of him he would only see the flash. He was now well into his eighties, but according to local folklore he was much older; it wouldn't have surprised anybody to learn that he had received the Queen's telegram. Very few people in Grapplewick had actually seen him but he was nevertheless extremely well known. The stories about him were legendary; some said that he had cut off his brother's head with a sabre and buried him in two places on his land; some said that in fact the body was buried but the head was kept in a glass case on his dresser at the farmhouse; others said that it was his parents and not his brother whom he had hacked to pieces.

There were even more lurid tales sufficiently gruesome to deter casual visitors to the farmhouse. In fact, older people would make a detour of miles rather than go past the place. However, like most rumours that circulate in small, suspicious communities, they bore little relation to the truth. Crumpshaw's parents had died peacefully and were respectably buried in St Mary's churchyard, while his brother had been respectably killed on the Somme.

Old deaf Crumpshaw neither knew nor cared what people said about him, being content that they left him alone. Although Sagbottom's Acres had only been part of his holding, he wasn't rich. Miles of dry black stone walls crisscrossed his farm, but he had neglected the land until it had deteriorated into its original wild state. Many years ago he had kept sheep, but again this fact had become subject to legend. One day he had a thriving flock, but come the dawn they were all gone. Some recalled a fleet of lorries groaning on to the moors during the night; others that a German bomber pilot had jettisoned his bombs in his haste to get back to Deutschland, thus wiping out the entire flock. The most accepted

– and most implausible – explanation was that old deaf Crumpshaw, sick to death of having to move his sheep from one pasture to another, had simply eaten them all. In any event, he was now a poor man living on social security. He was entitled to meals on wheels as well, but was unaware of this, and the social services didn't enlighten him as they were reluctant to drive the van over to his place. All his food and bits and pieces were obtained from a mobile shop that called every so often, but his store of money was now desperately low; in fact there was enough in the tin under the bed for about five pounds of potatoes and two tins of beans. The arrival of Superintendent Smith had been timely, to say the least.

The deal for Sagbottom's Acres had been negotiated by notes written on scraps of paper: 'Would you be willing to sell Sagbottom's?' Then Crumpshaw had written 'How much?', under which the superintendent had written 'Five thousand pounds.' He was delighted when Crumpshaw wrote back, 'Have you got the money with you?' Pulling out a wad of notes the superintendent had become the new owner; the deeds and receipt were handed over, but not until the farmer had laboriously counted out the money. Satisfied, Crumpshaw nodded and the superintendent saluted, desperately trying to hide his elation. Crumpshaw sucked on his one remaining tooth gleefully as he watched the policemen depart. He, too, had been trying to hide his elation. He knew that particular piece of land was useless, but if somebody with more money than sense wanted to buy it, well, that was their lookout.

He waited until the superintendent was well out of sight before he stuffed the money into his biscuit tin, which he then tied securely with a piece of string before sliding it under his bed. He decided that the next day he'd buy a tin of corned beef to go with his beans and potatoes. He could now afford to splash out a bit.

Early the following morning, three vans arrived at Sagbottom's Acres, disgorging practically the whole of Grapplewick's police force to prepare for the coming of the spacecraft. They were followed by carpenters and builders and a large transporter loaded with planks and scaffolding. They set to work with some urgency in a supremely well-organised manner supervised by Superintendent Smith.

In spite of all the activity it was late afternoon before old deaf Crumpshaw noticed all the activity. Because of his deafness, it wasn't so surprising he hadn't heard the clatter and bustle coming from Sagbottom's Acres – it was only when he shuffled across the yard to the privy that he became aware of the scores of people swarming all over the place. He frowned as a terrible thought occurred to him – was the superintendent going to build new houses on the land? No, it couldn't be. That was illegal. This was farm land in a green belt. Something funny was definitely going on, though, and he didn't like it. Furious, he flung on his cap and loaded both barrels of his shotgun. He left the farmhouse and made his way up the slight rise behind it, followed by Rex, his Welsh border collie. He was old and past his prime, too. He couldn't even remember what a sheep looked like.

The sergeant watched the farmer approach. He knew all about old deaf Crumpshaw. Like many other boys he'd been weaned on the legends but he'd never actually seen him before. He eyed the shotgun with some trepidation and hoped that Crumpshaw wouldn't do anything silly. Wheezing with the effort of the 300-yard journey, the farmer gave himself a moment to recover his breath while the sergeant waited apprehensively. Finally the old man spoke. 'What the bloody hell's going on?'

It was a useless question. He wouldn't be able to hear the answer anyway. The sergeant explained about the spaceship coming Wednesday, and was about to say more when he remembered Crumpshaw was deaf. He tried a second time, loudly and clearly, stretching his mouth around every syllable. Crumpshaw must be able to hear him. Only the dead were that deaf. Everybody else had stopped work and was looking at them, so the officer was glad when the farmer turned and shuffled across to the half-erected platform.

'What's this then!' He gestured with his shotgun.

The sergeant followed him. He didn't like the way the old man was waving the gun around. 'It's a platform!' he bellowed. 'For the VIPs!'

'Well, it looks like a platform to me,' grumbled the old man and again the sergeant tried to explain about Wednesday night and the aliens, except this time he used sign language. He pointed at the sky, then with the flat of his palm he simulated the landing. He then turned to the platform and shook hands with himself to indicate the welcoming committee. All in all it was a creditable performance and some of the carpenters applauded, although Crumpshaw didn't know this as they were behind him. The police officer continued, motioning to all the policemen dotted about the area who were knocking in signs and erecting the canvas shelters for the ladies and gents.

'Is it a missing person?' Crumpshaw eventually asked.

The sergeant shook his head in despair and slapped his hands against his flanks. Leaning forward he put his mouth to Crumpshaw's ear and bellowed, 'You're a stupid old bastard, aren't you!'

The farmer smiled triumphantly: 'I knew it was a platform all along.' And somewhat mollified he whistled for his dog. Rex was right behind him and barked a couple of times to let his master know he was at hand, but Crumpshaw turned in another direction and whistled again. The dog moved to heel and barked furiously.

'Where the dickens has he got to?' Crumpshaw muttered. 'He was here a minute ago.'

He whistled again and the sergeant took pity on him. He grabbed the old man's arm and pointed to the dog. Crumpshaw looked down and nodded.

'Oh, there you are. Took you long enough to get here,' and with that he set off down the hill to check on his biscuit tin.

Monday isn't the best day of the week for most people, but in Grapplewick it was different. The festivities had begun in earnest; absenteeism was the order of the day and the local school was closed for the lack of pupils. Pubs were well patronised but there were no ugly scenes of drunkenness. On the contrary, the streets were full of laughter, and on the few buses that were still running the conductors cheerfully declined to accept fares. 'Beautiful Grapplewick' badges were everywhere and there were still queues for the anti-fall-out hats. There hadn't been such a spirit of goodwill in the town since VE Day.

Bernard Whittaker moved over to the window and gazed down on the high street, shaking his head at the gay scene below. Normally the people in the street would be elderly, wandering aimlessly up and down like inmates in a geriatric open prison, but today throngs of young people in white Norman T-shirts were hanging around in groups, laughing loudly, while all the shopkeepers were standing in their doorways, smiling and waving. It was like Blackpool promenade on a rare hot day.

Aaron joined him at the window and together they surveyed the festivities below. They watched in silence for a moment, then the old reporter shook his head. 'There'll be tears before bedtime,' he said morosely. Whittaker turned away and sat down at his desk.

'I can understand them using it as an excuse for skiving off work, but look at the money they've laid out! They can't believe it, can they?'

Aaron shrugged. 'The special edition should be on the street in an hour or so. Let's see what effect that has.'

Whittaker sighed. 'That's if they have enough money left to buy a copy.' He turned to the old reporter. 'Did you want me for anything?'

'Oh aye . . . That "Beautiful Grapplewick" badge you found up at Kershaw's Croft?'

'Well, any reports on that?'

'Well, yes,' Aaron grinned. 'You'll enjoy this. I phoned the lab in Warrington this morning and they've tested the badge thoroughly; it would seem it's just ordinary plastic; nothing sinister apart from the words "Beautiful Grapplewick". They think that's hilarious!'

Whittaker smiled. 'It's a damn sight better than "Beautiful Warrington",' he observed and began to re-read his leader column for the extra edition. Aaron took this to be his dismissal and went back to his desk.

Before lunchtime the *Grapplewick Bugle* was on the streets, and so successful were the sales that Whittaker had to order a reprint of the edition. The headlines in thick black type screamed IT'S ALL A HOAX, under which there was a full-page warning to the people that the madness had gone far enough and that Grapplewick was in danger of becoming the laughing stock of Britain. It reminded people that over thirty small towns over the past year had received similar messages purporting to have come from outer space, and on each occasion no UFOs, in any shape or form, had made an appearance on Wednesday or indeed any other day.

The article went on to describe how the leading citizens had been duped by means of trickery and hypnotism into believing they were being addressed by a man from outer space who instructed them to prepare for the advent of fellow aliens. The article carried on relentlessly – the preposterous charade had now taken root in the minds of normally level-headed people, and the time had now come to call an end to these ludicrous preparations.

132

The article was followed by a detailed description of the man and the girl and was illustrated by two large Identikit pictures. The usual statement which said that if anybody knew of their whereabouts they should contact the police, was printed at the bottom of the page.

The article was effective. It was as if someone had thrown a large bucket of cold water over the whole of Grapplewick. Smiles disappeared and gleeful cries were now frowned upon. Yellow hats were furtively stuffed out of sight and the queue for badges outside Sutton's dispersed quietly. Everyone avoided each other's eyes and knots of people gathered on the high street outside the newspaper's office, anxiously awaiting more information on the scam. Shopkeepers whose tills had been pinging joyously now stood anxiously in their doorways. Jimmy Jackson was hurriedly packing a suitcase while the mayor was in a state of panic, wondering if he was now part-owner of several acres of nothing. The superintendent was having troubles of his own. As far back as a year ago a directive had been circulated to all police stations, stating that any information regarding the identity of the sender of the hoax letters was to be forwarded immediately to the Home Office. The superintendent had not only ignored this directive; he had actually spent three hours in close proximity with the man and had had ample opportunity to apprehend him. Whatever the outcome was to be, his career certainly lay in ruins.

Whittaker was astonished by the success of his article. He also felt a pang of guilt, as if he had taken a sweet away from a four-year-old child. This feeling quickly evaporated though, when at around four o'clock that afternoon an amazing incident occurred that completely reversed the balance of opinion in the town. An army convoy trundled down the high street and on to the moors. It wasn't a large convoy, just a jeep followed by six three-tonners crammed with squaddies from an engineering battalion who whistled at everything female under sixty – the prerogative of troops in transit. Their arrival was innocuous, an event which under normal circumstances wouldn't have merited a second glance, but in the present situation the townspeople seized on it as a vindication of their earlier beliefs.

Rumours spread through the town like an epidemic of cholera and this show of military might, witnessed by many people, assumed sinister proportions. In less than an hour it was a well-known fact that those troops were digging in round Sagbottom's

Acres, heavy nuclear artillery was on its way to shoot the saucer out of the sky as it circled in preparation for landing, and on the radio the Government had declared Grapplewick an open city. Nobody had actually heard this, but everyone knew several people who knew someone who had. It was the stimulus they needed to shrug off their despondency and embarrassment. They were more than ever convinced of momentous happenings due on Wednesday night.

With regard to the newspaper article, it had obviously been written on the instructions of higher authority in order to dissuade people from going up to Sagbottom's, but they had underestimated the Grapplewick folk. Fists were shaken at the windows of the *Bugle* and some of the hotheads wanted to form a vigilante group to march on Sagbottom's Acres and engage the troops. But a further rumour soon put a stop to that; the troops had supposedly been ordered to shoot on sight anyone approaching.

The sad truth of the matter was that the convoy, engaged upon a perfectly normal movement from Manchester to Catterick, was lost. The troops neither knew this nor cared, but the green lieutenant in the jeep leading the convoy was having difficulty with his map-reading and the grid references didn't include Grapplewick. It wasn't just a slight error on the lieutenant's part, it was a monumental cock-up, and if they hadn't turned soon they'd have probably ended up in Scotland. But, unwittingly, they had completely negated the effect created by Bernard Whittaker's article. On Tuesday, Jimmy Jackson unpacked his suitcase and opened Sutton's Iron Foundry for business as usual. Queues were already beginning to form for the anti-fall-out hats, and excitement was further fuelled by the rumour that Councillor Butterworth, having disappeared, was being held hostage by the spaceman. For what purposes nobody seemed to know, but it was enough to add to the mystery of the UFOs.

TWENTY-ONE

Superintendent Smith, the mayor and Norman were seated in the interrogation room at the police station. The policeman was in civvies, having been suspended from duty pending an investigation. Chief Inspector James of the Special Branch was conducting the interrogation with Sergeant Thompson in attendance.

'Are you sure, are you absolutely sure he asked for nothing in return?'

'Positive,' replied Norman. He was the only one present who absolutely believed everything the spaceman had said, and he couldn't wait for Wednesday to assume office.

The Special Branch man ran his fingers through his hair as he paced up and down. 'All right,' he said. 'Let's go back to the beginning . . . the barber's shop.'

His sergeant flipped over the pages of his notebook to the relevant one.

'How many times do I have to tell you?' blurted Norman. 'He sat in the chair and changed into a black fellow with a monkey on his shoulder.'

'Did he wave any sort of object in front of your eyes?'

'No, he didn't, but OK, say he hypnotised me. What about the blind man then?'

The Special Branch officer stared at him for a moment. 'That's easy. He could have been an accomplice.' Norman snorted and the big man raised his eyebrows. 'OK, let me put it to you another way. Grapplewick's a small place and you've lived here all of your life. Isn't it slightly strange that a blind man comes into your shop and you don't recognise him?'

Norman blushed. 'I don't know everybody, do I?' he mumbled.

Superintendent Smith cleared his throat. 'The following day, Thursday, I ran a check with the social services and the person Norman described to me was not registered amongst the blind.'

135

The big man nodded and for a while there was silence in the room. Suddenly Norman's eyes widened. 'Wait a minute. I think I've seen him again; yes, I thought I recognised him.' He swivelled around to his uncle. 'Do you remember the mob that broke into your office looking for badges?' The mayor looked back at him uncomprehendingly. His spirit was crushed; whatever happened he was a broken man who would probably be removed from office, and if that wasn't enough, his nest egg was gone too.

'The badges?' he asked.

'Yes,' said Norman excitedly. 'The blind man. I spotted him in the crowd. I knew I'd seen him somewhere before.'

The Special Branch men exchanged glances while Norman looked anxiously from one to the other. 'That doesn't prove he's not an accomplice, though, does it?'

DCI James eyed him sympathetically. 'No it doesn't, Sonny Jim, and it's rather odd behaviour for a man who's just been granted the gift of sight.'

Norman pondered this for a moment. 'Ah, yes, but if he was in cahoots with the spaceman he wouldn't have stormed into the town hall, knowing I'd be there and might recognise him!'

The Special Branch man looked at him coolly. 'How was he to know that you would be there? How could anyone have guessed?' Norman's shoulders sagged. His ace had been trumped. 'Kershaw's Croft,' the man went on, 'you were obviously under hypnosis.' He nodded to the mayor who instantly perked up.

'That's right!' It might be quite a good defence plea. 'He must have been good because normally I . . .'

'Yes, yes,' broke in the Special Branch man testily.

'He didn't hypnotise me, though,' said Norman. 'When I looked out of the window I could see the lights of Grapplewick twinkling below.'

'It could have been a photo on a black background.'

Norman shook his head. 'I'm sorry to disappoint you but it couldn't have been a photo. I distinctly remember that the lights were twinkling.'

The superintendent sniggered.

'Something amusing?' asked the interrogating officer, and the superintendent glared back at him. He wasn't used to being interrogated and he objected to being treated like a suspect and being forced to listen to the damn fool answers Norman was coming out with. The lights were twinkling, for God's sake. The next minute he'd be talking about sleigh bells ringing.

'With due respect,' he began, 'we've established that the man is a gifted hypnotist and he used his powers on these two.' He waved his hand in the general direction of the mayor and Norman as if to dissociate himself from them. 'But what rational explanation can be given for the Indian woman and the burning down of his shop?'

'Ah yes, the shop, that's easy. Only a guess, mind you, but we're back to the accomplice. As for the woman, I'm afraid that is still a mystery.'

Again Norman interrupted. 'Yes, somebody could have been there to set light to the shop, but how would he know the exact moment to do it?'

The big man stared at him for a moment. 'What are you getting at?'

Norman was triumphant. 'The spaceman predicted it. Before it happened he put his hands to his forehead and a bit after that we heard the fire engines.'

They sat back to await an explanation, but the big man appeared to have other things on his mind.

'Now this girl Oomi, was there anything odd or different about her?'

The superintendent shrugged. 'I never met her so you can leave me out.'

Norman opened his mouth to speak but was interrupted by a peremptory knock at the door.

'Yes,' growled James.

Sergeant Buckley came in and hurried across to him to whisper in his ear. Norman and the superintendent strained to hear what was being said but with no luck.

Finally James nodded. 'Thank you, sergeant, I'll be right with you.'

He turned to the three of them. 'Well, I don't think there's any need to detain you further. If something crops up I'll let you know.'

Gratefully they all rose and shuffled out. As they were crossing the charge room nobody noticed the lady in conversation with the desk sergeant.

The Special Branch man popped his head out after they'd gone and beckoned to her. 'Would you like to come in here, madam.'

He stood to one side while she entered the room. 'Sit down, please,' he said, indicating a chair.

When she was settled he began, 'So you think you recognise the Identikit picture in the paper?'

He wasn't optimistic: there had been a score of claimants in the police station since Bernard Whittaker's article, and up to now all of them had proved to be dead ends. One of them, a stunted bearded man, came to turn himself in insisting he was the spaceman. It was a farce and Chief Inspector James was bored with it all. It was a degrading assignment for Special Branch anyway. It was 'bobby on the beat' stuff, and he had more important things to do than chasing up and down the country like a travelling salesman. However, the instructions were from the Home Office and until the letter writer was apprehended it would continue to supply the Opposition parties in Parliament with ammunition with which to taunt the Government. He was in a no-win situation: if he wasn't successful it would be a black mark on his record, and if he did make an arrest and the sender turned out to be a spotty Herbert he'd be a joke for not having caught him sooner.

The woman seemed composed, almost resigned. 'Oh yes, I recognise him and he's no more a spaceman than you are. His real name is Heinrich Adlon.'

He stared for a moment, realising that he hadn't been paying much attention.

'I'm sorry,' he said. 'What was the name again?'

'Heinrich Adlon.'

'A German?'

'Well, German parents, but he was born just outside Birmingham.'

The chief inspector looked at her, with the first stirrings of excitement coursing through his body. The first letter had been delivered to a small town just outside Birmingham, so there was the faintest of hopes that there just might be a connection. 'Now then, er . . .'

'Lesley, Eunice Lesley.'

'Thank you. Do you live in Grapplewick?'

'I run a dancing academy. Madame Lesley's.' She smiled and dropped her head. 'Not very successfully, I'm afraid.'

Chief Inspector James nodded sympathetically. Deep within his gut he had a feeling about this one, a feeling that he was about to achieve a major breakthrough. 'And you're absolutely certain that you can positively identify this man?'

She looked at him steadily. 'I should hope so . . . he's my husband.'

TWENTY-TWO

The wave of optimism that emanated from Grapplewick police station quickly reached Special Branch headquarters in London. At last an ointment had been discovered for the festering sore that had troubled the bureau for nearly a year. To date all they had achieved was to collate an extremely large file of 'Strictly Private and Confidential' marked letters, all similar and all useless, which had been delivered to various towns around the country. But now the hoaxer had made a serious error and Special Branch had a face, a name, an occupation, and most important of all, irrefutable evidence that the man was mortal.

Back in Grapplewick, having questioned Eunice Lesley for over two hours, the officers had learned the full story of their alien hoaxer. Eunice had told them of her younger days. Back then, she had been a dancer in the summer season at Bournemouth. She had been different from all the other girls in that she had inherited £50,000 during the run of the show. This was no secret; in fact on hearing the news she had taken the whole troupe out to dinner. Neither did having the money make any difference to her choice of lifestyle – twice nightly she had still enjoyed bouncing around with the rest of the girls to the tune of 'The Sun Has Got His Hat On.'

Unfortunately for Eunice, topping the bill at Bournemouth had been The Great Firenzi, a hypnotist of great skill and charm. All the girls had fantasised about him; he was cultured, aloof and untouchable, so it was hardly surprising that Eunice, gauche and not especially pretty, had nearly fainted when he had asked her if she wanted to be his assistant. By the end of the season they had married, although it would have been more honest to say that Firenzi had acquired for himself a slave. Eunice had given him her heart, her soul, her body, and sadly, her £50,000 inheritance. On his part, he had been charming, witty, attentive, and, after securing the inheritance, invisible. She had never seen him again.

When the Special Branch officers asked Madame Lesley for photographs of her husband, she refused. In fact, she didn't have any. She had destroyed them all. It didn't really matter to the officers too much; after all they could look through old copies of *Spotlight* and summer season souvenir brochures. Within a couple of hours photocopies of the wanted man would be faxed over to Grapplewick police station.

'What a bastard. Fifty thousand pounds was a lot of money in those days,' commented the junior Special Branch officer.

Chief Inspector James nodded wryly. 'It's a lot of money now.' Outwardly he remained calm, even indifferent to this mass of information coming in about the hoaxer, but this was just a policeman's facade. Inside, more than ever, he was burning to get his hands on the man. He knew now he wasn't a pimply-faced youth from a deprived background, but a cultured, devious and clever con-man. How many other women had he married and left penniless? But the jackpot question was, Why the spaceman masquerade? – *that* was the bottom line. What was he hoping to achieve with this elaborate con? Perhaps this was a job for Special Branch after all.

Wednesday morning dawned bright and clear. The citizens of Grapplewick knew nothing about the advances made by Special Branch, and nor did they care. Even if the true facts had been broadcast on breakfast television they wouldn't have believed them; no one was going to rob them of this day. From very early in the morning the traffic was all one way to Sagbottom's Acres. On a normal day a ten-minute drive would have taken Bernard Whittaker from his home to the office, but on this Wednesday after nearly an hour he was still on the road and he was still in first gear. On a normal day the streets of Grapplewick were never blocked; even during the rush hour the volume of traffic was negligible – like a quiet Sunday morning in the City of London.

Whittaker was astonished by the assortment of vehicles, family cars, mini-buses and even horses and carts bedecked with flowers. Indeed, he was crawling behind one charabanc crammed full of youngsters wearing Norman T-shirts, who shouted goodnaturedly to the pedestrians as they passed by. As he looked out of his car window, Whittaker was even more astonished to see people leaning out of the upstairs windows of their houses, cheering loudly and waving Union Jacks. Union Jacks, for God's sake! Two days back nobody in the town would have been able to lay their hands on one of those little flags but now it seemed that everybody had one. In front of him the charabanc stopped and one of the lads blew tentatively on a hunting horn while the others all cheered. 'Beautiful Grapplewick' badges were everywhere and Whittaker imagined that come the next day, Jimmy Jackson along with many other profiteers would be on their way to the Costa del Sol for a well-earned rest. Deep in thought, Whittaker went past his office but had no difficulty in doing a U-turn across the road. There was nothing at all coming in the other direction.

Once behind his desk he marvelled at the collective hysteria which had gripped Grapplewick. He knew Hitler had managed it in Germany in 1938 but then he had had an objective – world conquest. Here there was nothing, just a euphoric lemming-like rush towards the cliff edge. It was quite remarkable. The town's inhabitants were being drawn to Sagbottom's Acres as people are to the scene of a bad accident.

At this stage Whittaker too had no idea that the identity of the spaceman had been established. His own line of enquiry seemed to be struggling through treacle and he felt that he was running out of time. Wearily he picked up the phone. 'Hello, Doris? Get me the station master at Grapplewick Central.' He waited until she acknowledged, and was about to put the phone down when Billy burst into his office.

'Don't you ever knock?' growled Whittaker but his young reporter didn't appear to have heard.

'I think I'm on to something, chief,' he said eagerly, rummaging through the capacious pockets of his raincoat.

The phone rang and the editor snatched it up. 'Yes?'

'The station master,' said Doris and put him through.

Billy pulled out a wodge of rubbish from one of his pockets and then delved back in to find some more.

'Hello George, yes, Bernard Whittaker here . . . yes, I'm well, how are you? Yes . . . no . . . nothing's bothering me, George, but I was hoping you could help. I'm trying to trace a man between fifty and sixty, and a girl, much younger . . . they may have bought tickets in the last few days . . . Yes, I know, but these aren't your ordinary everyday people; he's smartly turned out and from all accounts the girl's a bit of a looker. No disrespect George, but they'd stand out on your station like a Chippendale in the waiting room.'

Billy leaned across the desk and tapped his arm. 'The girl,' he hissed, but his boss ignored him.

'I know it's the busy season, George, but try whoever's in the booking office. Ask him if he remembers any strangers.'

Billy shook his arm again.

'Hang on a minute, George.' Whittaker put his hand over the mouthpiece. 'Well, what is it?'

'Nothing on the man, Mr Whittaker, but a girl – and I'm sure it's the one we're looking for – has been staying at the Duke of Wellington for the past six days.'

Whittaker's eyebrows shot up. 'Good, Billy, that's great.' He returned to the phone. 'George,' he started, 'can you hang on a bit longer ... thanks.' He hooded the mouthpiece again and looked at Billy. 'Do you know when she checked out?'

'Early this morning; if I'd got there yesterday ...'

Whittaker shushed him and went back to the phone. 'We're getting there, George. Now, does anyone your end recall seeing a girl at the station this morning, buying a ticket?' He waited a moment or two before replying. 'No, I don't know where to, but there can't have been that many people about. We're talking about Grapplewick Central, not Gare du Nord.'

Billy tried to interrupt again but the editor waved him off whilst continuing his conversation with George. 'Yes, I understand that, but the people off on holiday and commuter folk presumably have bought return tickets. This person certainly won't be coming back ... yes, well, ring me if you hear anything. I'd send someone down but we're pushed for time. Thanks, George, see you soon.' He put the phone down, feeling that he'd just had a wasted conversation.

'Tell you what, Mr Whittaker,' Billy piped up, 'one of my mates is a porter down there. Any talent on the platform and he'd spot it all right!'

Whittaker looked at him thoughtfully. 'OK,' he said, 'get down there and have a talk with him. If he does remember the girl then he may just remember her destination.'

Billy puckered up his forehead. 'You mean the girl who checked out of the Duke of Wellington this morning?'

'Yes,' said Whittaker, inwardly despairing of his young reporter. He flicked down his intercom and got Doris again. 'See if you can find the whereabouts of Norman Waterhouse. If you locate him, I'd like a word.' He looked up to find Billy still standing there. 'What are you waiting for now?'

143

Billy hesitated. 'Well, the thing is . . . that girl . . . well, she's gone back home.'

Whittaker waited very quietly for Billy to continue.

'Well, the manager gave me her forwarding address.'

Whittaker regarded him for some time then sighed and shook his head. Slowly he reached forward and switched on the intercom again. 'Forget that call,' he instructed, and leaned back in his chair. 'You've got her home address?' he asked incredulously.

'Yes, sir, it's here somewhere.' Billy's hands shot into his raincoat and patiently his editor watched the ever growing mountain of debris from Billy's pockets – chocolate wrappers, bills, Polo mints and receipts – and that was just his raincoat. By the time he'd been through all his pockets there was enough litter on the desk to fill a decent-sized dustbin.

'Ah, here it is!' said Billy triumphantly, and passed over a crumpled piece of paper showing Oomi's address or, to be more exact, Ann Taylor's address, which was Yew Tree Close, Bogsea, Sussex. Remarkably, there was a telephone number there as well. 'Is that what you're looking for?' Billy asked hopefully.

Whittaker smiled, and keeping his voice as noncommittal as possible he replied, 'It's a start, Billy lad, it's a start.' Inside, he could hardly contain his excitement but it wouldn't do to make too much of this information in front of his reporter. Next thing he knew, Billy would be asking for a rise. He looked up to find Billy looking at him as though that might just be what was on his mind. 'Is there anything else, Billy?'

'No, sir, it's just that I thought we should have somebody up at Sagbottom's. You know, human interest and all that.'

'By God, Billy, you're right! Get up there as quickly as possible and circulate.'

'Thank you, sir,' and Billy was gone before anything more specific could be asked of him.

As soon as the door closed Whittaker switched on the intercom, but almost instantly he had second thoughts. It was useless ringing now; the girl wouldn't have got home yet, and that was if she was going direct. She might have stopped off in London for some sightseeing or shopping. He slammed his desk in frustration; he didn't have the resources to check her out and he didn't want to leak the story to his pals on the big dailies. Grapplewick would quickly be confirmed as an open asylum. They would also elbow him out of the biggest story of his career.

Outside, above the noise of the traffic he heard the sound of the hunting horn and realised that the charabanc must have only moved fifty yards or so since he made his U-turn to the office. He frowned. Another sound was missing. There was no noise coming from the outer office. He turned to look through the glass partition. No wonder he hadn't heard the clack of typewriters – the desks were empty, the machines covered, the photocopiers switched off and the phones silent. He walked over to his door and flung it open. Only Aaron was in the office, busy on the telephone. As Whittaker approached he cupped his hand over the receiver. 'Thought it might be a good idea to hire a helicopter to take pictures of the harvest festival.'

Whittaker thought for a moment. 'No, Aaron, cancel it.'

The old reporter looked at him for a second or two then turned back to his desk. 'Forget it, Bob, some other time.' He put the phone down.

'You didn't tell him what it was really for?' enquired Whittaker.

'No, we were just haggling over the price.'

'Good. The fewer people outside Grapplewick that know about this the better.' He looked around the deserted office. 'Where is everybody?' he asked.

'Where else?' replied Aaron. 'Badges, gumboots, the lot.'

The old editor sighed; he shouldn't have asked, he could have guessed. 'Oh, by the way, young Billy managed to trace the girl; she's gone home.'

'To Androm?'

Whittaker smiled. 'She caught a train early this morning to the south coast.'

'A train? I'm surprised our spaceman didn't give her a lift in Kershaw's Croft.' He slapped his thigh. 'Oh, I almost forgot; he can't. Kershaw's Croft isn't there any more; well, most of it's gone.'

Whittaker frowned. 'What are you talking about? It was there on Friday.'

'Well, it isn't now. Some enterprising Johnny has been dismantling it and would you believe, the stones are now for sale as souvenirs.'

Whittaker stared at him. 'I do believe it, and I also believe that the whole town has gone stark staring raving bonkers!'

TWENTY-THREE

The town hall, which was normally bustling with queues of enquirers, was utterly deserted. The only signs of life came from the mayor's office on the first floor, where an emergency meeting was being held, chaired by the head of the Conservatives, Councillor Davies. The only other people present were the mayor and Norman. It should have been a full council assembly but the rest of the members were strangely unavailable, either too ill to attend, or abroad. In other words, nobody wanted a part in this meeting. Councillor Butterworth, one of the original gang of four, was safely tucked away in a nursing home; at least, the nursing home's address was on the notepaper tendering his resignation. Ostensibly Councillor Davies had called the meeting to discuss the present situation and to find out what the hell was going on. He was totally unaware of the events of the last few days, having spent the past two weeks in Marbella on a fact-finding mission. He had returned late on Tuesday night, so the atmosphere in the town had knocked him for six.

The mayor filled him in with an up-to-date appraisal of the facts, cleverly easing the burden of responsibility on to others; Norman had been hypnotised at the barber's, he had accompanied Norman to Kershaw's Croft against his better judgement, and after the meeting in his office – which he had merely organised – rumours started circulating that the man was an alien who was proclaiming that a spacecraft was going to land at Sagbottom's Acres on Wednesday. The mayor finished his appraisal with a shrug as if to say, 'What could I do?'

It was a masterly whitewash but Norman listened with only half an ear. He was a demasted ship in the doldrums. All his dreams were up the spout; the Utopia of which the man had spoken was a brilliant concept and would have certainly been welcomed by the ordinary people of the world, but if he was being honest with himself he would have to admit that the main reason for his depression was Oomi. Not only was she part of this chicanery, but he'd never see her again.

'It's incredible,' muttered Councillor Davies as he rose and walked over to the window. Outside the traffic was thinner than earlier; presumably most of the spectators had already reached Sagbottom's Acres. 'And do you mean to tell me,' he continued, 'that they all believe a spacecraft will be landing today . . .'

The mayor shrugged again. 'I don't know whether they believe it, but they're all going up to Sagbottom's.'

The councillor looked at him, visualising the crowds packed on every vantage point like an old Biblical depiction of the Sermon on the Mount. Finally he spoke. 'And what happens afterwards?'

'Afterwards?' echoed the mayor.

'Presumably they'll be up there all night. What's going to happen on Thursday morning?'

This was a question that had bothered the mayor for the past five days. 'I don't know,' he said unhappily. Inside the office there was a deep silence, broken only by the distant noises in the high street. Both the mayor and Norman sat staring at the carpet in utter dejection until finally the councillor cleared his throat. 'What time will you be going?' he asked.

The mayor looked at him vacantly. 'I haven't made up my mind whether to go or not.'

The councillor looked aghast. 'You must go.' He looked at them both. 'Don't you see? If you're not there the crowd will assume that you knew all the time that there'll be no UFOs and they'll come storming off the moors like Genghis Khan's mob in search of blood – your blood.'

The mayor could easily imagine this, but he wasn't going to give way to Councillor Davies so easily. 'Yes, but if we do attend, they won't have to come storming off the moors. We'll be there.'

Councillor Davies thought about this for a moment. 'OK, but it's the lesser of two evils. If you're there they'll think you've been taken in as well and you may even get some sympathy.'

The mayor mulled this over. Inwardly he agreed with the councillor that it was the best course of action. The more he thought about it the better he felt; after all, he was the mayor and a leader of men. Yes, he'd go to Sagbottom's Acre in the full panoply and majesty of his office. To hell with sneaking in like an urchin under a circus tent flap, he'd go in style, with trumpets blaring. All he needed now was to organise this. He rose purposefully to his feet and strode to the door, calling in the town clerk.

By late afternoon most of Grapplewick's citizens were at Sagbottom's Acres, with a three-mile tailback stretching to the outskirts of the town. The area around the assumed landing site was already crowded with the early arrivals – groups of young folk in Norman T-shirts waving scarves above their heads, families with spread blankets littered with half-eaten sandwiches and bits of shell from hardboiled eggs, and elderly people dozing in light collapsible chairs. Only the very old could sleep through the incredible cacophony of sound that surrounded them: the two carousels on which bobbed fierce horses that clanked around to tinny music and crashing cymbals in desperate competition with several amateur pop groups who had made just enough money to buy mind-blowing sound systems but not enough to pay for music lessons. There were shrieks of laughter and joyful screams from the many side shows surrounding the area, and the mouthwatering smells from numerous fish and chip stands, hot dog vehicles and candy floss stalls permeated the air. It was quite amazing how, within one week, the town's citizens had been transformed from a shambling, listless bunch of no-hopers into a co-ordinated force of goodwill and high spirits.

Billy Grout forced his way between these groups of people. He already had a few interviews in his notebook, but they weren't very meaty. He wished he had a photographer with him. Most of the people surrounding him had cameras but to capture the atmosphere of Sagbottom's Acres called for a wide-angled lens. Even then it would be impossible really to capture the immensity of this carnival. Behind him he heard the tinkling of bells, and on looking around saw donkeys giving donkey rides. He wondered where on earth they had come from. It was really all too much for one reporter. He didn't know where to begin, and hoisting his bike on to his shoulder he struggled through the crush towards the way out. He had to get to a phone: Mr Whittaker wasn't going to believe this. A new sound joined the cacophony and to the right of the official platform the town brass band embarked on a rendition of 'The Dambusters March' in a futile attempt to lend dignity to the proceedings.

* * *

148

Just after dark an unmarked police car swept out of the station yard and up Radcliff Street.

'You still got the brake on?' asked Chief Inspector James.

The local detective constable automatically felt for it before he recognised the sarcasm and he put his foot down. There was no reason why he shouldn't, the streets of Grapplewick were deserted. It was an eerie experience, like driving through a ghost town. Most of the houses showed lights, but this was the customary obvious ploy to persuade marauding villains that the dwellings were occupied. Conversely and even stranger, all the pubs were dark and closed. As they sped up the high street Chief Inspector James suddenly realised it wasn't just the lack of traffic that was noticeable, it was the complete absence of buses. He felt conspicuous as the car drew up behind what appeared to be the only other vehicle in town. He heaved himself out and leaned back into the car.

'Wait here,' he said. 'Put your lights out and keep your eyes skinned. If you see anybody suspicious see what he's up to.' He straightened, looked up and down the street then bent back in again. 'If you see *anybody*, see what he's up to,' he added, and he made his way into the newspaper office.

The constable doused his lights and stepped out of the car. Apart from the switchboard girl, he was the only local police officer left in Grapplewick and he was impatient to get up to Sagbottom's. Turning in that direction he could discern a faint golden glow illuminating the sky. A firework burst into tiny droplets of light. If he didn't get there soon he'd miss all the fun.

Up in his office the editor poured out two glasses of Scotch and handed one to the Special Branch man, who nodded his thanks and drank deep.

'I've been trying to get in touch with you,' started the editor. James nodded again. 'I've been busy. What's on your mind?'

Mr Whittaker accepted the brusque manner; the policeman had an unenviable task, but then again he himself hadn't exactly been enjoying a week's package holiday either. And he didn't actually enjoy being spoken to as he did to others.

'We're almost certain that the man posing as a space alien is an illusionist who used to do a stage act under the name of "The Great Firenzi".' That should have brought the policeman to heel but it didn't.

'You're right,' he replied. 'He was an illusionist, and his real

149

name is Heinrich Adlon.' He shrugged. 'But he's probably used another dozen aliases since then. Well, is that all you wanted me for?'

The editor was nettled, but he still had a high card to play. 'Not quite,' he said. 'We've traced the girl, his assistant.'

The chief inspector stared at him for a moment. 'Oomi?' he asked, deceptively calm.

'Her name is Ann Taylor.' The editor was in the driving seat and he was tempted to throw in 'but she's probably used another dozen aliases since then', but he resisted the childish impulse. 'Yes,' he went on, 'we have her home address and telephone number.' He paused. 'Unfortunately the number has been reported as being out of order.'

James eyed him with new respect. 'Good work,' he said. His lethargic facade dropped away and he was all business. 'Do me a favour, will you?' He slipped a card across the desk. 'Ring that number and ask for Superintendent Cranleigh. If he's not there have him located, priority one. Tell him you're acting under my orders and to send two of our lads like the clappers of bastardy to this girl's address . . . and tell him, no arrest, just keep the house under observation.'

Mr Whittaker nodded. The Special Branch man strode to the door. 'Oh, and by the way,' he said, turning to the editor, 'thanks for the information, it could be the best lead yet,' and he was gone.

Mr Whittaker, well pleased with himself, winked at the closed door and pulled the phone towards him. After he'd dialled the number he heard the screech of tyres from below as the police car headed fast for Sagbottom's to witness the last act.

Late in the evening, lights were blazing in the mayor's office. At short notice, Sidney, the town clerk, had done a splendid job. A table set up along one wall was loaded with bottles of drink, plates of sandwiches and cake, now sadly depleted, cigarettes and one or two Havana cigars, even two jugs of Tetley Bitter. All this for no more than the expected half dozen dignitaries. It surprised and heartened everyone as they entered the room, and with smiles and much handrubbing they selected their particular fancies. After the initial assault on the hospitality, the mayor, resplendent in his robes of office – black, red and ermine – belched behind his hand as he surveyed the others.

150

Superintendent Smith was now back in uniform, dress uniform with medal and white gloves; Norman was morose and dejected. Florrie wasn't much better, overdressed and made up but still miffed at not having had time to have her hair done. Sidney came from the table and set down a fresh gin and tonic before her. It was her third and she perked up a little. Two more gins and she'd be in the maudlin stage . . . 'having to walk three miles to school barefoot'. Sidney himself added to the splendour in his own medieval town clerk's get-up. His tricorn hat and mace were on another small table in a corner. The Reverend Copthorne had yet to arrive, and unfortunately Councillor Davies, having instigated the get-together, had been unexpectedly called away to Leicester where his brother had been taken ill.

Norman suddenly blurted out, 'Why do we have to go up there if it's all a joke?'

Up to then the conversation had been amicable – football, the weather, the exorbitant price of most things; anything, in fact, that avoided the subjects of aliens and flying saucers. Now the last in the pecking order had had the temerity to throw a large rock into the placid water.

The mayor stared coldly at him. 'It's hardly a joke, Norman, when the whole town is up at Sagbottom's.'

'Oh, no,' replied Norman hotly. 'They're all up there waiting for a spacecraft that won't arrive because he said he was from the planet Androm when all the time he's just an ordinary con-man!'

The mayor smiled. 'That's what we've been told, Norman, but just because somebody looks like him doesn't prove that's the right person.'

Superintendent Smith picked up the drift. Norman had to be up there on the platform with them. If the crowd turned nasty and wanted somebody to point at, Norman was their man. The superintendent still had the remains of his career to think about. 'Oh, yes,' he added aloud, 'we've had numerous cases when a suspect has been positively identified and it's turned out to be somebody else.'

'That's right, Norman,' continued Florrie. 'It's not definite that he's the trickster; we've only been told he is. But if he is, what's he getting out of it, eh? Answer me that! As far as I can see he doesn't stand to gain anything at all; nothing financial any road!'

Norman digested all this information for a second or two. His aunt did have a point. 'Yes, what's he getting out of it?'

he repeated. 'There's been a fortune spent on badges, fall-out hats, gumboots and all that, but I can't see him being in cahoots with Jimmy Jackson and all the others.'

The mayor spread his hands: 'Well, there you are then.' But Norman wasn't wholly satisfied.

'It must be something to do with Sagbottom's Acres,' he said. The mayor buried his face in his tankard while the superintendent turned and helped himself to another dying sandwich. The conversation had taken a very embarrassing turn. He had been looking forward to making a tidy little profit from the land, but Sergeant Buckley had told him only two hours ago that the latest figure for car parking alone was £80,000. That wasn't just a tidy little profit; that was big league stuff, and when it came to light – as it undoubtedly would – the Serious Fraud Squad would have a field day.

Florrie giggled. 'Don't tell me the man's in partnership with old Crumpshaw! They would have heard the argy bargying in Blackpool!' She giggled again and the mayor decided that she'd had enough to drink for one function. He was about to steer the subject away from Sagbottom's Acres when there was a discreet knock on the door and Reverend Copthorne sailed in. It would be hard to describe his entrance in any other way; he could have been on a unicycle underneath his cassock, so effortless was his glide to the table of goodies.

'Evening all,' he said, eyeing the remnants. 'I hope I'm not late.' Judging by what was left on the table, he decided that he was.

'No, reverend, we've agreed to make a start at eleven,' said the mayor. He had decided upon that time earlier as, counting fifteen minutes to get there, that would leave them with only three quarters of an hour until Thursday, and what happened then rested in the laps of the gods.

The vicar nodded and smiled at all of them in turn. 'You know,' he started through a mouthful of madeira cake, 'I've got a theory about this spaceman.'

They waited while he tucked the crumbs into his mouth with a very white little finger.

'I don't think he's a spaceman at all.'

Again they waited. His face was glowing with excitement.

'I fervently believe that this is the second coming . . .'

They stared at him in open-mouthed disbelief.

'Yes,' he went on, 'I've given the matter some considerable

thought and I feel convinced there is every possibility that tonight we could be witnessing the manifestation of Jesus Christ our Lord ...'

They were stunned. They'd come a long way from con-man to the Son of God, but on reflection it wasn't too far fetched. The first time round had been a little town in Bethlehem so why not Grapplewick? But before anyone could challenge this theory, something even more dramatic occurred – an incident that shocked them all: a dull boom broke the silence. The mayor half rose to his feet and they stared at each other in puzzlement. The superintendent was halfway to the window when there was an-other boom – this time louder, bringing a small shower of plaster from the ceiling.

Norman looked up at the slightly swaying chandelier.

'The two sonic booms,' he whispered, hardly able to keep the jubilation out of his voice. 'They're coming,' he gasped joyfully.

Florrie hurriedly gulped down the rest of her gin and the super-intendent stared stupidly at the white dust on his sleeve. The vicar was all for a prayer of thanksgiving but there wasn't time. No one knew how soon the spacecraft would be landing. Their only desire was to get up to Sagbottom's as quickly as possible.

There was so much noise and revelry on Sagbottom's Acres that nobody heard the sonic booms. It wouldn't have mattered if they had, as most of the crowd had forgotten the reason they were up there in the first place. Every few yards it seemed there was a bon-fire surrounded by red animated faces and silhouettes, the bright flickering flames dominating the sickly white lights of the dozens of stalls where almost anything, from beer and hot dogs to badges and fall-out hats, was still available. The carousels indefatigably made their rounds, more pop groups now adding to the indescrib-able cacophony, and the night sky was rent with cascades, coloured balls and bangs from a seemingly inexhaustible supply of fireworks. Nearly everyone was partaking in the festivities, the exceptions being the sleeping young, the drunk and the dead. At half-hour intervals huge floodlights were switched on to a loud cheer, and an even louder one when they went out again. The lights were an intrusion: better the blackness in the middle, giving the appearance of a land-locked harbour surrounded by a busy holiday port.

153

Chief Inspector James surveyed the scene. It was grotesque, and something somewhere didn't quite fit. Circulating amongst the revellers were half a dozen men from the Liverpool Special Branch and some from Manchester. All carried pictures of The Great Firenzi and their job was to find him. They were diligent and at least thirty men between fifty and sixty-five years old had been manhandled to dark spots outside the area of festivities and questioned thoroughly. But it was hopeless, and deep in his bones, James knew it. A nut case might hang around to enjoy his success but Heinrich Adlon most definitely possessed all his marbles and would be miles away by now. But why? . . . What was it all about? James shook his head in frustration and decided to get himself a beer. Before he reached the stall the floodlights were switched on again and this time they were pointing to the entrance where a motorcade bearing the official party bumped down the grass to stop in front of the platform. For a moment all the chatter and the singing died down as word sped round that the mayor and the official welcoming committee had arrived.

At least it was a diversion and a derisory cheer went up, thousands of little Union Jacks were waved, and parents held up their offspring to witness the arrival. The Grapplewick brass band drum-rolled into the National Anthem but it was hopeless against the screaming obscenity of a rock band not fifty yards away. Even the bandmaster was having difficulty in hearing his musicians so a steady beat would have to suffice. A few of the town's leading citizens were already on the platform, and a gust of wind blew the strains of 'send her victorious, happy and . . .' They rose to their feet but the mayor, unable to hear the band at all, graciously waved them down again, proud that they should stand for his arrival. He was also impressed by the fact that on the seats they were to occupy were badges and anti-fall-out hats, a touching gesture. As he settled himself he, like all the others, was absolutely amazed at the incredible sights around him. He'd also noticed the vast sea of vehicles in the car park as they arrived and at five pounds a time he didn't need a ready reckoner to know his ship had come in. He leaned across Florrie and tapped Norman's knee. 'You all right, Norman?'

Norman frowned at him, missing the words in the general hubbub. The mayor held up his thumb and Norman nodded and smiled back. He was convinced now that the Special Branch had made a mistake. Just look at the extraordinary spectacular

154

extravaganza before him. How could the man from Androm possibly be a mortal, a common confidence trickster? Who else in the world could inspire a gathering such as this? And even if the whole thing turned out to be a gigantic hoax, what did it matter? He felt better and more mature for having met the man in the first place. The barber's shop in Coldhurst Street seemed a million miles away and even Benidorm didn't measure up. For the first time in his life Norman was actually thinking.

Some of the floodlights came on again, directed at the platform, and the dignitaries cringed, screwing up their eyes in the harsh white glare. And amid the general cacophony a chanting was being taken up, 'ee ... ee ... ee ... ee ... ee.' The bandmaster was still waving his baton for the National Anthem although most of the band had finished some time ago. The two carousels slowed to a halt, and the chant taken up by other sections of the crowd increased in volume.

'Speech ... speech ... speech ... speech.' The mayor licked his lips. The small Welsh garrison must have felt like this when confronted by the might of the Zulu hordes. 'Speech ... speech ... speech.' The cry was not accompanied by handclaps. Manfully the rock group tried to compete until somebody pulled the plug leaving them gyrating and striking noiseless guitars. It was several moments before they realised their tasteless mime was no longer backed up by the tape played through the enormous loudspeakers. The chant was louder now and the dignitaries on the platform rose and applauded.

The mayor, still seated, looked round at them and, realising what was expected of him, got to his feet. With an increased heartbeat that would have killed him if he'd noticed, he walked the three paces to the microphone. Thankfully the sheer mass of his audience was invisible behind the lights, but when the chanting died away it felt strangely lonely. He blew into the microphone to satisfy himself it was working, then he began.

'Fellow citizens of Grapplewick, we are all gathered here to welcome some very important people from afar.'

He was desperately trying to avoid words like spacecraft, modules and aliens, he hadn't expected to make a speech, and he realised that this was probably the most important address in his life. Indeed it might actually be *for* his life. He switched to neutral political ground.

'When I was a lad ... many years ago,' he added but nobody

laughed. 'Many years ago I lay in this very field and looked up at the sky and thought, what is life, who am I and what am I doing here?'

A wag in the crowd shouted 'Trespassin'!' and a great roar of laughter went up. The mayor beamed at the unseen hordes. That's the ticket, he thought, keep it light and friendly. He turned to where he thought the interruption came from and said, 'You're right and I'm not ashamed to admit it. I *was* trespassing.'

This got a laugh as well from people who hadn't heard the interruption. The mayor was more relaxed now.

'No, but to be serious for a moment . . . as I lay in this very field, I never thought I'd live to see the day when the whole of Grapplewick would congregate here in a body . . . with such good fellowship and community spirit in your hearts.'

This raised a cheer and he took out his handkerchief to blow his nose. It wasn't an act, he was genuinely moved.

'And I tell you this,' he went on, 'I'm proud . . . yes proud and humble to be your mayor.'

Some of the people round him clapped but he didn't hear anything beyond the lights so he went on, which was a mistake – they were getting restless. Faintly from the distance he heard, 'You'll neeeever walk alone' from the football supporters' club, and a rocket swooshed into the air. Behind the stage the heavy metal group and their road manager were frantically scurrying around with torches trying to locate the plug only to find that some bastard had cut the wires as well.

The mayor droned on about what a happy week it had been and this was a day one would be able to relate to one's children and one's children's children. He was waffling and regretted not sitting down when he'd said the proud and humble bit.

Norman fidgeted uncomfortably. 'Sit down, Uncle,' he thought, willing his uncle to do just that. If he'd been doing a turn at the music hall he'd have had the hook around his neck by now. He felt a tug at his sleeve and looking down he saw the editor. 'Oh, hello, Mr Whittaker,' he said.

'I think you'd better come with me, Norman.'

The lad frowned. 'Not now, Mr Whittaker. They could land at any moment. Didn't you hear the sonic booms?'

Whittaker looked away in exasperation, then turned his back to the platform. 'Look, lad,' he hissed, 'I haven't got time for games. I want to show you something before this lot string you up from the nearest lamp post.'

Norman hesitated for a moment, then jumped down while the editor cleaved a path through the crush and led him through to the car park. Meanwhile, the mayor was still struggling, sweat pouring down his face. His mouth was in a rictus of a smile as the crowd began to give him the slow handclap. Another chant began which the crowd soon took up: 'Nor-man, Nor-man, Nor-man.'

Thankfully, Norman didn't hear it; he was jolting back to Grapplewick in Whittaker's old jalopy.

'Yes, Mr Whittaker, just because he looks like the stage hypnotist doesn't necessarily mean that it's him.'

'It's him all right, The Great Firenzi. Oh, and by the way, his real name is Heinrich Adlon.' He glanced over at his passenger but Norman didn't like what he was hearing so had turned away. 'Oh yes, and we now know the identity of the blind man. God, he must have had a busy week!'

'How d'you mean?' asked Norman reluctantly.

'Well, it's my guess he not only set fire to your uncle's shop, but he's been up and down the town like Wee Willy Winkie, spreading all the new rumours and keeping the old ones going.'

Norman stared along the beams of the weak headlights, mulling this new information over, searching for flaws. 'OK then,' he said after some time, 'answer me this. If he was running about, spreading all these rumours, why did the spaceman insist that we all kept the secret?'

Whittaker turned on to the cobbles of Linney Lane. 'Psychology,' he muttered.

Norman frowned. 'I'm sorry? I'm not with you.'

'Clever, I'll admit, but if the mayor and the rest of you told everybody what had transpired at that meeting, they wouldn't have believed you. They would have thought that you'd all gone round the twist. By maintaining your secrecy and even denying that anything unusual had been said, you fuelled the rumours – especially when you went around wearing the badges.' He looked across to see how Norman was taking the news. 'By the way, I also talked to Jimmy Jackson, and somebody – I suspect you'll find it's your blind man – put the idea into his head about manufacturing "Beautiful Grapplewick" badges for the public at large.'

'So you think they were getting a rake off?'

'No . . . That was pin money to them, but the badges did have a purpose. They weren't just window dressing but more of a yardstick. The more badges that were on display, the more people would turn up to Sagbottom's.'

This all fitted but Norman didn't want to be convinced. 'What about Kershaw's Croft?'

'Ah yes, Kershaw's Croft.' Whittaker pulled up at a stop sign and looked right and left before entering the high street, although for all the traffic about his could be the only car in the world.

'Tell me, Norman, when you saw the pair of them in Kershaw's, did they sparkle? I mean their space costumes, did they sparkle?'

Norman couldn't see what he was getting at but he remembered last Wednesday distinctly.

'No they didn't, just plain white like plastic, but I'm certain they didn't sparkle . . . Why?'

The editor nodded with satisfaction. 'That's it then.'

'What's what?' said Norman, exasperated.

Mr Whittaker looked at him. 'Last week I found a couple of sequins at Kershaw's and I assumed they'd come off their costumes. But now I know I was wrong: you've cleared up another little loose end.'

'What loose end?' asked Norman impatiently.

The editor was in no hurry. He pulled into the kerb almost opposite the town hall and rasped on the handbrake.

'You told Chief Inspector James that when you hovered about in Kershaw's Croft, you looked down on the lights of Grapplewick and they were twinkling.'

'They *were* twinkling,' protested Norman.

The editor shook his head. 'They were twinkling, yes, but they weren't the lights of Grapplewick. They were sequins dangling on a black velvet background.'

Norman just gaped at him. 'Sequins,' he croaked eventually.

'Oh, yes, I spoke to a film director pal of mine and he put me on to it. Apparently it's an old studio trick to simulate distant lights in the background.'

Norman gazed unseeing through the windscreen. On reflection he had to admit to himself that the man hadn't allowed them to get too close, and he'd soon slid the cover back into place.

'But why?' he asked.

'Why what, Norman?'

'Well, if it was all a con trick, what did he get out of it? And why was it necessary to get everybody up on Sagbottom's Acres?'

The editor raised his hands. 'Just look around you, do you see anybody, any cars about?'

Norman shook his head.

'Well, that's it. It was imperative that Grapplewick was deserted.'

Norman looked at him blankly.

'Come with me for a minute, lad.'

He got out of the car and waited for Norman to join him.

'You'll not be fully convinced until you've seen this.'

They walked the two or three paces to the corner into Trafalgar Street, and Norman stopped dead in his tracks. Two cars were standing outside Lloyds Bank. Inside the bank, all the lights were blazing.

'Come on, lad, I want to show you what was in it for your spaceman.'

He took Norman's arm and together they walked through the impressive portals of the bank. The first person they saw was Chief Inspector James.

'Oh, it's you,' he said, lighting a cigarette.

Over his shoulder Norman could just make out other men; one was taking photographs, another dusting the twisted remains of a round steel door with a small brush. A blue fug still clung to the ceiling.

'By the way,' went on the inspector, 'thanks for the tip.'

The editor smiled. 'It was luck. I must have been the only man left in Grapplewick and even then if I hadn't taken the wrong turning getting up to Sagbottom's I'd have missed it.'

The Special Branch man nodded.

'Any leads on where they've gone?' asked the editor.

'Not yet, but it's only a matter of time. Airports are sealed up, road blocks and so forth, but I'm not optimistic, they had too much of a start. Still, at least we now know that all the letters weren't just the product of a diseased mind.'

The editor shook his head in admiration.

'What a build-up though: twelve months of UFOs Are Coming Wednesday until everybody gets fed up with the joke, then ignores it altogether.' He chuckled. 'He must have had his sights set on Grapplewick for a year.'

Whittaker looked at Norman pityingly. 'Come on, son,' he said. 'Let's get you sorted out.'

He was about to leave when he turned to the Special Branch

man. 'Oh, by the way, I'd appreciate it if you could let me know how you get on.'

'Of course . . . we owe you one.' And they shook hands.

Out in the street the editor jerked his thumb towards the bank. 'That was the first sonic boom. The second was Barclays just up the road.'

Norman was numb. He returned to the car like a slow programmed robot. At the back of his mind he'd clung to the belief that they were all mistaken and the man was genuine. But after the devastation in the bank he was finally convinced: nothing mattered now. Wrong again – a tight feeling squeezed his stomach.

'What about Oomi?' he asked fearfully. 'Was she . . . er . . . was she part of the gang?'

'No, no,' smiled the editor, 'not in the way you mean. I spoke to her on the phone about an hour ago.'

'Spoke to her?' asked Norman.

'Yes, she's an actress and your spaceman asked her to play the part of his assistant . . . the money was good and as long as she stayed in her hotel room, apart from when she had to play Oomi of course, it was a doddle, money for old rope. She hasn't any idea that the whole thing was a set-up. She's under the impression that it was a documentary programme dealing with the gullibility of a small town, and the effects of mass hysteria.'

Norman's relief was almost audible and the editor glanced quickly at him. 'By the way,' he said, 'time's getting short if you want to pack a few things.'

'Pack?' asked Norman. 'What do I want to pack for?'

The editor put his indicator out unnecessarily and turned left towards where Norman lived. 'Listen, lad, in a few hours there's going to be a lot of very angry people looking for someone to hit, and I've got the feeling that you're the patsy, so your best bet is to make yourself scarce.'

He took one hand off the wheel to delve into his inside pocket, bringing out a wad of notes which he passed over to Norman.

'Take this, you'll need a bit and as everybody else seems to have made money out of it, let's just call it your share.'

Norman stared at the fistful of crispness in his hand. He'd never even seen so much money in his life. He looked at the editor suspiciously.

'What about you? You haven't made any money out of it, have you?'

'Not yet I haven't, but whichever way this story breaks I have an exclusive and that should make the *Bugle* solvent.'

'But I don't need all this,' protested Norman.

'Oh, yes you do. There's your train fare for a start, milk train to Manchester, Manchester to London, change there for Bogsea.' Whittaker put two fingers into his waistcoat pocket and pulled out a card. 'Here's the address. I've written it down.'

'Why on earth should I want to go to Bogsea?' asked Norman, not relishing the thought of travelling the length of England on his own.

'Why?' repeated Whittaker. 'Why? So I'll know where to contact you when the story breaks. The address I've given you is Ann Taylor's address.'

Norman looked at the card, bewildered. 'Who's Ann Taylor?'

'Didn't I mention it?' said Whittaker innocently. 'You probably know her better as Oomi.'

Norman's face brightened and suddenly he felt very good. He wanted to hug Whittaker; he nearly did, but just as they were sweeping into Feathering Road an ambulance bore down on them, racing from the opposite direction. Whittaker swerved to the side of the road to avoid a head-on collision and with a screech of tyres they got away with a side swipe. The ambulance however was not so lucky. It mounted the pavement and crashed into a wall. The two drivers, shaken but otherwise unhurt, got out to ascertain the damage to their vehicles and to themselves. Both were relieved to find that apart from slight shock there was nothing serious, and the ambulance had only superficial denting at the side. Whittaker was missing his rear bumper but this was no great loss. He didn't have a front one anyway.

'You shot out of there without stopping,' said the ambulance driver accusingly.

'I'm sorry, but I didn't expect to meet anyone tonight,' replied Whittaker. He wandered over to the ambulance but apart from the few dents it seemed all right.

The ambulance driver seemed quite unbothered as well. 'Don't worry about that. I've got to get to the hospital as quickly as possible. I've got two heart attacks in there.' His mate jumped down from the back.

'What the bloody hell's going on?' He nodded to the stretchers inside. 'This hasn't done them any good, you know . . .' He was cut short as another ambulance came screaming around the corner.

161

'Busy tonight,' said Whittaker unnecessarily.

'And then some,' replied the driver as he grated his gears to reverse the wounded ambulance away from the wall. His mate clambered into the back to check on the patients, ignoring the editor. Whittaker's blood was up, though, and he was determined to find out what all the sudden activity was about.

Sitting in the passenger seat, Norman fidgeted impatiently. Already he had forgotten about the near-miss accident for he was floating on a bed of elation. Later on that day he would be meeting Oomi again, only this time she would be a more human Ann Taylor. He thumped the dashboard in frustration as Whittaker, talking outside to the ambulance driver was obviously in no hurry. At last he seemed to finish his conversation, and slowly he strolled back towards the parked car. Come on, come on, Norman urged silently although he still had hours before the train was due to leave. Suddenly he jumped sharply as another ambulance with sirens blaring came hurtling around the corner and careered past at such high speed that the parked car swayed in its backwash. As if reminded of the urgency, the damaged ambulance across the road suddenly shot forward, causing Whittaker to stagger out of its way. He watched the disappearing tail lights thoughtfully as he opened the back door and casually chucked in his back bumper. He then opened the driver's door and flopped into his seat behind the wheel, but he didn't start the engine. Instead he just stared out of the windscreen.

'Trouble?' asked Norman after a time.

Whittaker looked at him strangely. 'You could say that,' he answered enigmatically.

Norman waited and after what seemed like ages the editor shook himself out of his thoughts. 'I don't think you'll be going to Bogsea after all,' he said, turning on the car engine.

Instantly Norman was bewildered; shattered would have been a more appropriate description. 'Not going to Bogsea?' he asked.

Whittaker found first gear and released the handbrake. As they shot forward he continued. 'That's right, Norman, we're going back to the moors.' He paused and his next words hit Norman like a lorry-load of wet fish.

'A flying saucer has just landed on Sagbottom's Acres.'

CHAPTER

TWENTY-FOUR

A s the car struggled forward up the hill towards Sagbottom's, Norman craned forward in his seat to look up at the
sky. The same golden glow hung over the area, but there were
no fireworks now. The last time he had approached the field, a
jumbled cacophony of noise had greeted his ears, but now, the
straining noise of the clapped-out engine was intrusive in the
silence.

Reaching the crest, Whittaker stopped the car and switched off
the engine. They got out and apart from the sighing wind there
wasn't a sound in the air. Below them in the amphitheatre they
saw the same vast crowd as before, stretched out as far as the
darkness would allow, but this time it was still and silent, gazing
with rapt attention at a round sinister object in the centre of the
field. Norman gulped and looked at Whittaker, who was equally
overwhelmed. From their vantage point about half a mile away,
the UFO looked no bigger than a table mat, but once up close
they could imagine that it was very big indeed.

Leaving the car where it was they hurried down the slope towards the flying saucer. Their footsteps were muffled in the grass,
but such was the silence surrounding them that many heads
turned in their direction. Norman was eager to push his way forward to the platform, but Whittaker stopped him.

'Hang on a bit, lad. Let's see what's happening.'

Norman looked around him and for the first time he noticed
that everyone was wearing their anti-fall-out gear. To his left he
saw the platform where his uncle in his red robe and the vicar
were wearing their yellow plastic hats. Feeling a little conspicuous
he dragged his own from under his belt and put it on.

Whittaker, meanwhile, was standing on tiptoe staring at the
spacecraft. There was something menacing in the way in which it
just squatted there, with slits for windows around the side which

glowed faintly in the floodlight beams. He whispered to the man next to him. 'How long has it been there?'

The man eyed him suspiciously. ' 'Ast thou been asleep or summat?' he hissed, then reluctantly he added, 'About half an hour I reckon.'

Whittaker wasn't satisfied. 'Just landed without warning, did it . . . or did it hover over the field first?'

The man pushed him away. He wanted to watch the saucer, not answer silly bloody questions. Whittaker turned to another man in front of him, who turned his head but his eyes remained on the saucer.

'I've just got here,' whispered Whittaker. 'What happened?' The man stepped back alongside him so that he could talk and look at the same time.

'Fantastic!' he replied. 'Fanbloodytastic! One minute it was dark and the next, whoosh! All of a sudden there were these bright lights in the sky . . . I thought it was fireworks for a minute but it was too bright for that . . . Then the whole of the sky lit up and I've never seen owt like it! When they went out, there it was where you see it now.' He pointed towards the field. 'Bloody creepy, I can tell you. I never believed in flying saucers up to now, but what can't speak can't lie.'

The man was a good foot shorter than Whittaker and he had to tilt his head back and hold on to his yellow hat so he could look into the editor's face.

'Bright lights they were!' he continued, his eyes widening at the memory. 'Bright and white!' He jerked his thumb at the scaffolding holding the arc lamps. 'Makes this lot look like my granny's gas mantle!'

'Are you satisfied now, Mr Whittaker?' The editor looked across at Norman and smiled. In his yellow oilskins he looked as if he was just about to launch a lifeboat.

'Just hang about a bit, lad, until we know what's happening.' Norman decided that Mr Whittaker was a hard man to convince, but he stayed put and craned his neck to look again at the module.

Most surprisingly the person who lived within fifty yards of the spacecraft was totally unaware of the momentous goings-on at Sagbottom's Acres. Old farmer Crumpshaw, unused to the fresh air and excitement of the previous Sunday, was in bed where he'd been for the past three days. He didn't believe in doctors and so

164

when he felt poorly he just drew all the curtains and hauled himself under the blankets, surfacing spasmodically to help himself to whisky or to use the bucket. Only when he felt better or the bucket was full did he venture out.

It was his dog Rex who awoke him, with forepaws on his bed, licking his face. Blinking his eyes, Crumpshaw grimaced. 'Get off me, you dirty little bugger!' he muttered, pushing Rex away from him. Wagging his tail furiously the dog scampered to his empty food bowl. Old Crumpshaw had no idea how long he'd been in bed but it was obvious that Rex wanted feeding. He swung his legs out on to the cold floor and rubbed his face. He was feeling better now, the sleep must have done him good, and judging by the light streaming in from under the curtains, it looked like being a fine day.

First he staggered to the kitchen and opened a tin of dog food, forking it into Rex's bowl. The dog, not having eaten for about two and a half days, devoured it as it came out of the tin, most of it never even reached the bowl. Crumpshaw wondered whether he should open another, but then decided that the dog could wait. First he would empty the slops and then perhaps have a fried egg. As he went back into the bedroom to pick up the bucket he remembered the biscuit tin and his fortune under the bed. Immediately he cheered up and decided that he would have two fried eggs and possibly some bacon as well. Slipping on his boots he shuffled into the yard and emptied the bucket down a drain.

As he was coming back into the house he stopped, realising that something was very wrong. It couldn't be day as the sky was black, but it was light over at Sagbottom's Acres. He walked over to the wall and his mouth fell open in disbelief. The field was brightly lit up and there were hundreds of people in it, all staring silently at some sort of black object in the middle of it. He shaded his eyes and looked harder. There were people as far as he could see, and they were all wearing yellow oilskin hats. Thousands of 'em. What the hell was going on? He remembered the old tales that his father used to tell him; tales of dark satanic rites where people came on to the moors to dance naked until the cock crowed. But what the dickens was the thing in the field that everybody was worshipping?

Anger now replaced his apprehension. If they wanted to play silly buggers then they could, but let 'em do it elsewhere. Muttering to himself he hurried back into his house and with trembling fingers loaded his double-barrelled shotgun. Some of the crowd nearest to his house had heard him emptying his slops, and the clatter of the bucket, but they were totally unprepared for the furious onslaught of the old man when he reappeared, bulldozing a path through them. A few turned angrily to see what the commotion was all about, but they soon made way on seeing him, a bearded patriarch in shirt and long johns waving a shotgun. He was obviously not a man to be argued with.

Crumpshaw came to the rope bordering the field and, lifting it up, he staggered in. A collective gasp went up but it was lost on him. He looked around at the awe-inspiring scene and all anger left him. He was now frightened. He turned fearfully to the round black object, but facing it gave him a new confidence. It certainly wasn't some devilish creature with horns and cloven hooves. Instead, the thing in the field looked benign and innocuous, like some great fat mushroom without a stalk.

Up on the platform the superintendent watched the little white figure in front of the UFO. Very soon the vicar saw what he was looking at and came over to join him. The two of them in their oilskin hats looked like a comic double act, but the time had passed for any humour.

'Well, do something, superintendent,' wailed the vicar.

Superintendent Smith looked at him. Hell would freeze first before he would set one foot into the field below him. He had his hat and badge on, but was that enough? He picked up a loud-hailer and put it to his mouth.

'This is Superintendent . . . endent Smith . . . ith speaking . . . king. For your own safety . . . afety, leave the area . . . rea . . . immediately . . . tely.'

The mayor went over to the superintendent. 'He won't hear you; it's old deaf Crumpshaw.'

Word went around the crowd like molten lava: 'It's old deaf Crumpshaw, it's old deaf Crumpshaw . . .' Some of the older people genuflected in respect while very young children peered fearfully from behind their mothers' jeans. Crumpshaw indeed couldn't hear a thing but he noticed one or two uniformed policemen dotted around the field, so he guessed that whatever was going on must have had some form of official blessing. However, he was still undecided.

Back on the platform the superintendent, realising that he wasn't getting through to the old man down below, bent down to his sergeant. 'Go in there and get the pillock out!' The young sergeant gulped and turned to his right and left, but the two constables who had been behind him had magically vanished. It looked like he was the muggins.

'And sergeant, better give him one of these.' The superintendent handed him a sou'wester. The sergeant took it with ill grace and sidled slowly into the field, holding the hat before him as if it were a peace offering. The crowd waited expectantly. They weren't experts on neutrons or fall-out, but they all agreed that the sergeant was a brave man. Sweating now, and constantly pushing up his hat, which kept sliding down over his eyes, the young sergeant advanced slowly. If radiation didn't get him then there was always the shotgun.

Crumpshaw watched him approach and was confused. If he was going to be arrested then why didn't the man just get on with it? Why didn't he come straight up instead of crouching and tiptoeing towards him holding out that hat? Involuntarily the farmer took a step back and as he did so he stumbled over a tussock. As he fell his fingers closed on the trigger and a blast erupted from the barrel. People gasped and screamed and the sergeant fell flat on his face. He wasn't hit; it was just a reflex action on his part. In fact the shot hadn't even been discharged in his direction.

Crumpshaw was dazed. Still weak from his three days in bed, it took him a couple of minutes to struggle into a sitting position. In front of him the policeman was kneeling on all fours and gazing, not at him but over his shoulder. With a puzzled expression on his face, Crumpshaw turned and faced the great black mushroom behind him – which was now sagging and crumbling into a shapeless mass. The police sergeant was the first to recover. Rising to his feet he carefully approached the hissing, contracting black blob. The farmer and his shotgun forgotten, he raised his arm slowly to feel the object which was rapidly sinking into the field. With ever-growing confidence he brushed his hand over the surface and smelled his fingers. 'It's rubber,' he muttered. He moved over to one of the slitted windows that had reflected the arc lights and touched that surface. It felt tacky, and when he looked at his fingers they were glowing. Increduously he turned to the distant platform and shouted to his superior, 'It's luminous paint, sir!' He didn't know whether his explanation had been heard so he held up his hand to show his bright fingertips. This acted as a signal. Suddenly one flashbulb went off and soon camera flashes were rippling through the packed assembly like so many fireflies on a black summer's night. All the dignitaries were on their feet now, and a murmur was stalking through the crowd. They were still unsure about what was happening but convinced that whatever it was, it was definitely not in the script. The superintendent spoke into the microphone, calling for calm and insisting that everybody stayed where they were. He then jumped down and entered the field, warily approaching his sergeant. The town clerk laboriously helped the mayor down from the platform and he followed the superintendent into the field, together with the fire chief and the more inquisitive members of the public. The area seemed harmless enough and soon scores of people were scrambling over the ropes and moving into the field. The police, however, were quicker, and linked arms to form a cordon around the dying rubber space module.

Whittaker jerked Norman's arm. 'I think it really is now time I got you on that train,' he whispered, but Norman remained rooted to the spot, fascinated by the scene before him. Angrily the editor came back and whirled him around. 'Pull that silly bloody hat over your face in case anybody recognises you. You're coming out with me.'

Norman didn't argue and slowly and imperceptibly they backed out of Sagbottom's Acres. When it was safe to do so they turned and ran for the car. Behind them the UFO was now nearly flat on the grass. The superintendent and fire chief circled it cautiously, looking for any clues as to where it might have come from. One of the firemen who had also been examining the saucer called them over, pointing to the ground. Two or three yards away from the rubber mass was a piece of piping that just protruded above the surface of the ground. The fire chief knelt down and sniffed it. 'Well, that explains the lights,' he said.

'Lights?' asked the superintendent.

'The bright lights that preceded this thing.' He kicked the pipe gently. 'When we dig this up, we'll find it's an eight-inch mortar which fires a flare. We used to call 'em Bengal Lights.'

The superintendent looked at him. 'And this was the light in the sky?'

The fire chief shrugged. 'Oh, I think when we search the area we'll find one or two more of these, all set to go off simultaneously.'

'What was the object of that exercise?' asked the mayor, butting in. The fire chief ignored him and knelt again, lifting up a segment of the heavy rubber to scoop the dirt away from another piece of metal. He shone his torch at the exposed piece and examined it carefully. Finally he rose to his feet and dusted the earth from his hands. 'We'll soon have that dug out,' he said. 'But a pound to a pile of goat droppings that'll be one of the cylinders that inflated the damn thing.'

'You think there's more than one?' asked the superintendent.

'I should think so,' replied the fire chief. 'They'd have to be pretty powerful to inflate this thing in under two minutes.' He turned to the mayor. 'In answer to your question, sir, bright lights, everybody looks up, and for a time we're all blinded. By the time we get our vision back this thing has inflated like a bloody great chocolate souffle.'

The mayor nodded. 'Yes, I was blinded for quite some time.'

'And then to add to that lot,' continued the fire chief, 'each of them flares is equal to a million candle power.'

The mayor turned to the superintendent. 'Your lads have been up here since Sunday. They must have been walking around with their eyes closed!'

Superintendent Smith grabbed his arm and led him a couple of yards away so they wouldn't be overheard. 'The man, smart-arsed Jack, phoned me on Saturday night.' The mayor looked puzzled but the superintendent carried on. 'The spaceman,' he whispered, 'he warned me not to venture inside the landing area as it was already charged with neutrons or something like that. He said that a homing device had already been laid to guide down the module.'

The mayor nodded understanding and turned to Florrie, who by this time had pushed her way through the crowd to be beside her husband. 'How did it come down?' she whispered breathlessly.

The mayor raised his eyes to heaven. 'It didn't,' he hissed, 'it came up.' This left her more confused than ever.

Superintendent Smith gazed around at the sea of confused faces and decided that the moment had come for him to make a tactical withdrawal. At the moment the crowd was in a state of shock and bewilderment, but this moment wouldn't last and he didn't want to be around when it wore off. He turned to his hapless sergeant and whispered in his ear. Within seconds a gangway had been

169

cleared through the spectators and the superintendent strode purposefully through it as if he were off to make further investigations. He didn't fool the mayor, however, who scampered off after him, leaving Florrie to fend for herself.

In fact they needn't have panicked. The crowd was more interested in the pile of black rubber which was lying in the field, and some of the more adventurous ones were already carving it up for souvenirs. As it was, for three or four weeks after the event unscrupulous dealers were selling pieces of rubber from the fake spacecraft at exorbitant prices, although the amount of rubber that changed hands would have been sufficient to have covered at least ten miles of the M1.

The whole extravaganza had been brilliantly orchestrated, from the very first contact in the barber's shop to the carnival at Sagbottom's Acres. Every step had been carefully calculated and carried out with meticulous timing, but it wasn't over yet. The Great Firenzi was still at large with a fortune at his disposal. For him the world was a plateful of Whitstables, but there were forces out to find him. Interpol had already been alerted, but they would be of no use if he was still in Great Britain. Nobody could be sure of where he was; but one thing was for certain. He wasn't on his way back to the planet Androm in Kershaw's Croft.

PART THREE

BOGSEA – BEACHY HEAD, SUSSEX

TWENTY-FIVE

As the train pulled out of Manchester, Norman settled back in a window seat and opened his newspaper; *The Times*, no less. He'd no intention of reading it, it was merely to conceal himself from the other passengers and from the way everybody else flipped open their dailies, they weren't too keen to be seen either. He gazed sightlessly at the newsprint, thoughts tumbling in a shapeless, chaotic mess through his already over-taxed brain. Uppermost in his mind was the spaceman, or The Great Firenzi, or whatever. The sheer nerve and effrontery of the man was unbelievable. Had he been on the side of law and order what a great prime minister he would have made. But then again, had he been on the side of law and order he wouldn't have been a politician.

Norman smiled ruefully to himself when he thought of the dangling sequins in Kershaw's Croft. But they *had* looked like lights. Anybody would have been fooled, and even had he seen through the deception, there's no telling what might have happened. There was a ruthless streak to the man – the burning down of his uncle's shop, that wasn't an illusion, that was cold, calculated, wanton destruction. Norman tried to find logical explanations for the man's sequence of trickery but there still remained one or two imponderables. How had he managed the Indian lady? He couldn't have been able to see her, let alone predict her movements precisely. And there again it was never explained how his accomplice had managed to fire the shop at exactly the right moment. His thoughts raced on. Had old, deaf Crumpshaw not accidentally shot the space module, they'd all still be up on Sagbottom's Acres staring at it. And with at least eight hours' start, the man could have been anywhere. As it turned out, he'd been within a hair's breadth of being caught red-handed by the editor. Two unforeseen slices of bad luck, but still he'd managed to evade capture and disappear.

The train jerked into Stockport and Norman blinked out of his reverie. He was still holding his newspaper exactly as when he'd left Manchester and he was overwhelmed with embarrassment. People would think he was a slow reader and had just mastered the headlines. He flapped it open to the centre pages and hid himself again, and as the train eased out of the station his thoughts returned. How had the detective from Special Branch . . . James, that was him . . . how had he managed to identify the man so quickly? But then Norman was unaware of the vital information passed on by Madame Lesley. His weary brain, unused to overtime, shied away from the problems. All in all it had been one helluva week, and probably the most important in his life. Seven days in which he'd emerged from his chrysalis to become an adult. Never again would a package tour to Spain with a bunch of his mates appeal to him. The barber's shop which had been his world was no more, and rather sadly he had to admit to himself that the sun didn't rise and set on Grapplewick. It was a discovery that gave him no comfort.

Norman was genuinely fond of his uncle and aunt, and he had been reasonably happy living with them, just a pleasant empty vessel floating aimlessly from one meal to the next. Part of him wanted to get off at the next station and speed back home to hide his face in the bosom of mediocrity, but his new-found strength resisted the urge. The Great Firenzi had inadvertently pointed him in the direction of a harder, more competitive life, and it scared him a little. A wave of depression engulfed him, but lifted just as suddenly when he thought of Oomi, or to be more exact, Ann Taylor. The new name wasn't as exotic but it didn't matter. She was the same girl and, more important, she was innocent. She had been deceived just the same as everybody else.

Lulled by the mesmeric rhythm of the wheels, Norman dozed against the cool pane of the window, mercifully missing Rugby and Newport Pagnell. He awoke to see the dark, dreary, tall buildings of Euston Station beckoning to him. Immediately he was gripped by panic – he was alone in London! According to his uncle's atlas, London was the hub of the British Empire. He was amazed at the amount of people running, walking and dodging each other as if they all knew exactly where they were going, and all were obviously late for whatever it was they were hurrying to. A tannoy blared incomprehensibly and the tempo of the crowd quickened. Norman found himself swept along the concourse towards the Underground, but he soon figured out that that was where he wanted to go, so he didn't resist. He couldn't understand why everybody was in such a state. They weren't even content to stand still on the escalator and enjoy the adverts but had to push past him and leap down two stairs at a time. Did they know something he didn't? Was there some sort of emergency, or were Londoners like this all the time?

At the bottom of the stairs there were several openings to platforms with destination boards, but the rushing torrent of people didn't give him a chance to read them. Central line, Circle line flashed past, and what the hell was Bakerloo? He began to panic again so when he saw the large 'Way Out' sign he took it.

Back on ground level he breathed deeply to rid himself of his claustrophobia, and looked around. In the street it was just the same as below; thousands of men and women all looking worried and rushing around as if there was a curfew. Suddenly Norman remembered the money Whittaker had given him. He took it out of his back pocket and hailed a taxi, which turned out to be a very good investment. Forgetting his hunger and his tiredness he looked out of the taxi window and began to enjoy himself. He saw many large, impressive buildings that made Grapplewick Town Hall look like a gatehouse. His head swivelled from side to side as they drove over Waterloo Bridge. St Paul's was to the left and Big Ben and the Houses of Parliament were to the right. He was amazed at the width of the Thames; the river Ribble flowed through Grapplewick and he could spit across that.

Owing to the volume of traffic, the taxi never exceeded twenty miles per hour, so for Norman his trip was a wonderful sightseeing tour. On reaching Waterloo he wished his journey could have been longer – that is until the cabbie told him his fare. Good grief, he could have bought a suit for that back home!

After a wash and brush-up and a quick snack at the station, Norman boarded a suburban train for Bogsea. There weren't many passengers at that time in the afternoon and Norman dozed again until the station announcer woke him with an 'All change ... Bogsea, all change ... Bogsea.' His heart beat faster; this was the end of the line in more ways than one. He squared his shoulders and strode to the ticket barrier. He wasn't a hick any more. After all, he'd got here, hadn't he? And under his own steam too.

The big burly man at the gate clipped his ticket and it was only when Norman had passed through that he stopped. There was

175

something familiar about the man. Norman eased back ostensibly to read the destination boards, but he surveyed the railwayman covertly and suddenly he knew what it was. Pinned on his lapel was a *white plastic badge.*

Norman was staggered. He couldn't read the lettering from where he was standing and before he could edge nearer, the man turned his back and hurried through a door marked STAFF. It wasn't just a coincidence, though: other people were wearing badges. The woman in the newspaper kiosk was one of them. He waited until she was attending to a customer then he strolled across and was able to read the lettering: 'Bogsea is bracing.'

'Yes, luv, what can I get for you?'

He stared at her uncomprehendingly for a moment. 'Oh, er, have you got the, er, *Times?*'

'I'm sorry luv, not this late, they've all gone.'

He nodded and was about to walk away when he saw the headlines of the *Evening Standard:* BIG BANK ROBBERY. He took the paper and put the money on the counter.

'Fourteen million they got away with,' said the lady. 'How they could blow open two banks and get away without anybody knowin' is beyond me.'

It wasn't beyond Norman though. Nostalgia flooded his mind as he thought of Lloyds and Barclays banks in Grapplewick, dear little Grapplewick. He frowned at his momentary weakness and went out to the taxi rank. It wasn't far to Ann Taylor's address, just long enough to give him time to read the article. In fact he read it twice, but there was no mention of the spaceman, or Sagbottom's Acres. For some reason or other it was being kept out of the newspapers but why? And were the 'Bogsea is bracing' badges anything to do with UFOs, and if so when were they supposed to land? More than ever he was eager to see Ann Taylor; she would have the answer to that. He swayed forward as the taxi pulled up outside an ordinary semi-detached suburban house.

Ann had obviously been expecting him because just as he entered the front gate she was at the door. She smiled, but it wasn't particularly warm, it was the sort of greeting you'd give to a delivery man.

'Did you have a good journey?' she said, standing to one side so he could come in.

'Yes, thanks.'

He waited till she'd closed the door, then followed her into the lounge. A man with his back to him was talking quietly on the phone. His heart plummeted – was it her husband? Never once had he thought of her being married. But then again, why not? Red juicy apples don't hang on trees for long when some greedy bastard with a ladder comes by. But he needn't have worried. The man turned to look at him and Norman relaxed, then immediately he was uptight again. It was Chief Inspector James of the Special Branch.

'Right sir, I'll keep you informed.' And he put the phone down.

'Ah, so you got here then.'

Norman nodded and they all stood looking at one another like Act Three in a bad provincial theatre. Ann was the first to break out of the deadlock.

'Well,' she said with forced cheerfulness, 'have you had anything to eat, er . . .'

'Norman,' he broke in, amazed at his own temerity. 'No thanks, I had a meal in London.'

It sounded good and cosmopolitan. No way would he admit that his meal was a dead hamburger at the station buffet.

James sighed. 'Look, why don't we all sit down? I have a few things I'd like straightened out.'

Ann sat on the settee against the wall, and the two men in armchairs facing each other, but before the policeman could begin, Norman blurted out the question he'd pondered in the taxi.

'What about the badges "Bogsea is bracing"? Why are they wearing those?'

James shrugged. 'Same reason you had "Beautiful Grapplewick".'

Norman stared at the chief inspector, mouth wide open, then he remembered Ann was present and he shut it.

'You mean they think UFOs are going to land?'

The policeman smiled. 'Grapplewick did.'

Norman ignored this. 'Yes, but when? When are they going to land?'

'Tonight.'

'Tonight?' Norman was flabbergasted. 'Tonight,' he repeated. 'But how – I mean the man was up north yesterday. Well, he couldn't have left Grapplewick much before midnight.'

'Ah yes,' said Ann, 'but immediately after the meeting in the town hall at Grapplewick last Thursday morning, he came down here and set this one up.'

177

Norman couldn't quite take this all in. 'You mean, do the same thing here?'

Ann nodded. 'I'm afraid so, a carbon copy job except that he didn't burn down a barber's shop, he set fire to the mayor's house instead. The burgling and the banks were news to me. Chief Inspector James told me.'

Norman looked at the policeman who raised his eyebrows as if to say, 'Satisfied now?' but Norman wasn't. It was a bit too rich for his apprentice brain.

'But the blind man – Mr Whittaker told me he was in Grapplewick all the time.'

'He was, the man here was another accomplice, and also . . .' she hesitated and lowered her head, 'another Oomi.'

'Well obviously,' said Norman. 'You couldn't be in two places at once.'

Chief Inspector James sighed. 'I'm sorry to interrupt, but I have work to do.' He turned to Ann. 'To continue where we left off, how did you get up to Kershaw's Croft and back again?'

'He had a camper, you know, like a mobile caravan, which he parked round the back, then afterwards he ran me back to the town and dropped me off near the hotel.'

James nodded. 'That figures, we found the tracks out the back and it had to be either a camper or a four-wheel drive. We're checking that out now.'

Norman squirmed with embarrassment when he thought of that night in Kershaw's Croft.

'I'll bet you thought we were a right couple of Herberts,' he muttered bitterly.

Instinctively Ann reached out and touched his knee.

'Oh no,' she said earnestly, 'that's not true . . . Well, partly; he thought your uncle was a bit . . . well, a bit gullible, but he was impressed with you. As a matter of fact after you'd gone he said we had to go careful with you. He's the one to watch, he said, he's unpredictable.

Norman looked at her and it was Ann's turn to blush. The chief inspector sniffed. He hadn't missed the exchange but before he could continue his interrogation, a bleeper chirped twice and he took a radio from an inside pocket.

'James,' he said into it, and after listening for a few moments he said, 'OK, I'll be out shortly and we'll tour the banks. Out.' He stuffed it back into his pocket.

Norman's eyes widened. 'Do you think he'll do the banks here?'
'I hope so,' said the policeman, 'but I very much doubt it. Every
bank within a five-mile radius is being watched, but I think he's
smarter than that.'

'How do you mean?' asked Norman.

'Well, for a start only half of the town have made the pilgrimage up to Beachy Head. There's still too many people about.
Apparently they didn't fall for it.'

'And we did,' growled Norman, flagellating himself.

Again Ann shook her head. 'Don't feel too badly about it, Norman. There's an international match on telly tonight at half past
seven, live from Wembley, and that's more important to a lot of
people than a spacecraft landing. That doesn't say much for the
people of Bogsea, does it?'

Norman silently agreed, but he glanced covertly at his watch to
see if he'd missed it. Again the bleeper demanded attention.
'James,' said the policeman into his radio. He held it to his ear
while he listened, then said, 'Well, he's bottled up here somewhere
. . . yes, the minor roads are most important . . . OK, out.'

Norman was impatient with a question.

'How did you know that he'd be pulling the same stunt here?'
he asked.

'We didn't until last night,' answered the chief inspector, pick-
ing up his hat. 'Your Mr Whittaker gave us Miss Taylor's address,
and I assigned two of our lads to keep an eye on the house. Well,
they spotted the badges and the activity in the town and it didn't
take 'em long to piece two and two together.'

He turned to Ann. 'I'll be off now, but thanks for your help.'

She rose to show him out. 'See you later, Norman,' he said. 'I
must ask you not to leave the house. I may be back with more
questions.' He hurried down the short drive. It was getting dark.
As he got to the gate he stopped and walked back to the girl. 'Just
as a precaution,' he said softly, 'don't draw the curtains.'

Norman was still standing when she returned.

'Sit down, Norman,' she said. 'I appreciate you standing up
every time I do, but I think we know each other better than that.'

He blushed and lowered his head. Now the chief inspector had
left, all Norman's new-found poise and sophistication seemed to
have accompanied him straight out the door.

'Can I get you a cup of tea or something?'

'Tea will be fine,' he mumbled and she went into the kitchen.

He was about to sit down again but then changed his mind. In a momentary flash of insight he saw himself through her eyes, a bumbling stumblebum well placed for a gold medal in a prat show. Sternly he straightened his tie and strode in after her. She turned when he came into the kitchen and smiled.

'Do you like it strong?' she asked.

'It doesn't matter,' he replied. He had more important things on his mind than the strength of tea. 'Er, Ann . . . the man, well, you know . . . the spaceman . . . well, when he came to the meeting in the town hall he was suddenly there, and when he went he seemed to disappear. I talked to one or two other people but nobody remembers him. What I mean is, how did he manage to arrive without anybody seeing him?'

She smiled as she spooned the tea into the pot. 'Same way as I did,' she answered. 'An old man walked up the steps and into the toilet on the first floor near your uncle's office. In his carrier bag was a smart suit, and all he had to do was change and walk into the meeting. On the way out he did exactly the same, but in reverse.'

Norman's eyes widened. 'And you did the same?'

'Well, yes . . . except I used the ladies.'

He looked long and hard at her. The man was a genius – he hadn't missed a trick. There was still one burning question to be answered, though.

'What about the Indian woman on the street?' he began.

'That was me,' Ann replied.

'I guessed as much,' Norman replied hotly, 'but why Indian?'

Ann giggled and Norman frowned. Instantly she became contrite. 'Oh, Norman, I'm not laughing at you, I was remembering how I looked and felt when I spent that time traipsing up and down in front of that bike shop before I got the signal.'

'Signal?' he asked, and she put the teapot down and faced him.

'I had a bleeper on me, like Chief Inspector James's, only when mine bleeped I had to stagger to the wall. When I was bleeped again I had to fall down, and that's when they carried me into the shop.' She giggled again. 'I genuinely nearly did have a heart attack when they laid me on the floor. I was so scared that they'd hear the bleeper that I kept moaning to cover the sound of it.'

Norman smiled with her. 'I'll tell you something,' he said, 'it fooled us completely.'

Ann poured the boiling water into the pot. 'Before you ask,' she said, 'I had to be Indian because a long sari would hide my legs and the

180

pregnancy disguised my shape.' She put down the kettle and turned to face him. 'And you realise the brilliance of his thinking? I had to be coloured as no European could faint without first turning deathly pale.' She looked earnestly at Norman. 'Don't you think that's clever?'

He shook his head in wonder. 'He's going to be a hard man to catch.'

Across the street, Detective Chief Inspector James sat in the front of the unmarked police vehicle, receiving information and issuing orders. Not surprisingly a wide search of all the trailer parks and camp sites had drawn a blank. He'd also spoken to all of his surveillance teams positioned outside every bank in Bogsea, but everything was as normal. Suddenly his radio crackled into life. 'Team Three, Lloyds.' He pressed the button on his radio. 'Go ahead, Team Three.'

'A white Ford saloon has just parked about one hundred yards from the target.'

James thumbed his mike. 'Can you see who's in the car?'

There was a slight pause. 'No, the occupants are not visible from here . . . hang on . . .' The chief inspector waited. 'Yes, two men have got out and locked the car doors . . . They're moving in the opposite direction. They're too far away to identify . . . Over.'

'OK, one of you follow them but don't apprehend, just keep them in view. We'll be round there just as quick as we can. Out.' He lowered the radio from his mouth and spoke to the sergeant next to him. 'Where is Team Three?'

'Ashton Street, sir. About five minutes from here.'

'Let's go,' ordered James. 'Don't drive too fast, though, make it look natural.'

The local officer looked into the rearview mirror and eased away from the kerb. After fifty yards or so he turned left into a major road that led directly towards the bank. No sooner had he rounded the corner than a dark blue van pulled into the space vacated by him and two men in raincoats got out. One of them opened the back doors of the van and two uniformed policeman got out, taking their places in the front seats. No words were exchanged, but one of the men in the raincoats raised his hand and spread his fingers to indicate five minutes. Then the two of them walked across the road to Ann Taylor's house.

Norman was beginning to relax. The tea was doing him good

181

and Ann had switched on the electric fire, infusing the lounge with the warm glow of intimacy. 'Any more questions?' she asked mischievously from the armchair opposite.

He smiled. 'Not that I can think of.'

After a moment of silence he put down his teacup and leaned forward earnestly. 'You know, Ann, I think meeting you was the most important day of my life.' She looked at him seriously but before he could continue they were interrupted by the ringing of the doorbell and the spell was broken.

'That's probably Chief Inspector James,' Ann said as she went reluctantly to the door, but she was wrong. The hall light fell upon two men in raincoats.

'Special Branch,' one of them said, and proffered his card for identification. Ann didn't bother examining it.

'You'd better come in then,' she said and they stepped past her, waiting for her to close the front door. They then followed her into the lounge. She gestured towards Norman. 'This is . . .'

The taller of the two broke in. 'Yes, Miss Taylor, we know who he is. Chief Inspector James would like him down at the station to identify a couple of people. It shouldn't take long and Inspector Simpson will wait here with you to keep you company while he's gone.'

Norman rose to his feet and smiled at Ann. 'OK, I'll be as quick as I can.'

She took his hands. 'Quicker than that, I hope,' she said softly.

Norman looked at her, then whirled around, clapping the detective on the back. 'Lead on Macduff,' he said cheerfully, and practically skipped out of the house. Ann hurried over to the window to watch him go, but the police officer with her was quicker; he drew the curtains and faced her.

'Why did you do that?' she asked.

'I think it best if we sit down,' he advised, but she remained where she was.

Something was wrong, she only wanted to see Norman off. It wasn't against the law, was it? The man took her arm, not gently either. 'I think you'd better sit down,' he repeated and shoved her to the armchair.

'Who do you think you're pushing?' she said angrily. 'This is my house, and I'll . . .'

He plonked her down. 'Sit,' he commanded. 'Now don't give me a hard time, just keep your trap shut.'

She stared at him. 'You're not from Special Branch, are you?'

He leaned towards her. 'I won't tell you again, shut it.'

She waited until he was seated opposite, then leaped out of her chair to the door, but again he moved swiftly, deceptively so for his build, and grabbing her arm he pulled her round and backhanded her across the face. Eyes wide she stared at him, despising the tears that rolled down her cheeks. It wasn't so much the pain of the blow, but the desperation of knowing that Norman was in trouble, in deep trouble.

Chief Inspector James walked into the half-empty pub, wincing at the deafening pop music that was almost mandatory in places such as this.

'What are you having?' he asked his companion.

'I'll have a half of bitter, thanks.'

'Two halves of bitter,' he shouted to the landlord, although there was only the width of the bar between them.

The man nodded and as he took two glasses over to the pumps, the chief inspector turned and leaned his elbows on the bar.

'Where are they?' he asked softly.

The detective glanced casually round and as he lit a cigarette he murmured, 'In the corner by the juke box.'

They nodded to each other in silent toast as they took a mouthful of the flat, unexciting brew, carried their glasses casually over to where the two youths were sitting, pulled out a couple of vacant chairs and sat. The young men looked at them warily. There were other empty tables, why did they want to sit here? James took a long swig from his glass, then took his identification quietly from his inside pocket.

'Chief Inspector James, Special Branch,' he said, 'And this is Detective Sergeant McCumber.'

One of the youths looked wildly round but there was no way of escape. They were in the corner and to get out they would have to pass the heavies, and that wasn't a sensible option.

'What's up, then?' asked one of them with transparent bravado.

'Which one of you owns the white Ford?'

'What white Ford? What're you talking about? We don't know nothing about a white Ford.'

Chief Inspector James finished his drink. 'OK, let's continue this at the station. On your feet.'

One of them blustered, 'Hang on a minute, what about our rights? I mean I'm not going anywhere, I've done nothing.'

James leaned over the table. 'I haven't got time to play silly buggers. Now are you going to walk out of here nice and easy, or do I have to drag you out?'

Slowly they rose to their feet and as they did so, strong hands gripped their arms and they were hustled out and round the corner to the white Ford. Once there the detectives pushed them roughly against the car, slapped their hands on to the roof and spread-eagled their legs, searching swiftly until James delved into the side pocket of one of their bomber jackets and produced a set of ignition keys. He tossed them to his colleague whilst he held on to the collars of the two unfortunates.

'Try them for size,' he said.

The detective inserted one of the keys and the door opened smoothly.

'OK, cuff 'em,' and in a few seconds both youths were hand-cuffed and hustled into the front seats of the car.

Chief Inspector James slammed the door, then climbed into the back seat. 'Now,' he started, 'I haven't got much time so I want some quick answers, OK?' He leaned forward between them. 'Where did you get this car from?'

The two youths stared out of the windscreen, both acutely conscious of the chief inspector's face turning from one to the other.

James sighed. 'OK, you want it the hard way.'

He grabbed the long hair of one of the youths and jerked his head back viciously. The pimply face screamed, more with shock than anything else, and the detective outside the car looked quickly up and down the deserted street. The youth yelped again as James tugged once more until the man's head was arched over the back of the seat.

'It belongs to a mate of ours,' he gasped.

James yanked again. 'Listen, Sonny Jim, we've checked and this car was stolen not ten miles from here this morning.'

'Stolen?' the youth asked apprehensively. 'We didn't know nothing about that, honest, that's the God's truth. If we'd known it was stolen we wouldn't have had no part of it.'

James released the other man's hair and took out a handkerchief to wipe his fingers. 'OK, let's hear it.'

The youth didn't hesitate. 'We were in the pub about half past two and this bloke came up to us and asked if we'd just park the car for him.'

184

'This afternoon?' asked James quickly.

'No, he asked us this afternoon and said he'd be back this evening, and if we weren't going to Beachy Head to see the Saucer would we park it then – outside the bank.'

The words were tumbling out now and the other had joined in. 'Tall geezer, well spoken, he said not to ask any questions and he gave us a century each.'

The chief inspector looked from one to the other, then apparently satisfied he stepped out of the car slamming the door behind him.

'Book 'em,' he said to the local detective.

'Yes sir, what's the charge?'

Chief Inspector James shrugged. 'I dunno,' he said, 'parking on a double yellow,' and he crossed the road to where his own car waited.

'Any developments?' he asked as he eased into his seat.

'Not a dicky bird, sir.'

James grunted and stared sightlessly through the windscreen. Something was niggling him, some unformed thought at the back of his mind. The two youths were harmless Jack-the-lads overjoyed at the hundred pounds for the easiest job they were likely to get, but why? It had to be his man who'd put them up to it. But for what purpose? And suddenly he knew.

'Back to Ann Taylor's place,' he barked. 'And don't spare the horses.'

The driver screeched away from the kerb and Chief Inspector James thumped his knee impatiently, silently castigating himself. What a dummy, what a thickhead he'd been. Of course, the Ford was a decoy – that's all it was – and it had succeeded brilliantly. They had drawn him away from the house. He clenched his fists – if anything had happened to Norman or Ann he swore he'd make the man pay. All the frustrations and humiliations of the past twelve months welled up inside him. By God, he'd have the man if it was the last thing he ever did.

James was out of the car before it had stopped. 'Get around the back,' he spat at his driver, 'and are you armed?'

The local officer stared at him. 'No, sir, we weren't issued with any.'

James looked towards the house and tugged a 9 mm automatic pistol from his shoulder holster. He handed it over to the officer. 'Take mine. It's not standard but it's better than most.'

The officer hefted it in his hands. 'I'll manage, sir.'

'Good. I'll give you five minutes to get round the back. If anybody comes charging out, shoot, OK? Forget all that crap about fair play, just shoot first. Do you understand? We're dealing with a high roller!'

The officer hesitated for a moment and then hared for the corner of the street. James looked at his watch and waited.

There was silence in the room. Ann sat stony-faced staring at the glowing bars of the electric fire while the man, still in his raincoat, lounged in the armchair opposite, eyes half-closed, nursing a glass of whisky. He was, however, alert and instantly stiffened as the front doorbell chimed. He immediately jumped to his feet and his hand moved quickly to an inside jacket pocket, retrieving an ugly grey revolver. Ann drew a sharp breath and felt herself trembling. 'See who it is,' he hissed, 'and whoever it is, get rid of them.' Ann hesitated. 'It might be Chief Inspector James,' she said, halfway between hope and panic.

The man thought quickly. 'OK, just tell him your boyfriend's gone to the town to look for him, and I'm your Uncle Jack.'

'What if he doesn't believe me?' she wailed.

In response the man smiled without humour. 'Then it'll be too bad for you both.'

The doorbell chimed again and he thrust her towards the door. 'Don't forget now – don't be clever or I'll blow his head off.'

Ann opened the door slowly and Chief Inspector James smiled down at her. 'Mind if I come in for a minute?' he said. 'I'd like a few words with Norman.'

Ann felt the presence of the man behind her. 'I'm sorry,' she replied, 'but Norman's gone to town looking for you.' Although she was an actress this wasn't a role she relished, and to her ears her voice sounded false and stilted.

James peered over her shoulder and she turned. 'Oh . . . That's my Uncle Jack.' If this was an audition, she certainly wouldn't get the part.

Still smiling, James walked past her. 'Chief Inspector James, pleased to meet you.' He held out his hand. For a second the man hesitated, then they shook hands. The gun had been returned to its pocket. Ann was still holding the door open. 'Do you mind if I come in and wait for him then?' asked the policeman. 'I can only spare a couple of minutes so let's hope Norman hurries back quickly.'

Ann glanced at the man who gave a slight nod. 'Of course,' she said, closing the door. 'Come through.'

The three of them walked into the lounge where the policeman remained standing while the other man sat down in his armchair, outwardly relaxed but all spring and steel inside. Ann sat opposite, desperately trying to think of a way in which to warn the policeman, who seemed completely at ease, jingling loose change in his pocket. 'I suppose Ann's told you what the flap's about,' he asked casually. The man nodded and sipped his drink although his eyes never left the chief inspector.

'Ah well,' sighed James, 'I wouldn't have minded a glass of whisky myself but I think I'd better be off before temptation gets the better of me.' He took his hand out of his pocket to look at his watch and as he did so a few coins spilled out and fell on to the carpet. Instinctively the man bent down to retrieve them and James was ready for him. His knee jerked up, crashing into the man's face and sending him hurtling over the arm of the chair. Blood from his broken nose sprayed on to the carpet as James dived after him, pinning him down on the floor. It was an unnecessary precaution. The man lay limp on the ground amongst two of his teeth, gasping for breath through his bleeding mouth. James straddled him, removing the gun from the thug's raincoat pocket. He then bundled him over to go through his other pockets, hoping to find papers, a wallet, any source of possible identification. He spoke over his shoulder. 'Can you bring me some cold water and a rag?'

Ann didn't answer. She just stood in the middle of her lounge, white and shaking, hands over her mouth to suppress a scream. James looked over at her and rose to his feet to put his arm gently around her shoulders.

'Sorry it was a bit rough,' he said gently, 'but you don't mess around when the other feller's got a gun.'

'You knew he had a gun?' she asked, astonished.

'I guessed . . . when I went to shake hands with him he had to let go of something in his pocket before he took his hand out, and I assumed it wasn't a Mars bar.'

She shuddered. This wasn't her world and it frightened her. Up to half an hour ago she had treated the whole affair lightheartedly, and the appearance of Norman was a happy ending to a pleasant dream. But not now. This wasn't part of the pleasant dream. This was real violence, not at all like on television. There was blood all over her lounge; not ketchup, and the gun was real too. She turned away from the sprawled figure on the floor; her only experience of violence had been in her last two plays.

'Have a sip of that.' James was handing her a glass of whisky but her hands were shaking so much that she couldn't hold it. He helped the glass to her lips and as the spirit warmed her insides her trembling eased and she greedily gulped some more.

'You first alerted me that something was wrong before I even entered the house,' he said.

Ann frowned, trying to recall her few banal lines at the door.

'It was smart of you to draw the curtains.'

She stared at him in confusion. 'Oh yes, but I didn't draw them. He did.'

James's eyebrows shot up. 'Well, that was good of him, then.' He saw that she had finished the drink. 'Now be a good girl and fetch me that water.' She hurried into the kitchen and almost immediately she came back, ashen-faced.

'What is it?' he asked quickly.

Ann pointed in the direction of the kitchen. 'When I was in there I noticed something white outside the window and when I put on the light it ducked out of sight. I'm sure there's somebody out there.'

James tensed for a moment and then relaxed. 'It's OK. That'll be my driver. Stand at the window and wave a white cloth or something, but don't open the door until you see him approach or he may shoot you.'

Ann hesitated. 'Go on,' James said, 'I want him in here sharpish.' He looked down at the groaning mass on the carpet struggling weakly to sit up. James watched his feeble attempts for a moment, then bent down, grabbed the man's lapels and dumped him on the chair. There was no fight left in him and not much blood either, judging by the steady trickle coming from his shattered face.

James heard the back door close as the younger detective came in. 'Good. Now get him handcuffed. I don't think he'll be a problem but you never know.' Ann shuffled in with a basin of cold water and set it down on the floor.

'When he's secure,' continued James, 'clean him up a bit. I'm sorry, but I don't have any time.' The young officer drew out his handcuffs and looked with distaste at the ruined face. He'd seen a few traffic accidents in his time but he'd never heard of such ings-on in an average law-abiding semi-detached. 'Well, get with it,' growled James as he examined the papers he'd tal from the man's pockets. 'I want him bright eyed and bus. tailed.'

Norman had followed the detective into the back of the van. He had wanted to look back at the window but the van doors had been slammed shut and immediately his arms had been pinned behind him and a soft pad slapped over his mouth and nose. The ether had taken effect quickly.

Some time later – Norman had no idea how much later – he opened his eyes and a wave of nausea swept over him. Weakly he closed his eyes again but that only seemed to increase his dizziness, so he took a deep breath and steadied himself to rejig his senses. Wherever he was, it was dark and stank of fish and diesel oil. He tried to move and found that he couldn't because he was tied to a chair. Panic-stricken, he struggled and thrashed with every ounce of his strength, but it was useless. Tears sprang to his eyes, but they were born of frustration; they weren't the mewlings of an adolescent. With a sickening awareness he remembered Ann and groaned as he recalled himself skipping out of the house like a besotted twelve-year-old.

A bright light dazzled him momentarily, then went out. He tensed, mouth open to hear better, and then it dawned on him that the dizziness wasn't the after-effects of the ether but because the room was gently rocking. He was on a boat, but where and more importantly why? Claustrophobia overtook him. Like a frightened child he opened his mouth and screamed for help. He wasn't a seaman so he didn't recognise the sound of a hatch being opened, but he heard footsteps on a steel ladder and a shape suddenly loomed in front of him.

'One more peep and you're dead.'

The voice was strangely familiar but Norman was unable to recognise the speaker in the dimness, until the probing beam of a lighthouse flashed through the porthole, illuminating the man for a brief second. Norman's throat tightened. It was the spaceman.

'I knew we'd have trouble with you,' said the man, almost apologetically, but then he pushed his face close against Norman's and his voice became harsh. 'You should have stayed in Grapple-

189

where you belong. You're in amongst the big boys now and ner you live or die is immaterial to me. You are my hostage little insurance in case the police get too close. By now they st know that I've got their star witness, so you've really served ur purpose. You may be of further use, but if you give me any ouble, you're history. Is that clear?'

With that he turned and hoisted himself up the ladder. Norman saw his dark bulk against the starlit night and then the hatch slammed down, leaving him in blackness again. Again panic feathered his insides, but he made himself think of the girl. That seemed to give him strength. Suddenly the silence was shattered by the throb of engines, and from the increased rocking of his tiny cell, Norman knew that they were under way.

Although the pain from his smashed face must have been excruciating, the man was a hard nut to crack and Chief Inspector James wasn't making progress as fast as he would have liked. 'I'll ask you again,' he shouted. 'Where have they taken the boy?'

The man looked at him, hate in his swelling eyes. 'Get stuffed,' he muttered thickly.

James stood back and sighed. 'You know you're a berk. You amaze me, you honestly do. Do you really believe they'll be coming back for you?'

There was a flicker in the man's eyes. He obviously hadn't given it much thought and James was quick to press home his advantage. 'We've got you in the bag. Possession of a firearm, kidnapping, and if anything should happen to Norman, accessory to murder as well.' He ticked off his fingers as he spoke. 'And you really believe they're coming back for you. It's more likely to rain gold sovereigns,' he sneered, and stood back. 'Take him down to the station,' he said to the young officer. 'I don't waste time on pillocks.'

Up on Beachy Head the crowds were still gathering in anticipation but most of the townspeople had already decided that the whole thing was a practical joke and had started drifting off back to their homes. More sightseers were turning away when it happened: there were several bangs and the skies were lit with a blinding light. Instinctively the watchers looked up – as they were meant to – and, momentarily robbed of their vision, they missed the blimp as it struggled frantically to inflate. The two Special Branch men, however, were not blinded as they were equipped with night-vision glasses: had they not been so prepared they could well have believed that a flying saucer was actually quivering on the grass. Further down on the coast two of their colleagues were only interested in observing the sea, and from the white glare cast by the flares they spotted a boat travelling slowly and without lights in a westerly direction. It was a phenomenal stroke of good fortune. Without the light from the flares they would have missed it.

The harbour master's office was ablaze with lights as Chief Inspector James leaped out of the car and hurried along to the jetty. He was about to mount the steps when his radio bleeped. Quickly he snatched it from his pocket and pressed the switch. 'James,' he said.

'Control, we've got him. Sector Four have a boat in sight, maybe a forty-foot motor launch travelling slowly without lights in a westerly direction. Over.'

Chief Inspector James was wary. 'What makes you sure it's him?'

'Couldn't be anybody else, sir. Drifted out of an inlet on the tide until they were far enough out to start the engines without being heard from the shore.'

'Are you tracking him?'

'Yes, sir, we've notified the coastguard's boat and they have him on radar, following at the same speed, awaiting instructions.'

James thought for a moment. 'Tell the coastguard to intercept and investigate.'

'Will do, sir. Over and out.'

James was about to stuff the radio back into his pocket when he stopped and pressed the switch. 'James, patch me into Sector Four,' he instructed. He waited a second or two. 'Do you have night glasses, over.'

'Yes, sir, but even so we would have missed him had it not been for the flares. They lit up the whole area. Over.'

James nodded to himself. 'Of course. Well done. Out.' He lowered his radio thoughtfully. He'd seen the flares from the car on his way over. It had been a replay of the Grapplewick incident, right down to the inflating flying saucer, and that bothered him. Two and two weren't making four in his calculations.

191

Now, making his way up the stairs to the harbour master's office, he paused. Heinrich Adlon was brilliant. For twelve months he had meticulously planned every step of the operation. It was inconceivable that his own carefully rigged flares should be his downfall. It would have been a beginner's mistake and up to now, he hadn't made any at all. James gazed unseeingly over the black water and excitement suddenly gripped his bowels as a glimmer of understanding grew at the back of his mind. The art of the master illusionist was the art of deception. Flap the right hand about and do the real business with the other one. Adlon's timing was precise – his skill rested on that precision. He had known down to the last second when the flares would be released so it wasn't feasible that he should be sailing close to the coast only to be picked up by his own illumination.

James slapped the rail triumphantly. Another decoy – that boat was meant to be seen. He bounded up the last few steps into the office.

The harbour master, a Captain Fletching, whirled around as James entered. 'Coastguards are closing in on the boat now,' he said.

'Good,' replied James. 'Have the coastguards identify the boat; that's all, then get back here pronto – we haven't got much time.'

Fletching looked at him, not understanding. 'Well, chop chop,' said the detective.

'You don't want us to make an arrest?' asked the captain, puzzled.

'Oh yes, and I've a feeling we're getting close, but our man won't be on that boat.'

The harbour master shrugged and passed on the instructions to his radio operator. He then turned to James. 'What now?' he asked.

'Firstly, have you had any traffic in the last hour?'

Fletching picked up a pad. 'A sloop from Barcelona moored at 21.40 hours.' He flipped over a page, but James interrupted.

'I'm only interested in outgoing traffic.'

Fletching put down the pad. 'Nothing outward bound since this afternoon.'

The radio operator looked across. 'Excuse me, sir, but Jack Sprotly went out about twenty minutes ago.'

James was immediately alert. 'Who's Jack Sprotly?' he barked.

Fletching grunted. 'Oh, Jack's all right. He's one of the local

192

fishermen. He owns the *Molly Neek*, a trawler. We don't log their comings and goings. They tie up just outside the harbour in any case; not our pigeon.'

James looked at him keenly. 'Is it normal for one of these trawlers to go out at this time of night?'

Fletching shrugged. 'They're a law unto themselves that lot, but yes, it is a bit early. They usually leave for the fishing grounds at about two in the morning.'

James looked over at the radio man. 'Did you see him personally?'

'Yes, sir. I was having a drag outside on the jetty when he sailed past. He waved.'

'Waved, did he?' asked James thoughtfully. 'So you know him well?'

'He lives next door to me. I was in the same class as his wife at school.'

'In which direction was he heading?'

'Due east, sir ...' He stopped, a puzzled frown on his face. 'That's odd.'

'What is?' snapped James.

'They usually sail south or southwest for the fish.'

James snatched the radio and quickly contacted Control.

'Go ahead, sir.'

'Call off the bank surveillance teams in town – I want every man I can get down at the harbour, and I want two of my men round to ... hang on a minute ...' He looked at the radio operator. 'What's this trawlerman's ... er, Jack's address?'

'Thirty-six Crombie Street, just behind the harbour.'

James nodded and repeated the address into his radio, adding, 'There'll be a man in there and he'll be armed and dangerous. As soon as you've got him, let me know. Out.'

He looked at the perplexed faces around him. 'I'm only just beginning to understand how our friend works, and if my hunch is correct, then there's a man in that house holding Jack's wife hostage.'

CHAPTER

TWENTY-SIX

Norman tried to rub some life into his wrists as he emerged on deck. In the cold wind a thin suit was no match for the weather and the thought of a thick woollen sweater and gumboots overrode his fear. He staggered and grabbed for the rail as a wave crashed into the bows, but almost immediately he was prodded forward by the man who had just untied him. Norman's vision was just beginning to adjust to the night, and in the faint gleam of the port navigation light he recognised the man who was shepherding him along the deck. He was the man who had walked into the barber's shop in Coldhurst Street, only then he had been blind.

Norman was pushed forward again and he stumbled up the steps to the tiny wheelhouse. The skipper was behind the wheel, standing close to the spaceman. They both looked around as Norman was hustled roughly inside. It was impossible to shut the door; two people in that enclosed space were more than enough and three were definitely a crowd. Norman was just grateful for the warmth.

For a time nobody spoke and Norman was able to observe the skipper's face lit by the light from the binnacle. It was grim and afforded Norman no comfort. The skipper moved easily with the sudden lurches of the deck, dividing his attention between the compass and the clear screen. The boat ducked into a deeper trough and a flurry of white spray lashed against the window of the wheelhouse. Norman flinched at the fury of the sea, but after a couple of swells began to get used to it, learning to anticipate the pitch and yaw of the thrusting bows. It actually wasn't that rough a sea, but the stubby trawler was pushing through it with a fussiness that overdramatised the slight swell.

'How long now?' asked the man.

The skipper looked up to the clock on the bulkhead. 'Twenty-five minutes, roughly.'

Now that he was attuned to his surroundings, Norman began to think. Why had he been brought to the wheelhouse only to be ignored? Surely they would have been less cramped had they left him tied up below deck. He examined their reflections in the glass screen. Was the skipper one of them? The way in which he had answered the spaceman had given Norman a faint surge of hope. As soon as that thought had crossed his mind the skipper spoke again. 'If anything happens to my wife, I'll have you – wherever you run to.' The man ignored the threat but Norman's question had been answered. At least he had one ally.

Ten minutes later the spaceman's accomplice returned and leaned over Norman to tap The Great Firenzi's shoulder. Both men then stepped outside the wheelhouse. Norman observed them as suddenly they tensed. At a shout the skipper closed the throttle and Norman lurched as the boat shot forward. As he steadied himself he could see ahead: some way off the port beam was a small pinprick of flashing white light.

'Spot on,' muttered The Great Firenzi and walked on to the deck.

'I'll give him "spot on" if I ever catch the bugger,' muttered the skipper, busying himself between wheel and throttles so he could lay the trawler alongside a rubber dinghy. Swiftly The Great Firenzi stepped down into it, followed by his accomplice.

'You can go home now,' shouted the spaceman. 'Thanks for the lift.'

The skipper slammed the side window shut and pushed forward the throttle, spinning the wheel to make a wide sweep which caused the dinghy to wallow madly in its wake as he set a course for the harbour. He was impatient to get back to his wife.

In a more spacious bridge area aboard the coastguard boat, Chief Inspector James stood with legs braced as the ship bumped slowly over the oily sea at half speed, two miles behind the labouring trawler. Beside him stood the captain, leaning forward with his hands on the chart table.

'What I don't understand is if you're quite certain your man is on board the trawler, why don't we just catch up and nab him?'

Chief Inspector James shook his head. 'I don't think he's making his get-away in a trawler, even if it's only to France. He doesn't know which ports are being watched, and if it comes to

...ne crunch he couldn't outrun a pedalo in that thing. No, I've got a feeling he's leading us somewhere.'

'Sir,' a signalman at the radar console called to the captain, 'they've turned, sir, heading on a reciprocal course.'

The captain stepped across and looked over the signalman's shoulder at the screen to watch the sweep arm painting a small blip.

'What's happening?' asked the policeman, joining them.

'They've turned, heading for home.'

'Just like that,' mused James.

He rasped the bristles on his chin. He was tired and now wasn't the time. He had to out-think the man but whenever he took a piece off the board, the man had another move up his sleeve. Why was he turning back? What the hell was he playing at? He had to find out and quickly.

'All right,' he said. 'Intercept as quickly as possible.'

'Increase revolutions to full ahead both,' ordered the captain, and the boat surged forward like a dog let off the leash. In less than ten minutes the ship's spotlight picked out the trawler forcing its way in the opposite direction. As they closed within hailing distance, the captain took up the microphone.

'This is the coastguard: heave to and stand by for boarding party.'

Crouching behind the guard rails eight armed policemen of the Special Branch waited tensely for anything that might happen. The trawler's screws whirled frantically in reverse until the boat was wallowing and dead in the water. The coastguard boat, circling warily to keep the trawler in the centre of its searchlight beam, drew alongside, bumping gently against the fenders as they made fast.

James was the first to board, and even though it was only a gentle swell he had to time his jump to meet the rising deck of the trawler. The eight policemen followed in line and scuttled over the deck, guns outstretched, safety catches off. Norman, shielding his eyes from the bright light, picked his way across the deck to where Chief Inspector James was standing.

'Inspector,' he called, 'it's me, Norman.'

Jack Sprotly came out of the wheelhouse. 'What the bloody 'ell's goin' on?' he roared. 'I 'ave to get back ... my wife ...'

'First things first,' said James curtly. 'I'm Chief Inspector James, Special Branch. Were you carrying any passengers?'

Norman broke in. 'Yes, the spaceman; well, you know, and th
man that was in Grapplewick with him – the blind one!'

'And where are they now?'

'They got into a dinghy with an outboard motor.'

One of the SB team hurried up to James and took him to one
side, speaking in a low voice.

'Can't we just dump the lot overboard?' asked James. The officer shook his head and tapped his watch.

James nodded. 'OK, everybody aboard the other boat – *now*!'

Immediately the black-clad officer clambered over the rail and
James pushed Norman after him.

'Hang on a minute,' said the trawler skipper; 'I'm not leaving
my boat. There's nothing wrong with her!'

'I haven't time to argue,' replied James. 'Your boat will be
blown to smithereens any second, so move yourself!'

Sprotly got the message and leaped for the rail. James was close
behind him and barely made it to the other boat, which had already begun to pull away. In the captain's small cabin James quizzed Norman and Sprotly and his puzzlement deepened; why
should the two criminals transfer to a small dinghy in mid-ocean?
Granted, a small rubber dinghy wouldn't be picked up on any
radar screen, but they were only ten or so miles from shore, and
James was convinced they weren't going to attempt crossing the
Channel in it.

He looked at Norman. 'Ask the captain to come in here, will
you?'

Norman sprang to his feet; he was getting used to the sea now
and was beginning to feel like an old sea dog. James had assured
him that Ann was well and he couldn't wait to get back to her.

The captain ducked into the cabin. 'You wanted to see me?'

'Yes,' said James, 'I'm assuming our man isn't planning to
spend the next couple of nights in a dinghy, so he has to be
making a rendezvous at sea.'

The captain nodded.

'Therefore, it would seem that he's waiting for a ship of some
kind,' carried on James. 'Now, did your operator see anything in
the vicinity on his radar?'

The captain thought for a moment. 'No. I looked as well but
didn't notice anything – mind you, we were only on a five-mile
wave and we didn't actually get to the periphery, so there may be
something two or three miles out that we missed.' He looked

ross to the trawler skipper. 'If the transfer position is correct, e can have another sweep from there.' He left and went back to ne bridge.

'Are you sure about my boat?' asked Sprotly.

James shrugged. 'No, I'm not, but my man believes there are explosives packed in the locker. The fact that Norman was pushed on to the bridge for no apparent reason makes me think that he was transferred there so he wouldn't see the explosives being set. In any case, if the boat doesn't blow within the next couple of hours, you can pick her up in the morning.'

The skipper snorted. 'That's if something doesn't run into it in the middle of the night.'

Both men left the cabin and, bending double into the wind, made their way along the deck. There were still about three hours left to daybreak but the adrenaline of the chase and the biting wind revived James. He was about to mount the ladder up to the bridge when a brilliant white light lit up the horizon. This was followed a couple of seconds later by a dull rumble. Both men whirled around and watched as a bright red glow illuminated the underbelly of the cloud base.

James patted the skipper's shoulder. 'Sorry about that. At least you won't have to worry about somebody running into her.'

Norman was in the wheelhouse, excited by the thrust of the bows as they bumped over the swell. The sea wasn't lashing at the windows of this boat; it now had more respect. They had all seen the flash of the explosion but Norman had shrugged it off as sheet lightning. It was only when DCI James and the skipper had come in that he learned the truth, and the shock of it was almost palpable. Up to now the whole thing had been an exhilarating chase which would end with the capture of the villain – and he couldn't be far ahead; Norman had last seen him boarding a rubber dinghy, for God's sake. Suddenly, though, the scenario had taken a turn for the worse and it wasn't a *Boy's Own* adventure any more. A trawler had been blown out of the water and it was only the sharp thinking of the chief inspector which had prevented Norman and Sprotly from going up with it.

'Sir!'

Everybody jumped and glared at the signalman.

'A ship coming up now at about six miles, and there's another one, sir. Probably a freighter.'

The captain watched the screen. 'There's another one coming up, a big one. An oil tanker, I think.'

'What is it, an invasion?' asked James, trying to inject a light note into the tense atmosphere.

The captain didn't take his eyes off the radar. 'No, we're coming into a bit of traffic here, but they're moored in the roads, waiting for a berth, I fancy. Either Southampton or Portsmouth.'

'Well, that's it!' exclaimed James. 'It has to be one of them!'

'Another two, sir, about ten thousand tons.'

The captain turned to the policeman. 'You've picked a busy night, inspector.'

James folded his arms and looked at the deck. He knew in his bones that Heinrich Adlon was aboard one of them, but the trick was to find out which one. He looked up. 'Is it possible to talk to the skippers of these ships?'

The captain thought for a moment. 'Yes, but I think it may be advisable to contact Southampton or Portsmouth first. They'll know who's moored and why.'

DCI James nodded. 'And in the meantime let's get in amongst them and have a close look!'

Aboard the *Kendo Maru*, Heinrich Adlon lay on his bunk, hands clasped behind his head, but he wasn't relaxed. He had twelve million pounds in the hold but he wasn't home and dry yet. He wasn't worried about Norman or the skipper – they were old news – but Chief Inspector James bothered him still. He couldn't figure out how the man knew he was at Bogsea – and where was James now? What was he up to? Had he been fooled by the decoy boat? Perhaps he had caught up as far as the Sprotly woman, although that was unlikely. Still, he was dealing with a high-ranking officer in Special Branch, not the lollipop man, so he had to expect changes to his carefully laid plans.

Adlon ran through his mental itinerary – on the following afternoon the ship would sail into Southampton to offload a cargo of iron ore and then proceed to Lisbon where it would load up with olive oil and timber. All in all this was a perfectly normal itinerary for the ship. She was registered with Lloyd's and her bills of lading were all in order. From Lisbon she would sail to the South Atlantic, and only then would he relax. Adlon suddenly jerked to a sitting position as a bright light flashed through the porthole, but then it moved on. He crawled over to the porthole and was now able to observe that the light was a searchlight from another

ip. Immediately he was on the alert. Something was terribly
wrong.

The coastguard boat circled the *Kendo Maru* slowly, bathing the
decks in a harsh white light. The captain had obtained all the information pertaining to the ships entering and leaving the port of
Southampton and there was nothing out of the ordinary on any
of them. They were all bona fide merchant ships with correct
papers, and there was a total of eight of them in the area. Slowly
the coastguard boat cruised in and out of the moorings, examining each ship in turn. The *Kendo Maru* was the last one.

'That's the one!' proclaimed James excitedly. 'It has to be!'
The captain stared at him. 'How can you be so sure?'

'I'm sure,' said the policeman. 'It must be. All the ships here,
once unloaded, are bound for different ports in the UK – except
for the *Kendo Maru*, that is. Her next port of call is Lisbon. After
that he's away and that'll be it. We'll have lost him and he'll go
somewhere where we can't touch him.'

The captain was still uncertain but James was impatient. 'I'll
get a boarding party together.'

He was on his way to the door when the captain stopped him.
'Belay that,' he said. 'You can't just board a ship like that on
the high seas, it's piracy. I'm sorry, but as captain of this vessel I
refuse to go alongside without the proper authorisation.'

'The trawler didn't bother you.'

'That was different, I knew the skipper. In any case, if we board
this ship and it turns out to be what you think it is, there's likely
to be bloodshed – and if it doesn't turn out to be what you think
it is, I'll be hiring out deck chairs on the promenade.'

James stared at him for a moment, then rooted in his pockets
for a card.

'Get me this number and tell whoever answers it's Chief Inspector James, Special Branch.'

The captain hesitated for a second.

'You'll be lucky to get that job with the deck chairs,' muttered
James softly.

The captain nodded and hurried away. James sighed. Excitement
and anticipation surged through him, but to a casual observer he
might have been idly contemplating what to order for breakfast.

'Your call, sir.' A seaman handed him the phone.

200

'Good morning, sir, James here. I'm sorry to wake you at thi. hour, but I think we've got our man.'

He spoke quietly for a few minutes then put down the phone. 'Problem solved,' he said to the captain. 'In forty minutes a detachment of Royal Marine Commandos will be choppered here, so we're to stand off until we hear them approach, then put on all your deck lights. Any questions?'

The searchlight went out and the boat picked up speed into the night. But Adlon was uneasy: somebody had been interested in the *Kendo Maru*, curious enough to circle slowly examining the decks with a powerful light. Whoever it was appeared satisfied enough to switch off and move on, but this did nothing to allay his suspicions. More than ever now it was imperative he stayed one jump ahead of the pack. At the back of his mind he knew they were closing in. He was certain he'd covered every angle but apparently so had the opposition. He had to find an alternative escape route.

Swinging his legs over the edge of the bunk, he put on a reefer jacket and made his way along the passage to the deck. The wind hit him, setting him back a pace, and he hunched his way forward to the ladder up to the bridge wing in order to give him a better vantage point. But there was nothing to see, the night was at its darkest and only the faint small navigation lights of the tanker at the next mooring were visible. All was black and silent apart from the busy wind and the occasional slop of the sea. A lesser man would be comforted, discounting the searchlight as a routine inspection, but instinct made Adlon uneasy. Somebody had been nosing around and he knew that he was the centre of attraction. Shivering in the night air, he turned up his collar and made his way back down to the galley for a mug of hot coffee, tea, cocoa, anything that would help him to think. But again his luck turned sour. Wrapping his hands around a mug of stewed coffee as he sat in the warm, humming boiler room, he missed the throb of the rotors as two helicopters passed close by.

The coastguard boat was in position, a freighter and a tanker hiding it from the *Kendo Maru* as the marines abseiled on to the deck. With the ship's lights ablaze, it was a spectacular sight for the few men lining the rails of the rusting freighter moored some fifty yards away. The manoeuvre completed, the helicopters

201

eeled away and all lights were again doused, bringing a smatter
f applause from the insomniacs on the ship nearby.

'Slow ahead both,' ordered the captain, and the coastguard
boat crept towards the target. They steamed to within three hundred yards and then the telegraphs rang for just enough revolutions to keep her head into the swell. When she stopped, two
marines pushed a rubber dinghy over the side and climbed down
into it. After adjusting their paddles in the rowlocks they bent
their backs and pulled strongly and silently into the darkness towards the Kendo Maru.

Aboard the coastguard boat there was no talking. All was silent
except for the low rumble of the engine. The strong wind was
now carrying all sound away from the target ship. All heads were
turned anxiously towards the navigation lights of the Kendo
Maru in the distance. James gripped the guardrail and leaned out
to listen for the splash of oars and the return of the two marines.
He listened in vain. Suddenly they were shinning up ropes to
board the boat behind him, clambering on to the deck. They
weren't a special unit for nothing.

Now that the preliminaries had been taken care of, the game
was about to begin in earnest. The marine lieutenant knew what
he had to do and ordered his men to move towards the rail and
stand ready with grappling lines. Soundlessly they moved over to
the side of the boat like a collection of ghosts all in black – black
jumpsuits, black balaclavas and blackened faces. They looked sinister enough even without the evil lightweight sub-machine-guns
they all carried. Whatever happened, they were going to be a huge
shock to somebody's system.

The coastguard boat surged forward, two searchlights illuminating the Kendo Maru. With a crunch they were alongside, grappling lines clutching the rail of the bigger vessel. Almost before
the captain gave out the order for the engines to be cut, the
marines were fanning out on board the deck of the freighter. One
marine crept along to the wheelhouse, the rest went below deck.

James boarded the Kendo Maru in a more sedate manner – he
was no spring chicken any more and not up to the antics of the
younger, highly trained men. Once on board he waited a few moments. Very shortly an assortment of crew, clad variously in dirty
singlets and shirts, blinked their way up on deck, hands clasped
behind their heads. James noted thankfully that he hadn't heard
any gunfire, but the smoothness and the success of the operation

made him vaguely uneasy. Four marines were still searching the vessel for the proceeds of the bank raids, whilst another emerged from the hatch to report that all crew members were now on deck.

The captain of the *Kendo Maru*, a wizened Oriental, seemed subdued and this gave James fresh heart. If the Oriental had been the captain of an innocent freighter plying an honest trade, he would have been surprised, angry, anything but cowed. James turned his attention to the line of crewmen scrunching their eyes against the harsh glare of the searchlight. 'OK, Norman, let's see if there's anybody you know.'

Norman had been daydreaming; he'd decided that as soon as he stepped back on to dry land he was off to the recruiting office. He wanted to be a marine. He'd been watching the quiet, deadly efficiency with which they went about their business, and now as Chief Inspector James was about to thrust him on to centre stage again, his chest swelled with pride. Norman at last realised that he wasn't just an average Herbert, he was one of *them*, an integral part of the operation. Slowly and carefully he went down the line, unaware that James behind him was holding his breath. As he passed the assortment of men without recognising any of them, his heart began to sink. What if Chief Inspector James was wrong? How was he going to tell him that the spaceman wasn't here? He remembered that the man was a master of disguise and glanced quickly back to the Oriental captain, but his hopes there were dashed. He might have altered his face but there was no way in which he could have shortened his legs.

Then, at the next man, Norman could hardly keep his exultation in check. It was the blind man who had walked into his uncle's shop in Grapplewick. He turned to James. 'That's one of them,' he said casually, surprising even himself; he hadn't meant to sound like Mr Cool. James breathed a huge sigh of relief and stood aside as one of the Special Branch men reached over and snapped a pair of handcuffs on the man, who stood in the line looking dazed. He made no protestations of innocence. James put it down to his being amazed at seeing Norman very much alive and well.

James stepped forward and looked into the man's eyes. 'All right, sunshine, where is he?'

The man craned his neck up and down the line and shrugged. 'I dunno,' he eventually mumbled.

'He should be here, though, shouldn't he?' The man hesitated, avoiding the detective's hard gaze. 'I'll ask you again,' continued James, 'and if I'm not satisfied, you're going over the side with an anchor chain around your ankles.'

Fear sprang into the man's eyes. He wasn't sure that the policeman would carry out his threat but as a betting man he wouldn't touch the odds with a ten-foot pole. 'I dunno,' he repeated, and as James turned away he blurted out, 'He's on the ship somewhere, but I don't know where.'

James nodded. 'OK. So where's the loot?'

The man's mouth snapped shut. For him the money obviously added up to more than his life.

'OK,' said James resignedly. 'Fetch me a length of chain.'

The man hesitated just long enough to realise that he had got his sums wrong, and that his life just had the edge over the money. 'It's in the hold,' he muttered.

James turned to one of his men. 'Take him below and have him point it out.' As the man was hustled out of the line James walked over to the stern and looked down at the oily black waters beneath. He was joined by a marine lieutenant.

'I'm sorry, sir, but there's no sign of anybody else.'

James sighed. 'Ah well. You've done a great job and I'll certainly mention it in my report.'

'Thank you, sir. What's the next move?'

'As soon as it's daylight, get the crew to bring this ship into Southampton, and make sure that nobody goes ashore unless I say so. OK?'

The young lieutenant hesitated. 'Need any help with the big one, sir?'

James shook his head. 'Nah, he's mine, and I've looked forward to this for a long time, but thanks again for all your help. It's good to know we're on the same side.' With that he strode briskly along the deck to clamber back on to the coastguard boat.

Norman scuttled off after him, perplexed as to why the chief inspector seemed so calm. Granted, they had the accomplice and the money, but what about Mr Big? The whole object of the exercise had been to bring him in, but they had missed him yet again. Surely this was a smack in the face, to put it mildly, yet James was behaving as if he was going away for a weekend's fishing. Surely it would have been better to stay aboard the *Kendo Maru* until daylight when they would have a better chance to

search the vessel more thoroughly. However, not for the first tim
Norman had underestimated the Special Branch detective. Under
neath that calm exterior bubbled a cauldron of excitement.

The coastguard boat steamed out of the roads in a westerly direction. 'Get a fix?' asked James calmly, sipping a mug of hot,
sweet tea.

The captain nodded. 'According to my charts, the tide changes
at about five o'clock and it's a riptide coming in from the Solent.
That's always a bit tricky in this area.' He ran a slide rule over a
chart and pencilled a dot. 'This should do it, as near as dammit,'
he said.

James put down his mug and yawned; he hadn't slept for nearly
a day and a half now, and that wasn't good. 'OK,' he said, 'I'll
leave you to it. I'm going down below to stretch out for a bit. Let
me know what transpires.'

'Will do,' replied the captain, and gave orders for the change of
course.

Norman hadn't had his full quota of sleep either, but no way
was he going to close his eyes now. He sat down on one of the
bridge chairs, determined to see out the last act. Within five
minutes his head fell forward and he went out like a light.

Four hours later the captain shook Chief Inspector James, who
was instantly awake. 'Congratulations, sir, you were right.'

James rubbed his eyes and grunted. 'Well done.' He swung his
legs off the bunk and followed the captain on deck, who handed
him his binoculars and pointed out to sea. James lifted the binoculars to his eyes and after a moment his face split into a wide grin.
'I don't know who's going to be best pleased on seeing the other;
him or me. By the looks of it he's had a long, hard night too.' He
handed the glasses back to the captain. 'Just like a fly in a web,'
he murmured.

The captain nodded. 'But how could you have been so certain?'

James rested his hands on the rail. 'First thing I noticed when
we went round the *Kendo Maru* was the dinghy tied up astern.'

'Yes, I noticed that too.'

'Bit unusual, isn't it?'

The captain thought for a moment. 'Yes, I suppose it is.'

'When those two marines rowed across, they emptied the petrol
from the outboard motor on the dinghy and filled it with sea
water.' He shrugged. 'Well, you know the rest: when we were on
board I looked over the side and the dinghy was gone. He had to

t some distance to be out of earshot before he started the en-
ɪe, but they don't run very far on sea water. Game, set and
.atch: all we had to do was wait for him to join us.'

They both leaned over the rail to watch as The Great Firenzi
was hauled on deck more dead than alive. James stood over him
and looked down at the shivering, sodden illusionist. 'Welcome
aboard Limbo Two . . . you miserable bastard.'

EPILOGUE

After reporting to his superiors, the chief inspector repaid a debt. He phoned Bernard Whittaker, editor of the *Grapplewick Bugle*, giving him the biggest exclusive of his career. Not only was it taken up by the major British dailies, but newspapers all over the world carried the story. From the sting to the final arrest of the 'spaceman', the story captured the public's imagination, and Norman featured prominently in the incredible saga. It was serialised in several magazines and Norman was interviewed and photographed, even appearing on the cover of *Time*. That was the last straw. He fled to a quiet resort in France until things quietened down. He wasn't alone, though: he took with him his wife, Mrs Ann Waterhouse.

Auntie Florrie died from a surfeit of riches – fridge, washing machine, new carpets and a fur coat. But it was the three weeks in Scarborough that brought about her final collapse. In a typically English summer she died of pneumonia. Her last words were, 'Tell me honestly, Albert, where did you get the money from?' He couldn't tell her the truth – he thought the shock would kill her – but now somebody up there would probably have enlightened her regarding the night on Sagbottom's Acres when her husband and Superintendent Smith became more than solvent.

Albert missed Florrie, he'd nothing to ignore any more, and after a decent interval he married Madame Lesley. It remains an amicable relationship – she doesn't have to give him dancing lessons and he doesn't have to buy her a box of chocolates every week. They now live in Farmer Crumpshaw's house so they can keep an eye on Sagbottom's.

Old deaf Crumpshaw died a week after he'd shot the spacecraft. He'd had enough and couldn't wait to hand in his life membership. Two days later the delivery man found him stretched out on the bed in a clean shirt clutching his will. It was a remarkable few lines, leaving £5000 to his dog.

Eunice Waterhouse, née Lesley, also enjoyed a fair amount of notoriety, being The Great Firenzi's first wife. Appearing on television chat shows she came across so well they gave her a six-week cookery series, which was a mistake. However she had an unexpected windfall when a Sunday newspaper suggested that she had supplied Heinrich Adlon with information regarding the town, and implying she was working hand in glove with him. First she was furious but after weeks of litigation she was somewhat mollified by an out-of-court settlement of £150,000.

Superintendent Smith retired shortly after the big night and took his riches to Marbella in Spain where he moved into a sumptuous villa near San Pedro. He also acquired a popular restaurant called La Lampara Azul, and along with some Spanish businessmen he bought a half share in a hotel. This was in his early days as a resident when he was known among the locals as El Hombre Rico because of his lavish lifestyle. So on a policeman's pay and a dodgy deal to buy Sagbottom's, one wondered if he hadn't any other little earners going before he emigrated. However his luck eventually ran out. He was no match for the Spanish mafia and when a great section of the hotel fell down, he was horrified to learn that it was his half. Now, sadly, his magnum of champagne is reduced to a Campari and soda, and the palatial villa has gone. He is now in a rented room at the back of the village. He doesn't own the restaurant any more, but he still carries a bit of weight with the council and due to his experience as a police superintendent, they have decided to be generous and give him a job as a traffic warden.

Grapplewick itself has prospered. It is now arguably the most famous little town in the world. Hollywood, Lourdes, Salem, Niagara Falls – all trail miserably in its wake. Lancastrians abroad no longer tell people they are from Manchester or Liverpool. They all live on the outskirts of Grapplewick. And every year on the first of May, thousands make a pilgrimage to Sagbottom's Acres – space societies, interplanetary societies, geographical societies – they all congregate to celebrate the landing. The fact that it was all a scam and the spacecraft was just an inflatable rubber contraption that resembled a saucer doesn't seem to matter. Every year Albert Waterhouse dons the mayor's robes of office, and along with members of the council they re-enact the scene as midnight strikes. All the side shows and refreshment tents are silent while flares are fired into the sky. But there the resem-

208

blance ends. Four searchlights shoot out and converge on the sp
where the spacecraft was reputed to have landed, and Norma
walks across the field and places a wreath in the centre of light
Why is a mystery, but no one is complaining. The tills are pinging,
the pubs are full, and most of the houses take in some of the thousands of overseas tourists that flood these shores to visit Sagbottom's, Big Ben, Stratford and St Paul's – in that order.

Every other shop sells mementos, the most popular being stones
from Kershaw's Croft, although enough stone has now changed
hands to build several pyramids.

It is generally accepted that when UFOs land, it will be on a
Wednesday, and the venue has to be Grapplewick.

There is a very interesting footnote, however, and one that is
inexplicable to this day. The spaceman or Heinrich Adlon or Firenzi, the great illusionist, was transferred ashore from the coastguard boat, more than half dead. When he opened his eyes some
time later he found he was in a prison hospital. But he never did
anything by halves, and closing his eyes again he quickly completed the journey. An hour later a doctor wrote out a death cer-
tificate and the body was transferred to the mortuary. It was the
end of possibly the greatest stage illusionist since Houdini . . . or
was it?

Chief Inspector James reflected on the man's brilliance. His
thoughts were mixed as he sat in the front pew of the little chapel
in the crematorium in order to pay his last respects to his adver-
sary. Certainly his old animosity was gone and he could not help
but admire the sheer ingenuity of the man. The patience and
planning of a twelve-month scam undoubtedly ranked high in the
annals of crime. The illusions and tricks, the split-second timing
of each miraculous event were surely the work of a master crafts-
man.

There were not many people in the congregation. He was the
only one as far as he knew with a personal connection to the dead
man. The others were extras: gravediggers, the crematorium staff,
passers-by, in fact anybody to make up the numbers. They all
stood now as the rollers began to revolve, moving the coffin forward. The organ piped out a background of genre music. Everyone craned forward as the little doors opened. Beyond them the
fire of the crematorium shone. The inspector was deeply moved.
It seemed such a stupid way to end one's days, after mewling into
the world at life's outset, only to end up a pathetic pile of ash.

...ne coffin was about to pass through the furnace doors when ...range thing happened – the rollers ceased to revolve and the ...ffin stopped. There was a rustle in the congregation and one of ...ne crematorium technicians stepped into the aisle, probably with ...he intention of giving it a helping hand, but before he could move forward the sides of the coffin fell outwards and the lid collapsed inside with a hollow thud. It was perfectly obvious to everyone in the congregation that the coffin was completely empty. Before anyone could scream or fall back in a dead faint the rollers began to revolve again, the coffin resumed its last journey into the flames and the doors slowly closed, blocking it from sight.

Chief Inspector James remained standing for several minutes. He badly needed a drink.